Reading and Writing Connections

Edited by

Jana M. Mason

University of Illinois at Urbana-Champaign

Allyn and Bacon

Boston   London   Sydney   Toronto

Series Editor: Sean W. Wakely
Production Coordinator: Annette Joseph
Editorial-Production Service: The Book Department
Cover Administrator: Linda K. Dickinson
Cover Designer: Susan C. Hamant
Manufacturing Buyer: Tamara McCracken

Library of Congress Cataloging-in-Publication Data

Reading and writing connections.

Proceedings of a conference held at the University of Illinois in October 1986.
Includes bibliographies and indexes.
1. Reading (Elementary)—Congresses.
2. English language—Composition and exercises —Study and teaching—Congresses. I. Mason, Jana.
LB1572.9.R42   1989   372.4   88–7918
ISBN 0–205–11855–0

Printed in the United States of America

10 9 8 7 6 5 4 3 2 1   94 93 92 91 90 89

Contents

Preface

A conference on reading and writing connections was held at the University of Illinois in October 1986 in response to a collaborative agreement between the Center for the Study of Reading at Illinois and the Center for the Study of Writing at the University of California at Berkeley. The agreement was funded by the U.S. Office of Educational Research and Instruction (Grant No. 23429–1). Individuals attending the conference included JoBeth Allen, Richard Anderson, Bonnie Armbruster, Kathryn Au, Bertrum Bruce, Linnea Ehri, Marcia Farr, Violet Harris, Alice Kawakami-Arakaki, Martha King, Sandra Murphy, Gay Su Pinnell, Barbara Powell, Taffy Raphael, Louise Rosenblatt, Andee Rubin, James Squire, Janice Stewart, Dorothy Strickland, Elizabeth Sulzby, and William Teale.

As the product of that conference, this book reflects the value of demonstrating connections between reading instruction and writing. The book shows practitioners how writing can be blended with reading instruction and how writing activities can be used not just to augment reading but also to establish and bolster emergent reading.

The book is divided into two parts. Part One documents the connections between reading and writing; Part Two describes how writing can take place in the classroom in conjunction with reading. The introduction to Part One outlines some important research goals suggested by the studies presented in Chapters 1–6. Chapter 1, which describes the connections between oral and written language, provides a foundation for the studies that follow by showing how children's written language develops and how their writings can be analyzed. Chapter 2 documents children's first efforts to write and describes how they change over the kindergarten year. Chapter 3 continues the documentation of writing development from kindergarten into first grade, explaining how children's written responses reveal their level of understanding about how to read words. Chapter 4, which describes a two-year study of children, from kindergarten through first grade, provides important evidence of changes in the connections between writing and reading development. Chapters 5 and 6 focus on connections between writing and reading. The study described in Chapter 5 demonstrated these connections by analyzing children's reading and writing attempts after their teachers had read books to them. The study presented in Chapter 6 examined writing development, together with its connection to reading, as it occurred over a school year in whole-language kindergarten classrooms.

Part Two, which features examples of reading and writing instruction in diverse settings, begins with a commentary on some of the ties between the two parts of the book. Chapter 7 is an eloquent presentation of a theoretical underpinning for connections in reading and writing instruction. Chapters 8 and 9 document the pleasure that kindergartners take in the writing activity that can precede or accompany reading, as well as the power of that activity. Chapters 10, 11, and 12 explain effects of interventions through school-supported instructional change. Chapter 10 describes connections between children's emerging awareness of reading and writing and the support in their homes for literacy. Chapter 11 describes a program that blends reading with writing in its efforts to change a negative prognosis for academically at-risk children. Chapter 12 describes a series of instructional techniques empirically tested to further writing activity and the understanding of reading and writing in the elementary school classroom.

I wish to thank the conference attendees for their participation and time-consuming support of the conference and book. I would also like to thank the following: Sarah Freedman for originating the idea of collaboration between the two centers and for helping me conceptualize the conference; Barbara Powell for her unflagging efforts to organize the conference; Margot Jerrard and Sandy Setters for their diligent editorial work; and Delores Plowman and Nancy Diedrich for their never-an-error, lightning-quick manuscript typing. Finally, I wish to thank the reviewers of the manuscript: Sandra Hollingsworth, University of California, Berkeley; Lenore Ringler, New York University; and Arlene Saretsky, Chicago State University.

J.M.M.

Contributors

JoBeth Allen
University of Georgia

June Barnhart
Northern Illinois University

Wanda Clark
Public Schools of Manhattan-Ogden, Kansas

Muriel Cook
Public Schools of Manhattan-Ogden, Kansas

Peggy Crane
Public Schools of Manhattan-Ogden, Kansas

Lee Dobson
Simon Fraser University

Linnea C. Ehri
University of California, Davis

Carol Sue Englert
Michigan State University

Irmie Fallon
Public Schools of Manhattan-Ogden, Kansas

Dale C. Farran
University of North Carolina-Greensboro

Joyce A. Hieshima
Northwestern University

Laura Hoffman
Public Schools of Manhattan-Ogden, Kansas

Kathy S. Jennings
Public Schools of Manhattan-Ogden, Kansas

Alice J. Kawakami-Arakaki
Center for the Development of Early Education, The Kamehameha Schools Honolulu, Hawaii

Bonnie M. Kerr
University of Illinois at Urbana-Champaign

Martha L. King
Ohio State University

Becky W. Kirschner
Michigan State University

Miriam G. Martinez
University of Texas at San Antonio

Jana M. Mason
University of Illinois at Urbana-Champaign

Sandra Murphy
San Francisco State University

Madelline E. Oshiro
Center for the Development of Early Education, The Kamehameha Schools Honolulu, Hawaii

Carol L. Peterman
Portland State University

Gay Su Pinnell
Ohio State University

Barbara M. Powell
University of Illinois at Urbana-Champaign

Taffy E. Raphael
Michigan State University

Louise M. Rosenblatt
New York University

Martha A. Sours
Public Schools of Manhattan-Ogden, Kansas

James R. Squire
Ginn and Co. Publishers

Janice Stewart
Rutgers University

Dorothy S. Strickland
Columbia University

Elizabeth Sulzby
University of Michigan

William H. Teale
University of Texas at San Antonio

PART ONE

Tracing the Development of Reading and Writing

Introduction by James R. Squire

The studies presented in Part One not only document reading and writing connections by providing correlational data or descriptions; they also have important implications for the classroom. The inclusion on the research teams of teachers who sorted data, raised questions about findings, and pondered the implications did much to enhance the utility of these studies for practice. Not until researchers and teachers forge more permanent, continuing relationships are we likely to eliminate the gulf that currently separates the college from the classroom. The practices employed in these studies represent a good start— so good, in fact, that like Oliver Twist trying to relieve his hunger, one wants to call for "more": more interpretation, more extended studies, more relating to context.

The Need for More Multiyear, Multilevel Developmental Studies of Language Development. Although longitudinal studies can provide valuable background data against which to interpret individual studies, most of our current studies offer merely descriptive snapshots of children and young people in particular groups at particular times. Such studies cannot suggest with any degree of certainty where children have been or where they may be going. Several outstanding exceptions to this approach are found in this book, with speech and writing links over a three-year period presented in Chapter 1, and a number of one-year studies that explain reading and writing links presented in succeeding chapters.

Data indicating that linguistic processes and strategies do not operate identically at every developmental level underscore the need for more longitudinal studies. For example, in Chapter 3 Ehri presents persuasive data on the ways in which early instruction in invented-spelling patterns (phonetic spellings) can support beginning reading behavior, particularly by strengthening children's understanding of phonemic/graphemic relationships. Yet throughout the elementary school years, spelling must be related to writing, not reading (Squire, 1979). Spelling, after all, is a writing skill, not a reading skill, and associating it too closely with reading can make young readers think they should be able to spell all the words they can read—words, say, like "Illinois" and "Winnipesaukee," which almost any of us can read but not easily spell until we commit them to memory.

Similarly, in Chapter 2, Sulzby, Barnhart, and Hieshima suggest the existence of developmental patterns in children's copying activity. Phonics strategies, too, seem to operate differently at different developmental levels (Chall, 1983), as does the process of composing. A study like Sulzby et al.'s can suggest hypotheses on how older writers perform, but surely nothing definitive. This uncertainty about developmental patterns is apparently why Allen and associates talk in Chapter 6 about a weak sequentiality in writing development and why they suggest that the rich studies of "miscue analysis" be replicated with older readers. In a similar vein, the significant analysis by Mina Shaughnessy (1977) of college students' writing errors suggests how and why the writing of younger readers be studied.

The fact is we have had no substantial longitudinal study of children's reading and writing since Loban (1976) initiated a thirteen-year analysis in the early 1950s. And Loban's study was pre-Chomsky, pre–cognitive psychology, pre–comprehension process, largely pre-television, pre–writing process, and even pre-Bruner. Our present need is manifest.

The Need for More Careful Study of the Impact of Text Structures on Writing and Reading. In Chapter 5 Mason, Peterman, Powell, and Kerr recommend studying children's ability to understand and internalize different text structures. Their findings demonstrate the effects of text structure on reading and recall and, to a lesser extent, on writing. Clearly, our present insights into the impact of stories in comparison with the impact of informational texts, for example, need to be extended to embrace written and oral language. Moreover, such studies are needed with both younger and older children.

The comment by Sulzby et al. (Chapter 2) that the patterns reflected in storybook reading may influence subsequent linguistic behavior brings to mind the sometimes neglected study of Ruth Strickland (1962), which suggested that constant exposure to the simplified sentences in basal readers will stimulate only simplified sentences in children's writing. An extension of such studies to children's oral language is overdue, especially with the intriguing evidence now available in Miles Myers's work (1987) with older students. Myers has found that the degree of formality in the speech events in which learners have been engaged seems to influence the degree of formality and informality in their writing.

The work on text structures on which Calfee is engaged seems promising, the more so since he carries it into classrooms (Calfee & Chambliss, 1986). But Calfee, like so many others, focuses largely on reading comprehension and does not include composition.

Which linguistic and rhetorical structures are most important in the curriculum to advance the quality of children's reading and writing? And when and how should they be taught? Some answers may emerge from the findings of the international assessment of writing, currently under way. For this comparative study, rhetoricians from eighteen countries (some Asian, some Latin American, some African, some English-speaking) identified fifteen modes of discourse, each involving distinct rhetorical structures that might be introduced through schooling. Yet preliminary data indicate that what schools teach and value varies from culture to culture, even when children are being taught to write in their native tongues (Purves & Takala, 1982). Only in the United States and Israel, for example, is logical analysis seen as the highest value in expository prose (unity, coherence, emphasis). Hispanic countries, in contrast, tend to value the rich embroidery and metaphorical quality of texts. One cannot but speculate that some of our difficulty in teaching new Americans who come from Hispanic cultures to read and write may derive from such diverse cultural values.

The Need for More Tolerance of Diversity in Language Learning. All the studies presented in Part One sense the presence of individual variation, although Allen and associates (Chapter 6) report such variation most explicitly with well over one hundred different patterns of development. Dobson (Chapter 4) provides interesting examples of differences in development.

No single description of language patterns and no single approach to language teaching can, of course, account for the complexities of language learning. As Jerome Bruner (1985) reminded the American Educational Research Association, every theory of learning contains an element of truth and no single theory can account for all the complexity of human learning. Our approaches to teaching in the classroom must be of a kind that admits such a rich eclecticism.

And yet today there are forces pressing—often in the name of excellence—for a single standard, a single approach to learning, a single instructional cycle with virtually identical instructional materials for all. Moreover, most research in reading and writing has tended to apply only to the education of mainstream children: valid perhaps for the groups being studied but surely not applicable to all children. This bias was the major, valid criticism of *Becoming a Nation of Readers* (Anderson, Hiebert, Scott, & Wilkinson, 1985), a research-based statement dependent on the largely mainstream research of the past fifty years.

According to Heath (1983), nonmainstream children now approach 50 percent of our student population, and their early instructional needs in reading and writing differ from those of mainstream children. Reading and writing are no less important for them, but the kinds of processes and instruction needed seem very different. A study of native Hawaiian children by Kawakami-Arakaki, Oshiro, and Farran and a study of black children by Stewart and Mason help redress the imbalance evident in the current research; both studies are presented in Part Two (Chapters 9 and 10).

We need to study the implications of such observations in research, as well as in the classroom. What we do not seem to need is a Procrustean, one-track, one-text, single instructional system.

The Need for More Valid Assessments of Reading and Writing Performance. The nation's specialists in reading and writing recognize that our assessment instruments largely determine what we teach. As long as standardized survey tests, state and large-district assessment tests, and program-related criterion tests in commercial systems continue to stress single skills and discrete elements of reading and writing, we will find these skills and elements stressed in our classrooms.

The assumption that seems to underlie much of the research presented in this book is that reading and writing are parallel, interactive processes. If that is the case, then do we not need to use measures of interactive linguistic processes, rather than the suspect standardized tests, to assess the results of our research? If writing samples are useful in indicating children's competence in writing, should we not consider ways of obtaining parallel reading samples?

Fortunately, at least three states are now moving to create state-wide assessment models that reflect a view of reading as a dynamic process. These models may offer insights for research (Wixson, Peters, & Weber, 1987). But we clearly need to think through a whole series of related questions:

- How do we assess developmental stages in reading and writing? The writing analyses of Sulzby et al. (Chapter 2) and of King (Chapter 1) suggest useful beginning steps.
- How do we describe the context for reporting the results of a study that focuses on only one aspect of the total process? If

misunderstood, Ehri's work with invented spellings (Chapter 3) could lead to more isolated daily drills in the classroom.
- What can children's writing tell us about their reading? And what can their reading tell us about their writing? Dobson's research (Chapter 4) offers intriguing answers.

We have thought too little about such questions. The time has come to address them.

The Need for More Compatibility between Models of Teaching and Models of Learning. We have learned much during the past decade about language learning and language development. The applications of Piaget's and Vygotsky's theories to American classrooms, coupled with a long series of studies of cognitive development, have clarified our conception of reading and writing as process—dynamic, interactive, meaning-oriented, self-correcting. In short, we have learned much about how children learn language, and much of what we have learned derives from cognitive psychology. Our models of learning become ever more clear.

Our models of teaching are, however, very different. Because our energies have been directed toward learning and development, we have left the study of teaching behavior to other specialists. The result is that our models of teaching, like our modes of testing, derive from the older behavioral psychology.

Studies of teaching effectiveness have presented particularly powerful behavioral models (Office of Educational Research and Improvement, 1986), and these models have been rightly popularized in our classrooms. (They have been especially effective in preparing children to score on behaviorally oriented tests.) Even the terms we use to talk about teaching—time on task; direct instruction; massed and spaced practice; congruence of objective, activity, and test; criterion-referenced check—reflect the distance from cognitive psychology.

The point is not that one perspective is right and one wrong but, rather, that as long as our teaching models are so different from our learning models, we run the risk of confusing and alienating those who should be the beneficiaries of our work—the classroom teachers.

How can we begin to view teaching and learning as twin dimensions of schooling that must be made compatible? One way, of course, would be to demonstrate sound teaching and sound learning in demonstration/observation centers throughout the country. The ideas of Allen and associates and of Sulzby et al. are apparently being implemented in classrooms, but are the classrooms open for observation? To what extent are teachers participating with Ehri, King, and Mason et al.? Is Dobson, herself a teacher, able to promote her ideas in other classrooms? The decline in the quality of American education during the past thirty years seems to parallel, in part, the decline in opportunities to see outstanding learning and outstanding teaching in the classroom. There are not enough of us with the intelligence, experience, and imagination to envisage teaching and learning as exciting as King would have them. What we need are demonstration centers of excellence to show us models in operation.

Could the Center for the Study of Writing and the Center for the Study of Reading join together with schools throughout the nation to establish a network of observation/demonstration centers? Why not? Given that our present reach exceeds our grasp in schooling, we should profit enormously from such concrete illustration and illumination of desirable practice.

R E F E R E N C E S

Anderson, R., Hiebert, E., Scott, J. A., & Wilkinson, I. A. G. (1985). *Becoming a nation of readers.* Urbana, IL: Center for the Study of Reading.

Bruner, J. (1985). Models of the learner. *Educational Researcher, 14*(6), 5–8.

Calfee, R. C., & Chambliss, M. (1986). *The structural design features of large texts.* Unpublished manuscript, Stanford University, Stanford, CA.

Chall, J. (1983). *Stages of reading development.* New York: McGraw-Hill.

Heath, S. B. (1983). *Ways with words.* New York: Cambridge University Press.

Loban, W. (1976). *Language development through grade 12.* Urbana, IL: National Council of Teachers of English.

Myers, M. (1987). Oral language: Its relation to reading, writing, and response to literature. In J. R. Squire (Ed.), *The Dynamics of Language Learning* (pp. 126–146). Urbana, IL: National Conference of Research in English and ERIC Center.

Office of Educational Research and Improvement. (1986). *What works: Research about teaching and learning.* Washington, DC: U.S. Department of Education.

Purves, A. C., & Takala, S. (1982). An international perspective on the evaluation of written composition. *Evaluation in Education: An International Review Series, 3,* 207–368.

Shaughnessy, M. P. (1977). *Errors and expectations.* New York: Oxford University Press.

Squire, J. R. (1979). *Instructional focus and the teaching of English.* Lexington, MA: Ginn.

Strickland, R. (1962). The language of elementary school children: Its relationship to the language of reading textbooks and the quality of reading. *Bulletin of the School of Education, 38,* Indiana University.

Wixson, K. K., Peters, C. W., & Weber, E. M. (1987). New directions in statewide reading assessment. *The Reading Teacher, 40,* 749–755.

1

SPEECH TO WRITING

Children's Growth in Writing Potential

Martha L. King

This chapter considers pervasive strands in langauge development from speech to literacy, paying particular attention to writing. It draws upon studies of early writing development at Ohio State University that identified and described (1) links between speech and writing and (2) particular features in children's spoken and written texts that indicate growth. The focus is on text and the constitutive function of language. Examples of early reading, story retelling, and writing illustrate development in terms of story structure, cohesive elements, and social and cultural contexts.

The great debate in literacy learning now centers on writing as well as reading. Raising questions about "connections" between these two forms of language, the debate opens the way for new or revised theories about how literacy is learned and used in the everyday world. Researchers have made great strides in understanding critical aspects of reading and writing. Significant insights have come from studies of early learning, or "emergent" literacy; the reading and writing processes; the cognitive demands of the tasks; the structural features of various forms of written discourse; and the cultural and historical uses of both oral and written language.

The focus of this chapter is on language development—from speech to literacy with particular attention to growth in writing. The research described here, conducted at Ohio State University,[1] was concerned with identifying and describing (1) links between speech and writing and (2) the particular features of children's spoken and written texts that indicate growth. The central question was, What is it young writers must learn to *do* in order to make the transition from speech to writing and then to extend their competence beyond the few sentences they write in the early years of school? Although the research focused mainly on the relationship between speech and writing, reading and listening became integral parts of it because we asked our students to retell traditional tales as well as to write stories. All four modes—speech, writing, reading, and listening—are language; insight into one—speech, for example—should therefore aid our understanding of another.

SPEECH AS THE BASIS FOR LITERACY

Once reading and writing are viewed as language, it is clear that understanding their relationship will necessarily involve assumptions about language learning and language use. Both skills are simply different modes of representing meaning within the larger system of language, which is manifested first in speech. While each mode has its own conventions, all are subject to particular constraints that operate within the system as a whole. This holistic view of language, in which particular rules and relationships can be expected to govern reading, writing, speech, and listening, allows one to make predictions about and to investigate aspects of the learning process across the four modes of the linguistic system (King, 1978).

Reading and writing are more than new sets of skills learned in school; they are a continuation of a process of language learning already well established in speech. Literacy, as Vygotsky (1978) has explained, develops as a part of "a unified historical line" of the development of symbolism, from speech through play and drawing to reading and writing. Reading and writing differ from speech in regard to the functions they serve and the symbol systems involved. Reading and writing use a second-order—visual—symbol system that has its origin in speech and other first-order symbols, such as drawing and symbolic play (Vygotsky, 1978). It is in these early modes of representation that children begin fulfilling a basic human need: to transform experience into various forms of symbolic representation (Langer, 1968).

The Social Context of Learning Language

Children learn to use language to fulfill personal needs within their own families and cultures (Cazden, 1983; Wells, 1981). Infants' first contact with speech is associated with the multiplicity of actions that comprise the care and attention they receive from their parents and other caregivers. Although the way language is used differs among and within cultures and families, all families and cultures provide sufficient demonstrations of talk for young children to form a system of language and its uses. Babies very early begin to make distinctions about the significant people, objects, events, and talk that surround them. Bruner (1975, p. 10) points to the rituals and play of bath and feeding times, for example, as the basis for the ontogenesis of speech acts; the distinct routines, gestures, and intonations draw "the child's attention to the communication itself and to the structure of the acts in which communication is taking place." Toward the end of the first year, the child's perspective on objects and events changes, and he or she deliberately seeks to incorporate them in the interactions with caregivers. A new integration occurs in which aspects of the physical environment are brought into acts of communication, previously limited to people. This important achievement in communicative competence is called *intersubjectivity* by researchers (Trevarthan, 1980; Bruner, 1975) and provides the basis for negotiation of meaning between parent and child. The child begins to act intentionally and develops an awareness of the intentions of others and of what can be shared in communication with them. The caregiver is intimately involved, according to Halliday (1975), and actually participates in the child's construction of a system of language and meaning.

But child-rearing practices differ in families and cultural groups, and this same kind of parent/child interaction is not universal. Heath (1983) especially has documented many substantial differences in the ways children are socialized into family life, culture, and the uses of language and literacy. For example, she describes in detail a black working-class rural community in the South wherein children from birth are a part of the social life of an extended family. They are seen as able to learn what they require in that global social context. The baby is constantly with adults, and instead of talking *to* the infant, the caregiver talks *about* the child to other adults. Surely, her body responses, intonation, and other aspects of the situation draw attention to particular utterances and actions that are significant and repeated. Since they are always present when accounts of events are shared, toddlers pick up and repeat bits of talk and later repeat them with variation. They learn to rely on nonverbal cues in the context, to negotiate meanings with several adults, and to adapt their language use to the changing situations. They learn to be flexible and creative in their use of rhymes, metaphors, and verbal play. Such language competence, however, is often ineffective in the first years of school where children are expected to answer questions and to learn letter names, words, and attributes (color and shapes) of objects (Heath, 1983).

Despite cultural differences in ways of learning and using language, virtually all children learn during their second and third years to take part in some form of extended discourse (Halliday, 1975; Wells, 1986). It may be in dialogues with parents, as Halliday and Wells report, or in pretend conversations in play and monologues, as Heath (1983) describes. Whatever their experiences, children's language develops, along with their sense of what can be shared in talk, as well as in actions, and what will engage the attention of an intended audience. This awareness of sharable topics in relation to the intentions of an audience—that is, *intersubjectivity*—is basic to all communication. It is the I-thou-it—or speaker-listener-subject (and writer-reader-subject)—relationship that functions across all forms of discourse. Talk becomes an increasingly important part of communication and plays a significant role in children's play. Children talk to get attention, to tell about themselves, to ask questions, to imagine, and to accompany their play. Their talk serves more than simply as an accompaniment to play; it mediates and extends the actions, as do other tools and objects used in symbolic play (Vygotsky, 1978).

How Children Learn to Construct an Oral Text

Talk in the preschool years, in which there is an effort to understand others and to be understood, is essential to children's learning the adult linguistic system. In such situations, where meanings are shared or negotiated with participants in the communication, children learn to construct an oral *text*. That is, they learn in a supportive situation to produce language of more than a single sentence that forms a unified whole (Halliday & Hasan, 1976, p. 1).

Halliday (1975) claims that dialogue is an important part of children's language growth at this time because it requires attention to words out of immediate context and a search for appropriate grammatical forms to express meanings. These skills are necessary in the adult system, where language serves three *integrated,* superordinate functions: *ideational,* in which language is used for thinking, organizing, and expressing ideas; *interpersonal,* in which language resources are used for interacting with others and for expressing oneself in various ways; and *textual,* in which language resources (words, sentences, and other language options) are used for creating texts that express meanings intended for a particular audience. These three functions provide the language resources needed to construct words, sentences, and texts that make sense within themselves and within a particular context-of-situation (Halliday, 1973, 1975). Function is no longer simply equated with use, as was the case in the child's linguistic system built during the first year or so; instead, a typical utterance includes both interpersonal and ideational components.

Language learning is rapid during the preschool years. Talk increasingly carries meaning between children and others. It is often ancillary to the action. The focus of attention is on *what* is being said, not on *how* the utterance is structured; however, the routines, repetition, and intonation call attention to the language itself. The process is facilitated when the child's own intentions come into play and meanings are not imposed from one person to another but are shared.

A vital part of what children are learning to do at this time is to construct *texts*, the fabric of all discourse and the place where connections between speech and writing or reading and writing can best be made. Although some aspects of reading and writing are not texts—names, labels, lists, signs, and the like—one cannot become a reader or writer or sustain a conversation without the ability to construct and reconstruct texts that are meaningful within a given situation. As children's worlds expand to include people and experiences beyond the home, they must use language more explicitly to tell about experiences not shared with their audience. In nursery school and kindergarten, children may be expected to listen to stories read or told and to share experiences with a group of children; to do so requires the ability to respond to or to produce a *sustained* text. For various reasons, some children are better prepared than others to meet these expectations (Heath, 1983).

MOVING INTO LITERACY

Most, if not all, children growing up in a modern society, where they watch television, go to restaurants, and accompany adults shopping, have experience with written language. They see writing used in signs, labels, names, grocery lists, and notes written to family members. All are very practical uses of writing and are largely dependent for meaning on the environment in which they exist. This highly *contextualized* writing, especially when it is part of an action ("Yes, that says *stop*," or "Now, help me find the Cheerios"), enables children to make inferences about both the functions of writing and the relationships between visual symbols and speech sounds (Cochran-Smith, 1984; Harste, Woodward, & Burke, 1984).

But literacy requires experience with another kind of written language, one in which meanings are independent of the situation and environment in which they occur. In such *decontextualized* writing, meanings are made explicit within resources of the language itself, through syntactical and lexical features and the conventions of a particular form of discourse. While the function of some kinds of writing (e.g., shopping lists) is to facilitate or accompany an activity, in other kinds (e.g., stories) the written language dominates or constitutes the activity itself. The resources of language make it possible to represent the properties of any situation within the text alone. Such texts are marked by conventions or regularities that are embedded in the culture, that reoccur over time, and that are expressed in language that becomes invariably associated with a particular activity. Texts are understood, Rosen (1984) avers, because "behind every text are other texts, not simply by way of specific references but also in the way it is constructed, how it transforms other texts, pillages them, echoes them—in a phrase, how it *belongs*" (p. 30).

Every story presupposes the existence of others; threads and connections of many different kinds exist and tie a story to other narratives and other verbal acts, forming what narratologists call *intertextuality* (Genette, 1980). Roland Barthes, a French narratologist, claims that "narrative is present in every age, in every place, in every society; it begins with the history of mankind and there nowhere is nor has been a people without narrative" (1977, p. 79). It is these predictable conventions of reference, structure, and symbols that shape and convey a sense that a text is a story and that make it predictable and comprehensible.

When children participate frequently in particular forms of discourse, such as television commercials, or enjoy repeated encounters with a favorite nursery rhyme or story, they are able to abstract a frame of reference or a conceptual perspective that guides their expectations and interpretations of similar texts in the future. For stories, they develop schemes—internal conceptual structures or sense of story (Applebee, 1977) that represents their understanding of such texts. By school age, these structures appear to be nearly fully represented in memory as dynamic schemata (Mandler & Johnson, 1977; Stein & Glenn, 1979). Further, there is some evidence that four- and five-year-old children's descriptions of common events, such as eating at McDonald's (Nelson, 1978), rely heavily on such schematic organization, suggesting a gradual acquisition of a story schema for firsthand experience beginning with scriptlike chronicles. Wells (1986) contends that infants construct a mental model of their world based on regularity of experience. This model later helps them make sense of their linguistic experiences. By reference to it, they construct mental stories about their own behavior, birds eating berries, or Mummy preparing dinner. In this way, "stories are woven into the tapestries of the child's inner representations, producing patterns that give it significance" (Wells, 1986, p. 200).

Parents often help children make links between the personal stories of their own world and those in books by reading storybooks to them and sharing their enjoyment. Example 1.1, which describes two-and-a-half-year-old Emily and her mother sharing *Rosie's Walk*, by Pat Hutchins (1968), shows how in these early interactions children become actively involved in constructing a text around a book.[2] Notice in the example that talk is an accompaniment to playing a game or doing something where language is subsidiary to the actions. Language is central; it constitutes the text, with the author/illustrator acting as a third participant.

As they share the picturebook, mother and child interpret the pictures and elaborate the text. Here are key features:

- They take turns, and the mother structures the exchange and keeps the focus on the text.
- Emily enjoys the pictures, as shown by her murmurings of "uhmm" as pages are turned, and with her mother's help she integrates the pictures and words to make a unified text.
- After the first pages, Emily seems to have learned the routine and initiates her own responses: "Trying to catch 'er"; "He fell into the flour."
- This is an unusual text of one sentence containing a string of prepositional phrases, with the story carried more in illustrations than in words. The words tell only of Rosie's walk, but the mother-child dialogue includes the actions of the pictured fox. The mother directs the child's attention to the fox, to his villainous intentions and resulting doom.
- Emily joins the author as she brings forward the story of the fox and emphasizes his actions: *banged* his nose, *gonna splash*, *fell* into the flour, *jumped* over, *landed* in the wagon, *went* home. Pat Hutchins's words attend to places: the *pond*, *haystack*, *mill*, *fence*, *beehive*.
- The mother mediates the text for Emily by extending Hutchins's prepositional phrase and at times filling in as narrator: "And Rosie just kept on walking." She encourages anticipation and prediction, a basic skill in all reading (Smith, 1979). Her collaboration in the task enables Emily to develop reading skill in the way Polanyi (1967) says all skills develop—with one's focal attention on the outcome of the global task. Emily takes control at the end: "Wham! The fox went home." The very instant *Rosie's Walk* is finished, Emily begs for "More," for "This One," and her mother asks, "Which one? This one? *Goodnight Owl?*" Then in a more formal "reading tone," begins:

EXAMPLE 1.1   A Shared Storybook Reading

Mother:	*Rosie's Walk* by Pat Hutchins.
Emily:	Pat Hutchins.
	(Mother reads that a hen named Rosie went walking in the yard.)
Mother:	What's happening?
Emily:	What?
Mother:	What's the fox doing?
	(Picture shows the fox jumping toward a rake.)
Emily:	He's trying to catch Rosie.
Mother:	Do you think he's going to catch her?
Emily:	No.
	(Mother turns page.)
Mother:	What happened?
	(Picture shows the fox hit by the rake.)
Emily:	He banged his nose.
	(Mother reads that Rosie walked toward a pond.)
Emily:	Uhmm.
Mother:	What will happen next?
	(Picture shows the fox falling in the pond.)
Emily:	He's gonna splash!
	(Mother reads that Rosie walked by a haystack.)
Emily:	Uhmm.
Mother:	What happened?
	(Picture shows the fox covered by hay.)
Emily:	He fell in a "stick" of hay.
Mother:	And Rosie kept right on walking.
	(Mother reads that Rosie walked by a flour mill.)
Mother:	There's the fox.
Emily:	Trying to catch 'er.
Mother:	Think he's going to do it?
Emily:	No.
	(Picture shows the fox covered with flour.)
Emily:	He fell into the flour.
Mother:	And Rosie just kept right on walking.
	(Mother reads that Rosie walked under the fence.)
Emily:	The fox jumped over.
	(Picture shows the fox jumping over the fence into a wagon.)
Mother:	And what happened?
Emily:	What?
Mother:	What happened to the fox?
Emily:	What?
Mother:	Where did he land?
Emily:	He landed in the wagon.
	(Mother reads that Rosie walked past a hive of bees.)
Emily:	Here—Wham! The fox went home.
	(Picture shows the fox running away from the bees.)
Mother:	Rosie got home in time for dinner.

> *"Goodnight Owl* by Pat Hutchins. This one's by Pat Hutchins, too. She wrote *Rosie's Walk."* And Emily replies, "She wrote it by Pat Hutchins!"

So the cycle is repeated. Emily is learning to engage actively in the reading process and at the same time to be aware of a third participant in their talk: the author not only of *Rosie's Walk* but of other favorite books as well. She is learning to attend to the *ideational* meanings of the text derived from her interactions with her mother and the text and its unseen author.

Henrietta Dombey (1983) studied the story-centered dialogue between a mother and her three-year-old daughter in terms of several linguistic and interactive features of the process that serve as "opening moves" for later involvement in reading. She attended to the layers of meaning that became apparent to the child as she and her mother shared the text. Dombey then made distinctions between book- and nonbook-centered conversations on the basis of meaning construction. Noting that in conversation children can take advantage of various aspects of the physical environment, she states:

> But when they learn to read they have to learn to ignore such sources of information as irrelevant . . . [and] to construct information from the interplay between the printed text, the pictures and those instances of common experiences which literary convention dictate the author has a right to invoke in the reader. This means paying close attention to the words on the page. [Dombey, 1983, p. 40]

It is clear that both Emily and Dombey's child were learning essential aspects of becoming a reader. With parents acting as mediators, they were establishing a transactional relationship with a written text in which a reciprocal relationship between author and reader was assumed.

THE SPEECH-TO-WRITING LINK: STORY RETELLING

In early experiences with stories, children build up a sense of what constitutes a particular form of discourse—a sense that contributes to their developing expectations and text-forming strategies. Retelling stories they have heard gives children the opportunity to produce sustained discourse within a frame of reference their listeners are likely to understand. Both Moffett (1968) and Britton (1970) argue that sustained discourse makes an important contribution to writing and that children take a first step toward it when they take over a conversation and maintain a topic independent of the feedback they ordinarily get in conversation.

Retelling stories provides a supportive link between speech and writing because there is a ready-made content previously experienced in language. This task differs substantially from giving an *account* in which firsthand experience must be organized and then coded in speech. Both story telling and retelling require that tellers make meanings clear through references within the text itself, rather than through the shared situational factors that often support other forms of spoken language. At the same time, they must draw on their linguistic resources at both the syntactic and semantic levels, as well as on their knowledge of story structure and conventions, to form a text that is appropriate for their listeners. The texture of discourse, as Halliday (1975) has explained, "depends not only on structuring the parts in an appropriate way and joining them together, but on doing so in a way that relates to context—as narrative, dialogue, or whatever generic mode is needed" (p. 111).

Researchers have analyzed children's story retellings as a means of understanding how stories are represented in memory and how related concepts develop over time. They have found that even when stories are deliberately rearranged with events out of order, children recall stories in prototypical form: setting, initial event, reaction/response, attempt/outcome, final event. The research suggests that traditional tales have conventionalized structures that can help children in remembering them and in producing original stories (Mandler & Johnson, 1977; Stein & Glenn, 1979). They serve not as templates to copy, though there is obviously some imitation, but as a basis for determining necessary and sufficient story elements.

Gardner (1982) and associates in Project Zero found that when a key element of a story is omitted, older children fill it in. They asked children to retell a story (written for research purposes) in which character motivation was omitted for half the subjects but fully included for the other half. They found that even when motivations were clearly included, first graders and third graders had difficulty understanding certain relationships between characters, the characters' goals, and why the characters behaved as they did. By sixth grade, however, subjects could supply motivation, handle syntax, and construct an adequate story. Those who heard a version of the story in which motivation was omitted actually included a good deal related to character actions. The longer the time between hearing and retelling the story, the more motivation they added.

Elements of traditional stories are represented not only in story retellings but also in original stories that children write or dictate. Botvin and Sutton-Smith (1977) observed that many of their subjects told fantasy narratives resembling the structure of fairy tales as analyzed by Propp (1968). Applebee (1977) reported that stock characters, such as witches and fairies, appeared in six-year-old children's stories, although fewer than half the children had firm concepts about the behavior of such characters; by age nine, however, the majority (86 percent) had clear expectations for witches, wolves, and so forth.

Much of the research on story structure and children's acquisition of its form and concepts was conducted within western mainstream cultures and reflects the experiences children in these cultures typically have and the stories they write. Researchers (Brewer, 1985; Cazden, 1983; Heath, 1983) have recently called attention to the differences among cultures and ethnic groups both in child-rearing practices (i.e., those pertaining to the sharing of stories) and in the kinds of stories indigenous to those groups. All agree, however, that the experiences of hearing the written language of stories read aloud and retelling them are highly important to all children as they move toward literacy.

Examples from first graders in the Ohio State speech-to-writing study illustrate the tie between story retelling and story writing. One aspect of that research measured children's growth in story retelling, another their competence in dictating stories, and a third their growth in story writing from the middle of first grade through second grade (King & Rentel, 1982; King, Rentel, Pappas, Pettigrew, & Zutell, 1981). In that study, thirty-six children were asked to listen to picturebook editions of folktales and to retell them immediately afterward to a "naive" listener ("a visiting teacher who likes stories"). They were also invited to dictate and to write stories. Written stories for sixteen of the children were studied through the beginning of fourth grade.

The story retellings of first-grade children varied greatly in length, from 3 to 69 T-units (the main clause plus all subordinate clauses; Hunt, 1965), with the mean at 16.50. The structure of the retellings, determined on the basis of Propp's (1968) identification of fixed elements, also varied in terms of the *type* and *number* of elements or functions included and the *order* in which they occurred. The children's retelling texts contained roughly twice as many functions and function types as the stories they dictated and about four times as many functions and function types as those they wrote. The number of function types used in their retellings increased significantly from first grade to the end of second grade, even though the stories retold in second grade contained the same number of function types as those retold earlier (see King et al., 1981). Retellings that were similar in length (T-units) and structure (as determined by function types) differed substantially in other text-forming structures, as is shown in Examples 1.2 and 1.3. Hillary's retelling of *Squawk to the Moon, Little Goose* (Preston, 1974) was one of the two longest in the collection.[3] Excerpts from the other retelling, by Bill, provide a basis for comparison.

EXAMPLE 1.2   Hillary's Retelling of *Squawk to the Moon, Little Goose*

1. Once upon a time there were four little ducks and their mother.
2. And the mother duck went to visit someone.
3. And she left the little ducks all alone.
4. And the littlest duck was a bad little duck.
5. So he went down to swim at the pond when his mother said to stay home.
6. And up in the sky was a cloud shaped like a fox.
7. And he thought the fox was real.
8. And it was gonna swallow the moon.
9. So the moon went behind the cloud-like-a-fox.
10. And the little duckling thought that the fox had swallowed the moon.
11. So the little duckling went up to tell the farmer.
12. And by the time he had gotten there and talked to the farmer, the farmer said, "Oh, then what's that up there in the sky?"
13. And the farmer pointed.
14. And the duckling hadn't looked up in the sky.
15. And there was the moon, big and round and right there.
16. So the duckling went down with her head held downward so she didn't have to see the moon.
17. But when she went there, when she got to the pond again, she saw the moon in the water.
18. It was only a reflection.
19. But *she* thought that the moon had fallen into the water.
20. Then she ran up to tell the farmer.
21. And the farmer said, "Stupid duckling, can't a man get any sleep?"
22. And, he said, "But farmer, the moon has fallen into the water."
23. And then the farmer said, "Then what's that up in the sky?"
24. And there was the moon, big and yellow and right there.
25. So the duckling went back to the pond with his head faced up so she could see the moon.
26. But while she was walking a fox caught her and took her down in the weeds.
27. And then he said, "Oh, now I'm going to eat you."
28. But the duckling said, "Please don't eat me."
29. And the fox said, "Well, will you give me juicy chicken meat?"
30. And she said, "No, no, no."
31. And then he said, "A duck?"
32. "No, no, no."
33. He said, "I'll give you a cheese as big as the moon."
34. So, the little duckling went down to the pond.
35. And the reflection on the water made it look like there was a cheese there.
36. And the fox hadn't bothered to look up.
37. So he said, "You don't have a cheese as big as the moon."
38. And then she said, "Then what's that down in the water?"
39. And he said, "A cheese as big as the moon."

40. And then he said, "I'm gonna eat up that cheese."
41. And he dives in the water.
42. Splash!
43. And the duckling ran home.
44. And he got a spanking for going out.
45. So the mother tucked him in again.

EXAMPLE 1.3 Excerpts from Bill's Retelling of *Squawk to the Moon, Little Goose*

1. Well, once upon a time there was three ducklings.
2. Well, I'm telling the story about the ducklings.
3. But they were goslings.
4. And they had a mother—like every other gosling would.
5. And I don't know where their father was.
6. And their mother went out on a trip. . . .
   [Little Goose appeals to farmer a second time.]
27. She went back to the farmer's house and squawked out in the farmer's garden.
28. "All right, what is it now?"
29. And the duck said, "The fox ate the moon!"
30. What, the fox ate up the moon—again?"
31. No, wait a minute [said to listener].
32. I'm mistaken [said to listener].
33. "The moon fell down in the water and down at the bottom of the sea."
34. "Could you get it?"
35. "Well—just a minute." . . .
   [Little Goose bargains with the Fox]
48. And she asked, "Give me a nice goose to eat?"
49. "No, No."
50. "I'll eat you."
51. "How about a nice chicken?"
52. "No."
53. "Then I'll eat you."
54. "How about a cheese as big as the moon?"
55. "Well—OK."
56. "Where is it?"
57. "It's down in the water."
58. "Well—OK."
59. "I'll try to get it."
60. Splash! . . .
67. And they lived happily ever after.
68. The moral to the story is, never get out of bed without your mother letting you.

As a storyteller, Hillary begins with a traditional story-opening line, "Once upon a time, . . ." even though the story as written by Edna Preston begins directly with the first event: "Mrs. Goose put all of her goslings to bed." Bill, too, begins in a traditional way but quickly changes stance to address the story listener directly (lines 2–5). Both children refer to the main character (Little Goose) as "Little Duck"; however, Bill pauses to explain that the story is about goslings.

Bill's entire story contains more T-units and words than Hillary's, but her T-units are longer: 10.5 versus Bill's 7.3. Much of the difference in complexity is due to the way each child handles dialogue. Hillary embeds the dialogue within the frame of the story and throughout makes clear who is speaking—except in lines 32 and 38, where she omits pronouns ("No, no, no" and "And then said, . . ."), and in various places where she switches pronoun gender in reference to Little Goose (e.g., lines 16, 22, 25, 33). Bill, on the other hand, relies more on voice change to indicate who is speaking. His sentences are short and often require the listener to infer each speaker's identity.

Hillary's text is more explicit than Bill's in several ways. She uses proportionally more specific nouns, verbs, and adjectives and fewer pronouns to make her story clear and cohesive. Although not evident in the excerpts from Bill's text, both children use a range of conjunctions, the temporal *then,* the casual *so,* and the adversative *but* about equally. However, Bill uses *well* extensively, both in his role as narrator and in the speech of his characters.

Hillary's text clearly retells the story. It is cohesive and coherent, and it shows her ability to assemble her language resources at both the discourse and the semantic and syntactic levels to reconstruct a text she had heard in a way that relates to the context of story telling— that is, as narrative, not dialogue. The development of this text-forming skill is most apparent in the written stories that she also produced as a part of the Ohio State Study.

ANALYZING STORIES WRITTEN OR DICTATED BY CHILDREN

In the Ohio State Study, stories that children produced were defined not as personal narratives (although some were), but as texts that are similar to the traditional stories young children typically hear at home and at school. Stories were so defined because we wanted to relate children's retelling competence to their writing. We limited the field to story in order to get texts that were similar in (1) structure, (2) the purpose for which they were told or written, and (3) the role of language in the form of discourse. In both the retelling and written or dictated modes, language functioned primarily as constitutive to the discourse, rather than ancillary, as is the case in much of children's speech.

Cohesion and Coherence

Story retelling differs from conversation in several ways but especially in respect to the relationships between the participants; story writing differs from retelling in regard to the medium of communication, as well as in respect to the relationships between the participants. Writers must create story content and structure for readers not present. To be meaningful, the texts must have unity, which, according to Halliday and Hasan (1976), is achieved through *cohesion*, or the kinds of semantic relations that occur when one element of a discourse presupposes another in the text because its meaning is tied to that word, phrase, or clause. For example,

> Abby wanted to walk on the rainbow.
> But she couldn't find one anyplace.

She in this short text is interpretable only through the referent *Abby*, and *one* through *rainbow*. *She* and *Abby* represent one type of reference tie, while *one* functions as a substitution for *rainbow*. Reference and substitution are two forms of cohesive ties; others include use of ellipses, conjunctions, and lexical ties. *Lexical tie* refers to the way cohesion is achieved through the choice of words—for example, through reiteration (Some people talk and talk, or laugh and laugh); synonyms and near synonyms (glides, soars, sails); antonyms (heat of summer; cold of winter); superordinates, or hyponyms (mice, snakes, deer/animals); and part-whole relations, or meronyms (animals with claws and paws, hooves and snapping jaws). These semantic relations convey meaning because they are based in languagewide, supratextual bonds founded in experience. Generally, any two lexical items that tend to appear in similar contexts (fish and chips; hamburgers and fries) generate a cohesive force (Hasan, 1980).

Children very quickly learn to make their stories cohesive and to form meaningful relationships within the text itself. Our studies at Ohio State of the written and dictated texts of first and second graders show that children first rely heavily on pronoun reference (using *I, my, his, they, it*), and to a lesser degree on lexical cohesion achieved through specific words. But from first to second grade, the proportional use of pronoun reference declines and there is a sharp increase in semantic relations formed by lexical ties.

These two classes of cohesion (reference and lexical ties) form separate chains of meaning, according to Halliday and Hasan (1980), and make a major contribution to the overall *coherence* of a piece. Chains of meaning formed through reference ties are called *identity chains;* such chains refer to the same person, place, or thing. Those formed through lexical cohesion are called *similarity chains;* they contain references to the same semantic field. In our studies, identity relations initially took precedence over similarity links, but by the middle of second grade children's narratives contained two similarity chains for every identity chain. This development can be observed in three of Hillary's stories written in first, second, and third grades.

In February of first grade, Hillary wrote "The Silly Tadpole" (Example 1.4) on two pieces of paper folded to make a four-page book. In her previous school experience, writing had been an activity that occurred as a follow-up to some special event. The words children might need to describe this event were first generated in talk and then listed on charts for the children to use in their writing. Although story writing had not been a common part of Hillary's school experience, her first story demonstrates considerable competence. It includes a formal beginning, a main character (whose thoughts or goals are revealed), an initial event with a complication, and a final event that promises equilibrium in the end.

In this brief text of six sentences, Hillary forms four identity chains (of reference) by using personal pronouns (he, they) and demonstratives (*the* mom, *the* watertower), as well as two chains of similarity as represented by repetition (sea, sea), and a weak meronomy chain (watertower, water, sea).

The next text (Example 1.5), written in November of second grade, is much longer than the first and contains a greater number of identity and similarity chains. In addition to using personal pronouns and demonstratives, Hillary now employs possessives and manages a full range of similarity relations. She uses reiteration (up, up; down, down) most frequently, but she also uses opposites (started, stopped; little, big); part-whole relations, or meronomy (room, house); and words that belong to the same semantic field (e.g., sounds of gum—pop, bubble, and blow). One gets the impression in this text that Hillary is simply

EXAMPLE 1.4 The Silly Tadpole

1. once there was a tadpole who lived in a watertower
2. and he thought that the watertower was the sea
3. one day water started to drain out
4. and he landed in a little boy's bathtub
5. the mom was cleaning the bathtub
6. and they took it to the sea

EXAMPLE 1.5 Hillary's Story of a Horse That Could Fly

1. once there was little girl
2. and she had a horse that could fly
3. one day she was on her horse
4. and someone said "U. F. O."
5. and she said to the horse "up up"
6. and the horse went up
7. they saw someone
8. and the horse started flying
9. stop it!
10. the horse stopped
11. it threw something
12. on up up and up they went
13. down down
14. oh there is the house
15. down down
16. when they got down the girl said "oh mommy I have been up up up and down down down"
17. "no no you didn't go up up nor down down down"
18. "yes I did"
19. "well you are going up up up to your room now"
20. but when she got to her room she got some gum and blew a big bubble and floated out of her room and down on the horse
21. pop!
22. it popped on the horse
23. but the horse chewed it off
24. and they were happy

playing with words—with contrast, similarity, and repetition—while indulging in a bit of fantasy. It is a story to please herself and any other interested reader who might encounter it, especially members of her class.

"Ellen and Her Magic Dragon" (Example 1.6), written in the spring of third grade, illustrates how an increasing variety and number of elements in Hillary's language repertoire combine to make a text that tells an interesting and cohesive story. Chains of reference and similarity are expanded both in frequency and type, and the proportion of semantic chains to reference chains increases as the writer structures meaningful relationships.

Ellen and Peanut, of course, make up the longest identity chains, but reference is also established through other elements (e.g., wolves, kingdom, and day/Wednesday). As the story builds, Hillary plays across a wide range of similarity relations, using reiteration most extensively

EXAMPLE 1.6 Ellen and Her Magic Dragon

1. Once in a far away kingdom surrounded by trees there lived Ellen.
2. Ellen was a smart eleven-year old with brown eyes and brown hair.
3. She was one of those everyday kids except for one thing.
4. She had a dragon.
5. The dragon's name was Peanut because the only thing he would eat was peanut butter and jelly sandwiches.
6. He always protected Ellen and got her out of any trouble she was in.
7. He lived in the house across from Ellen's house.
8. They had to break all the ceilings through so he could sit down.
9. One of their favorite things to do was to take a walk around in the forest around the kingdom.
10. When Ellen got tired of walking, Peanut would put Ellen on his back and carry her home.
11. One day Peanut was sick.
12. And that was Wednesday.
13. "Darn," said Ellen because this was the day they go walking.
14. "Oh well," said Ellen.
15. "I guess I'll just go by myself."
16. It was a bright sunny morning when Ellen started walking.
17. She walked and walked.
18. But there was something missing.
19. She missed Peanut.
20. Soon she got tired.
21. But there was no one to carry her home.
22. So she decided to rest awhile.
23. Soon she was asleep.
24. When she was sleeping a pack of wolves crowded around her.
25. Soon she woke up and saw the wolves.
26. She screamed!
27. At that very minute Peanut appeared.
28. He picked up all the wolves and blew them all away.
29. Then picked up Ellen and they went back to the kingdom.
30. He was awarded with all the peanut butter and jelly sandwiches he could eat.

(lived, lived; brown, brown; walked, walked; sleep, sleep). But she also uses near synonyms (go, walk; said, screamed; carry, pick up; saw, appear; kid, eleven-year-old), antonyms (sleep, wake; get-tired, rest), meronyms (house, ceilings; hair, eyes), and hyponyms (trees, forest; morning, Wednesday; eat, peanut butter and jelly sandwiches).

Story Structure

Children's knowledge of language enables them not only to form sentences and to express meanings in written and graphic form but also to select words and to weave them together in ways that fulfill their particular purposes and make meaning explicit within a text. A second source of knowledge that enables children to give meaning to their texts is drawn from experience with texts themselves. All speakers and writers, whatever their communicative purposes, rely on their knowledge of differences in the structure of various texts—stories, rhymes, television commercials, cartoons, and explanations. From these experiences, they intuitively and then sometimes consciously learn the form and conventions of a particular genre. Story structure thus provides another means of analyzing the stories that children produce.

Hasan (1984) contends that in all forms of discourse some elements are *obligatory* and must occur; other elements, while interesting, elaborative, or supportive, are *optional*. Stories for children, she claims, must have three elements: an initiating event, which must contain a particular character; a sequent event, normally recursive; and a final event. Such stories may also have a setting, which Hasan calls *placement*; a finale, or formal ending; and a moral. The placement, if it occurs, will either precede the initiating event or be part of it.

Hillary's story, "The Silly Tadpole," has two of the obligatory elements of a story: an initiating event ("one day water . . .") and a final event ("they took it to the sea"). There is also the optional placement, or setting, and if one considers pictures to be part of the story, there is a finale with the tadpole happily swimming about with his friends in the sea. What is missing, of course, is the middle, or sequent, event(s).

In comparison with her tadpole story, Hillary's story about the magic dragon is much more fully developed, as is shown particularly in the placement, for which she writes ten sentences, arresting the story development until line 11. There is a particular character, Ellen, and both temporal distance ("a far away kingdom") and impersonalization ("Ellen . . . a smart eleven-year old") are established. The story definitely occurs in nonreal time.

As she creates the setting for Ellen and the dragon, Hillary elaborates by giving information that is optional but important in this story. She sets up expectations by providing details about the habits and attitudes of both Ellen and Peanut, although attitudes are more implied than explicit: the dragon *habitually* ate peanuts; he and Ellen *habitually* walked; and he *habitually* carried her home, implying a careful *attitude* toward his friend. Many children as they are finding their way into writing stories give this same kind of attention to the beginning of the story, setting the stage for action. Sometimes they spend so much effort at this juncture they are unable to fully develop the middle and end of their story. From the perspective of Hasan's "structure of the tale," Hillary's magic-dragon story has, in addition to the elaborate placement, an initiating event (line 11), five sequent events (lines 16–17; 22–23; 24; 25–26; 27–28), a final event (line 29), and a finale (line 30). Hillary's text is coherent not simply because it has interrelated chains of reference and similarity but also because it has the *obligatory* elements of a child's story, as recognized in our culture. Several narratologists since Propp have proposed more elaborate story structures, but the simplicity of Hasan's scheme makes it especially useful in observing the development of children's stories.

Narrative Codes

Beyond the aspects of coherence and basic elements of plots, meanings in stories derive from various other codes that are historically part of the culture and that are known through previous experiences with a variety of discourses. Barthes (1974) maintains that everything in a narrative functions or signifies, but at different levels. In the ideal text, he says, the networks are many and interact without any one of them being able to surpass the rest; the text is a galaxy of signifiers, not a structure of the signified. Children bring to writing their knowledge of the world—what things are and what they do, how humans and nonhumans behave, how people feel and believe—all of which informs the text. Knowing about peanut butter and jelly sandwiches and the pleasures of walking in the forest were important aspects of Hillary's story. As we examine Hillary's last text, we can see that she assumes with other storytellers shared cultural knowledge and draws on common stereotypes:

- Ellen was an "everyday" kind of kid.
- The dragon ate peanut butter and jelly sandwiches just as any patient, kind animal or human would do.
- As Ellen walked in the forest, she felt "something was missing." A shared cultural knowledge of what it means "to be without" invites readers to share this feeling of loss. It both conjures up sympathy and helps create suspense about what is to come.

Hillary shows awareness of her readers when early in the story she begins to build up expectations. She uses contrast and other literary devices to create suspense and mystery:

- Ellen was an everyday kind of kid, "except for one thing. She had a dragon."
- Peanut was sick and couldn't go with Ellen.
- "She walked and walked. But there was something missing."
- "Soon she was asleep."

Hillary not only exploits the established codes and conventions of the genre to weave her tale; she violates the code as well. She gives the wolves in the story a conventional role, but the dragon is a kind and friendly dragon, rather than the typical fire-producing one.

In her role as narrator, Hillary assumes different communicative functions as she seeks to establish and maintain contact with her audience while shaping the events into an appealing story (Genette, 1980). While her main attention is on the relationship between the events and the overall structure of the story she is constructing, she *directs* attention and sets the stage for action in a long introduction. She *communicates* directly with the audience about the time sequence of the story ("that was Wednesday. . . . the day they go walking"), and she *explains* how a dragon could possibly live in a house.

Throughout, Hillary demonstrates that she can write a story with well-defined characters and related events that are located in the familiar world of trees and forest. It is a world with everyday kind of kids but where fantastic events occur. She can weave the events into a text that is coherent and that has a structure and other conventions that make it recognizable as a story.

CONCLUSION

Children are highly competent language learners whose entry into literacy can be traced to earlier developments in speech. The intent in this chapter was to show how children's language develops over time in predictable ways that signal later accomplishments. Literacy can naturally evolve from speech when children have a need to read and write and sufficient demonstrations from literate adults about how literacy functions for them in life. The point of highlighting some key concepts of language and learning, such as *intersubjectivity*, *intertextuality*, and the *constitutive function* of language, was to draw attention to their pervasiveness in all language use throughout life. The focus on *text* was, of course, to emphasize that any piece of meaningful language, spoken or written, is cohesive, has structure, and draws on cultural connections. These are the places where connections between the four modes of language can best be made.

NOTES

[1] Three studies, supported in part by grants from the National Institute of Education, are reported in King et al. (1981), King and Rentel (1981, 1982), and Rentel and King (1983a, 1983b).

[2] This example was contributed by Mary K. Holt, Emily's mother.

[3] Examples 1.2–1.6 are from the King and Rentel studies cited in note 1.

REFERENCES

Applebee, A. N. (1977). A sense of story. *Theory into practice, 16,* 342–347.

Barthes, R. (1974). *S/Z* (R. Miller, Trans). New York: Hill and Wang.

Barthes, R. (1977). *Image, music, text.* London: Fontana Paperbacks.

Botvin, G. J., & Sutton-Smith, B. (1977). The development of structural complexity in children's fantasy narratives. *Developmental Psychology, 13,* 377–388.

Brewer, W. F. (1985). The story schema: Universal and cultural-specific properties. In D. R. Olson, N. Torrence, & A. Hilyard (Eds.), *Literacy, language and learning: The nature and consequences of reading and writing* (pp. 167–194). Cambridge: Cambridge University Press.

Britton, J. (1970). *Language and learning.* London: Allen Lane, Penguin Press.

Bruner, J. (1975). The ontogenesis of speech acts. *Journal of Child Language, 2,* 1–19.

Bruner, J. (1983). State of the child. *New York Review of Books, 30* (Oct. 27), 84.

Cazden, C. (1983). Adult assistance to language development: Scaffolds, models, and direct instruction. In R. P. Parker & F. A. Davis (Eds.), *Developing literacy: Young children's use of language* (pp. 13–18). Newark, DE: International Reading Association.

Cochran-Smith, M. (1984). *The making of a reader.* Norwood, NJ: Ablex.

Dombey, H. (1983). Learning the language of books. In M. Meek (Ed.), *Opening moves: Work in progress on the study of children's language development* (pp. 20–43). London: Bedford Way Papers.

Gardner, H. (1982). Making of a story-teller. *Psychology Today, 16,* 48–50 ff.

Genette, G. (1980). *Narrative discourse.* London: Blackwell.

Halliday, M. (1973). *Explorations in the functions of language.* London: Arnold.

Halliday, M. (1975). *Learning how to mean: Explorations in the development of language.* London: Arnold.

Halliday, M., & Hasan, R. (1976). *Cohesion in English.* London: Longman.

Halliday, M., & Hasan, R. (Eds.). (1980). *Text and context: Aspects of language in a sociosemiotic perspective.* Tokyo: Sophia University.

Harste, J., Woodward, V., & Burke, C. (1984). *Language stories and literacy lessons.* Portsmouth, NH: Heinemann Educational Books.

Hasan, R. (1980). The texture of a text. In M. Halliday & R. Hasan (Eds.), *Text and context: Aspects of language in a sociosemiotic perspective* (pp. 43–59). Tokyo: Sophia University.

Hasan, R. (1984). The nursery tale as genre. *Nottingham Linguistics Circular,* 13.

Heath, S. B. (1983). *Ways with words.* New York: Cambridge University Press.

Hunt, K. (1965). *Grammatical structures written at three grade levels* (NCTE Research Rep. No. 3). Champaign, IL: National Council of Teachers of English.

Hutchins, P. (1968). *Rosie's Walk.* New York: Macmillan.

King, M. (1978). Research in composition: A need for theory. *Research in the Teaching of English, 12,* 193–202.

King, M., & Rentel, V. (1981). Conveying meaning in written texts. *Language Arts, 58,* 721–728.

King, M., & Rentel, V. (1982). *Transition to writing* (Ed. Rep. No. 240 603). Columbus, OH: Ohio State University.

King, M., Rentel, V., Pappas, C., Pettigrew, B., & Zutell, J. (1981). *How children learn to write: A longitudinal study* (Ed. Rep. No. 213 050). Columbus, OH: Ohio State University.

Langer, S. (1968). *Philosophy in a new key.* New York: Mentor Books.

Mandler, J. M., & Johnson, N. S. (1977). Remembrance of things parsed: Story structure and recall. *Cognitive Psychology, 9,* 111–151.

Moffett, J. (1968). *Teaching the universe of discourse.* Boston: Houghton Mifflin.

Nelson, K. (1978). How young children represent knowledge of their world in and out of language: A preliminary report. In R. Steigler (Ed.), *Children's thinking—What develops?* Hillsdale, NJ: Erlbaum.

Polanyi, M. (1967). *The tacit dimension.* Garden City, NY: Anchor Books.

Preston, E.M. (1974). *Squawk to the moon, little goose.* New York: Viking Press.

Propp, V. (1968). *Morphology of the folktale.* (L. Scott, Trans.). Austin: University of Texas Press.

Rentel, V., & King, M. (1983a). *A longitudinal study of coherence in children's written narratives* (Ed. Rep. No. 327 089). Columbus, OH: Ohio State University.

Rentel, V., & King, M. (1983b). Present at the beginning. In P. Mosenthal, L. Tamor, & S. Walmsley (Eds.), *Research on writing: Principles and method.* New York: Longman.

Rosen, H. (1984). *Stories and meaning.* National Association of Teachers of English Papers. London: University of London.

Smith, F. (1979). *Reading without nonsense.* New York: Teachers College, Columbia University Press.

Stein, N. L., & Glenn, C. G. (1979). An analysis of story comprehension in elementary school children. In R. O. Freedle (Ed.), *New directions in discourse processing: Advances in discourse processing* (Vol. 2, pp. 53–120). Norwood, NJ: Ablex.

Trevarthan, C. (1980). The foundation of intersubjectivity: Development of interpersonal and cooperative understanding in infants. In D. R. Olson (Ed.), *The social foundations of language and thought* (pp. 316–342). New York: W. W. Norton.

Vygotsky, L. S. (1978). *Mind and society: The development of psychological processes.* Cambridge, MA: Harvard University Press.

Wells, G. (1981). *Learning through interaction. The study of language development.* Cambridge: Cambridge University Press.

Wells, G. (1986). *The meaning makers.* Portsmouth, NH: Heinemann Educational Books.

2

FORMS OF WRITING AND REREADING FROM WRITING

A Preliminary Report

Elizabeth Sulzby, June Barnhart, and Joyce A. Hieshima

This chapter discusses how young children's emergent writing can be interpreted when compared with how children reread from their writing. Children's writing samples were collected in group writing sessions at monthly intervals during the kindergarten year. Children also wrote at three-month intervals in individual writing sessions through kindergarten and first grade. The researchers discuss (1) the forms of children's writing and rereadings of their writing and (2) developmental patterns over time, group, and setting. The chapter focuses on how these kindergartners wrote at the beginning of kindergarten, based on a preliminary analysis of the samples. Two surprising

This study was conducted under the direction of the first author; data were collected by the three coauthors. Roberta Buhle of Northwestern University and the Naperville, Illinois, schools did classroom observations. George Kamberelis and Liliana Barro, formerly of Northwestern University and now doctoral students in the Combined Program in Education and Psychology at the University of Michigan, have subsequently rescored all the data, using information from this preliminary study to clarify the analysis system. Kamberelis also helped collect the first-grade data. Many thanks are due to Northwestern University undergraduates Ann Branch, Stephanie Starcevich, and Pamela Hall, and to University of Michigan undergraduates Elizabeth Schneggenberger and Laura Melendez. Data analysis was partially supported by the Center for Research on Learning and Schooling (CRLS) and the Program in Curriculum, Teaching, and Psychological Studies of the University of Michigan. Our greatest thanks go to the children, teachers, principals, and administrators (particularly Dr. Christine Rauscher) of Community Consolidated School District 15, Palatine, Illinois, who made us welcome in their classrooms and shared their knowledge with us.

longitudinal results were explored: the endurance of scribble as a form of writing, particularly with advanced forms of composition and rereading behavior, and the late and tentative appearance of invented spelling. Examples are included in the chapter so that other teachers and researchers may use the classification system.

If one observed only the forms of writing used by young children, one might expect to see a nice, tidy developmental progression from "less mature" to "more mature" writing forms—from scribbling to letters to invented spelling to conventional orthography. However, such an inference would be misleading. A more accurate understanding of the forms of children's writing and how they develop can be gained by observing how children read from their own writing. In the fall of 1985 we began a large-scale, longitudinal study of the forms of writing and rereading that 123 kindergarten children used when asked to write stories. In this chapter we outline the impetus for the study and report preliminary findings. These findings focus primarily on the first data collection in early October 1985, although data patterns ranging throughout the kindergarten year into first grade are also noted.

IMPETUS FOR THE STUDY: SETTING AND RELATED RESEARCH

Researchers from Northwestern University had been working for a year in a collaborative effort in a large suburban school district (fourteen elementary schools, twenty-five kindergarten teachers, forty-eight morning and afternoon sessions) with a heterogeneous and growing school population. We had agreed to work with the district to improve their kindergarten literacy curriculum and to conduct kindergarten literacy research in their classrooms. After a year of research and in-classroom demonstrations of children's emergent literacy, many teachers had begun trying out ideas in their classrooms and were interested in testing the instructional efficacy of emergent literacy practices. In fact, the ideas were spreading so fast that we were in danger of losing any chance of having so-called control groups for an implementation study.[1]

The time was ripe for this research because kindergarten teachers nationwide were becoming aware of the significance of children's emergent writing and reading behaviors. In addition, many of these teachers were disturbed by anecdotal reports appearing in teacher magazines and journals, particularly by reports that included examples of long, interesting stories written by children in very readable "invented spelling." Teachers often interpreted these reports to mean that kindergartners "should" be using invented spelling. When they invited their own kindergartners to write, they were disappointed that many children either refused to write or used different forms of writing, such as scribble, drawing, or random-appearing strings of letters.[2] They wanted to know how to foster emergent literacy in their classrooms and what to expect from their children when they did so.

Recent research raises important theoretical and empirical questions about how children become conventional writers and readers. Although it appears that a growing number of researchers (e.g., Allen, Chap. 6, this volume; Bissex, 1980; Chomsky, 1970; Clay, 1975; Dyson, 1982, 1984, 1985; Ferreiro, 1978, 1986; Ferreiro & Teberosky, 1982; Gundlach, 1982; Gundlach, McLane, Stott, & McNamee, 1985; Harste, Woodward, & Burke, 1984; Kawakami-Arakaki, Oshiro, & Farran, Chap. 9, this volume; King & Rentel, 1981; Martinez & Teale, in press; Martlew, 1986; Mason & Allen, 1986; Read, 1970, 1975; Stewart & Mason, Chap. 10, this volume; Sulzby, 1981, 1983, 1985a, 1985b; Sulzby & Teale, 1985; Wolf & Gardner, 1981) have been investigating children's early writing development, the research has varied greatly in focus. Few investigators have taken a systematic look at the forms of writing used by young children over time with a sample size sufficiently large to deal with issues of development and of individual variation within development. Even fewer have examined the forms of writing by examining how children reread their writing.

Clay (1975) focused on the patterns that could be seen as underlying many different forms of writing. In her pioneering book *What Did I Write?* she displayed examples of children's use of the writing forms themselves, including scribble, drawing, strings of letters, copying, and readable invented spelling. She often used children's statements about their writing to infer the principles they were displaying, but she did not systematically study the rereading or the compositional intent of all the pieces of writing.

Ferreiro (1978, 1984, 1986), Ferreiro and Gomez Palacio (1982), and Ferreiro and Teberosky (1982) have studied forms of writing and children's interpretations of how different pieces of writing can be read. In the tasks Ferreiro designed, researchers asked Argentinian and Mexican children to write given words or sentences (dictation from adult to child) and to read these items back. Using a Piagetian clinical-interview method, the adults then asked the children about the relationship between the forms of their writing, their rereading, and the symbolic relationships involved. Ferreiro does not furnish an actual inventory of writing forms, but she does draw some conclusions about the forms that are most likely to accompany a given understanding about the relationship between speech or compositional intent and the writing forms.

Sulzby (1981, 1983, 1985a, 1985b; Barnhart & Sulzby, 1984, 1986) has investigated children's use of different forms of writing and how children reread from these forms. She has found that children will use different forms of writing for different tasks. Kindergarten children tend to use conventional or invented spelling to write short, familiar words and to branch out to less mature-appearing forms when asked to write sentences, and to even less mature-appearing forms when asked to write stories or other pieces of connected discourse. Barnhart (1986) found this to be the case when using tasks designed to replicate Ferreiro's and Sulzby's methodologies. She also found that children from the United States may produce invented or conventional spelling but give low-level explanations of the relationship between graphics, speech, and meaning.

Sulzby (1981, 1982) analyzed how two classrooms of kindergarten children reread from dictated and handwritten stories. She found that seven categories could capture all the rereadings in relation to these types of stories. Her category system depended on very few of the characteristics of the forms of writing, and although it furnished useful rankings of children and correlations with other measures, it lacked the precision needed to understand the relationship between writing and rereading. The results of a project involving a two-year longitudinal look at a small sample of nine children convinced Sulzby (1983) that the forms of writing and their relationship to rereading were critically important and that the developmental patterns were quite complex but understandable. The forms of writing children used when writing stories as a group classroom activity differed from those they used when writing stories outside the classroom in individual interviews. In a later analysis of data from twenty-four children, Sulzby (1981, 1985b) determined that kindergarten children used the following not-yet-conventional forms when asked to write stories in one-to-one interviews: drawing, scribbling, letterlike forms, well-learned elements (later referred to as "letters-patterned"), and invented spelling.

In further analyses of data across studies and from classroom and home observations, she (Sulzby, 1985b; Sulzby & Teale, 1985) noted that a less mature-appearing form might be paired with a quite complex form of rereading. Children would often use a less mature form of writing to accomplish a more mature compositional task, and their subsequent rereading would also be high level.

These studies had suggested three broad questions: (1) What are the forms of writing and rereading used by kindergarten children? (2)

What are the developmental patterns of writing and rereading? and (3) Do these patterns shift consistently over settings, in particular across group and individual interview settings?

For the current study, we collected eleven writing and rereading samples from each of 123 kindergarten children across five classrooms. The children produced eight of the samples in a group setting in their regular classrooms at approximately monthly interviews; they produced the other three in individual interviews, conducted quarterly. The samples were collected from early October 1985 through May 1986. (Children from two of these classrooms were also interviewed individually in September, January, and May of their first-grade year.)

Our preliminary report addresses three more specific points drawn from the broad questions guiding the study: (1) the patterns of writing and rereading that the children used for the first story-writing task of the study (the first time they were asked to write stories in kindergarten), (2) the fit between the categories of writing and rereading that we were expecting and those that we actually found across the kindergarten year, and (3) unexpected patterns in two forms of writing—scribbling and invented spelling—and the relationship of these two forms to rereading.

THE STUDY: METHOD AND FINDINGS

Subjects

All the children ($N = 123$) enrolled in five morning sessions of kindergarten in Palatine, Illinois, whose parents agreed to their participation took part in the study; children from two of these classes were followed through first grade as well. Researchers from Northwestern University and classroom teachers gathered the monthly group writing and rereading samples; the university researchers alone gathered the samples from individual sessions.

Teachers carried out two roles. They collected data to see if their judgments coincided with those of the university researchers, and they implemented emergent literacy techniques in their everyday teaching. The teachers were observed and interviewed monthly about the implementation and their reactions to what the children were doing. Full details of the implementation are described elsewhere (Buhle, 1987), but some findings about the teachers' judgments and reactions are included in this chapter.

Procedures

First Group Session: Modeling the Forms. The first group data-collection session was critical. In it we modeled five major writing forms used by kindergartners and stressed our acceptance of children's "writing the way kindergartners write." The five forms modeled were scribble, drawing, letter strings, invented spelling, and conventional writing (or "how grown-ups write"). These had been found to be the most prevalent forms in previous studies and in home and classroom observations of five-year-olds. In October a researcher visited each of the five classrooms to introduce story writing for the first time in the school setting.[3] After being introduced as an important visitor, the researcher explained to the children that she had some secrets. First, she wanted the children to write a story for her. Second, and usually after a child or two had said, "But I can't write," the researcher explained that another part of the secret was that she knew how five-year-old children (or kindergarten children) write and that she could read their writings. Then she added, "And, if I can't read it, I have you here, and you can read it for me."

The next step—a crucial one—was to elicit and model the five forms of writing. After the children expressed concern about being able to write, the researcher elicited topics that the children wanted to write about. She called on about half the children after allowing them a planning period to "put your thinking caps on and think about what you want to write about." After the children's topics were made public, the researcher selected one topic and asked the child volunteering it to suggest "how we could begin that story." This step gave children the opportunity to engage in composition. As soon as a beginning sentence was suggested, the adult restated it and asked how the children might write it.

If children volunteered all five writing forms, the researcher accepted their offerings; if any were not volunteered, the researcher mentioned them as examples of ways she had seen kindergartners write. The key issue here was to model the same five forms with all the groups and to emphasize to the children that the teachers and researchers would accept the children's ways of writing and that no one way was favored. An associated principle in the elicitation was not to present erroneous information to the children (i.e., to avoid telling them, for example, that scribble or drawing "said" the sentence being written). This was accomplished by having the adult point to any of the emergent forms (scribble, drawing, letter strings, invented spelling, etc.) and say, "Yes, some kindergartners would write [the child's sentence] like this." She then added, as she swept her hand left to right beneath the printed form, "And then they could read it like this." Conventional writing was referred to as "grown-up writing."

The researcher next asked more children about their writing topics, reminding them that if they needed to, they could always "put their thinking caps back on" when they got to their seats. She then asked the children's teacher to explain how they were to find writing material and how they should go to their seats. (The purpose of this step was to reestablish class control for the teacher, to involve her in the activity, and to get the children moving in established patterns to their seats.)

The next step was for the adults to keep quiet and out of the children's way until they were engrossed in their writing. In this session, as in all group sessions, the children were free to talk with each other, to look at each other's writing, and to offer aid and comments. After they were writing and some appeared almost ready to finish, the researcher announced that there were special chairs in the room: an "author's chair," where a child could come to read his or her story, and "waiting chairs," which allowed a child to wait for a turn without forming a crowded line.

Children then came up individually and read their stories to the researchers. The researcher's elicitation was, simply, "Read me your story." When the child was finished, the researcher responded with praise focused on the story content. The readings were tape recorded, and observations were noted on a checklist, entitled "Forms of Writing and Rereading" (see Appendix 2.1).

Subsequent Group Sessions. In subsequent group sessions, we again asked children to write stories on topics of their choosing, but did not model the forms of writing. In the first three sessions and in the final session, the researchers collected the data; in the intermediate sessions, the teachers collected the data. Researchers monitored the class during all the teacher data collections.

Individual Sessions. In November, February, and May, each child was seen individually and asked to write a story in a quiet spot near the classroom. As the child wrote, the researcher made observational notes of the order of composition and of other nonverbal behaviors, including barely audible speech. When the child was finished, the researcher elicited two rereadings: reading without pointing and reading with pointing. If the child did not point during the first rereading, the researcher, being careful not to introduce extra metalinguistic terms such as "point at the words," or even "point at what you are reading," then said, "Now read it to me again, and this time *point* while you read." If the child pointed voluntarily during the first rereading, the researcher simply asked the child to read the story again. The purpose of the two rereadings was to judge the stability of the speech used across the rereadings. The comparison across group and individual settings allows for a replication of findings from Sulzby (1983).

Story-Elicitation Procedures. Whereas in the group sessions the children chose their own topics, in the individual sessions topics were assigned. To replicate Sulzby's previous work, the children were asked in the first individual session to write about learning to ride a big wheel or bicycle. In the last two individual sessions and in the first-grade individual sessions, they were asked to write about "something exciting or scary" that had happened to them. The examiner's wording was always precise: "Write your story," and "Read your story." Occasional clarifications (such as a researcher's asking, "Is this part of your story?" while pointing to a section of graphics) were worded as neutrally as possible after rereading. All sessions were audiotaped, and the writings were collected.

Analysis. While the child was writing or immediately afterward, the researcher (or teacher) checked the appropriate boxes on the "Forms of Writing and Rereading" checklist. These judgments were based on the examples and explanations provided in a manual, "Forms of Writing and Rereading Example List" (see Appendix 2.1). All the forms of writing used were checked. For rereading, only one category was to be checked, except when a child initially refused to reread but subsequently agreed to do so.

After making judgments during the in-class data collection, the researcher made judgments another time by listening to the audiotape and comparing it with the child's writing in a quiet setting. Thus the first step was to calculate intrarater agreement. A second researcher then judged the data independently, and interrater agreement was calculated. For sessions in which the teacher collected the data, two interrater agreements were calculated: teacher-researcher and researcher-researcher.

Preliminary Findings and Discussion

In all cases of preliminary scoring of group data, intrarater agreement was higher than interrater. For writing, the intrarater agreement ranged from 92 percent to 100 percent and interrater agreement from 88 percent to 100 percent. Initial agreement was lower for rereading, with intrarater agreement ranging from 75 percent to 100 percent and interrater agreement from 71 percent to 87 percent.

As we had anticipated, the judgments for the first session were the most difficult and reflected the greatest number of disagreements during the year. (Agreements for both writing and rereading were in the 90–100 percent range for subsequent scoring.) After discussion of these points, the rules were clarified; some of those clarifications are noted briefly later in the chapter.

Forms of Writing and Rereading Used in October. Table 2.1 shows data pertaining to the first question—namely, what are the forms of writing and rereading used by these kindergartners? Definitions of these forms appear in Appendix 2.1. Although children used a wide range of forms of writing and rereading in the first group story-writing session in October, almost none of them used invented spelling at that time. The most common forms of writing were drawing, scribbling, and random or patterned letter strings. (The conventional category primarily represents the child's writing of his or her name on the paper. We are now treating "name" as a separate category; see Ferreiro, 1986.)

While all the children produced some graphics when asked to write, thirteen of them refused to read, saying "I don't know," or "no," making no verbal response, or shaking their head. However, of these thirteen, six did, in fact, later read. Researchers responded to a refusal by saying, "Well, would you like to go to your seat and think about it for a while? Then you can read when you are ready." Three children were inadvertently not asked a second time if they would read. Another three who had produced graphics said, "I didn't write."

The predominant form of rereading was written monologue. This reading behavior was paired with many forms of writing—drawing, scribble, or letter strings, as well as with more mature-appearing forms of writing. To be judged as having produced a written monologue, a child had to have uttered at least two clauses. The speech had to be judged to be predominantly in "reading intonation" (see Reuning, 1986; also Scollon & Scollon, 1981). Also, there had to be some indication that the wording was more appropriate to written prose than to oral conversation or storytelling. The predominance of the written monologue is some indication that, even though the children's writing forms appeared relatively immature, their reading attempts for these forms were quite advanced.

Some children used drawing as a means of writing, and they reread from it. Some indicated clearly that their drawing was not writing or was an illustration to the accompanying writing; others made no indication that the drawing was not writing. (From previous research, we believe that kindergartners do make distinctions between drawing and writing—distinctions that are complex and appear in different guises—but that they sometimes use drawing as a means of writing. Similarly, they write with scribble and letter strings.)

The distribution of forms of writing and of rereading found in Table 2.1 is quite consistent with data we have gathered in more

TABLE 2.1 Frequencies of Forms of Writing and Rereading Used by Kindergartners in October

Forms of Writing[a]	Classrooms					
	One (N = 30)	Two (N = 23)	Three (N = 23)	Four (N = 23)	Five (N = 24)	Total (N = 123)
Drawing	26	2	19	6	21	74
Scribble						
Wavy	1	9	4	8	4	26
Letterlike	0	4	6	7	3	20
Letterlike units	6	3	2	3	0	14
Letters						
Random	11	17	12	11	5	56
Patterned	11	9	10	11	9	50
Name-ele-ments	4	3	4	1	2	14
Copying (env. print)	0	1	2	1	0	4
Invented Spelling						
Syllabic	0	0	0	0	0	0
Intermediate	1	0	0	0	0	1
Full	1	0	0	1	2	4
Conventional[b]	16	4	12	9	6	47
Other	5	0	0	1	0	6
Forms of Rereading						
Refusal	4	2	0	5	2	13
"I didn't write"	0	0	0	0	3	3
Dialogue	2	1	7	5	0	15
Labeling/describing	14	4	1	1	1	21
Oral monologue	6	5	8	4	6	29
Written monologue	3	12	7	9	11	42
Naming letters	1	1	0	2	0	4
Aspectual/strategic	0	0	1	0	3	4
Conventional	3	0	0	1	5	9
Other	0	0	1	1	0	2

[a] Includes multiple coding for forms of writing and double-coding for 20 children in reading (oral and written monologue; refusal and subsequent rereading; naming letters and another form).

[b] Conventional here includes the writing of the child's name and any other isolated words (all recorded on the checklist). No child wrote story in totally conventional print.

than sixty kindergarten classrooms at the beginning of the school year or when children were first asked to write pieces of connected discourse.

Forms of Writing and Rereading: Expectations versus Findings. The forms of writing and rereading listed in Appendix 2.1 and Table 2.1 were our starting point for determining the adequacy of our category system for capturing development over time. Two points are important to understand. First, we did not know at the outset how important some of our distinctions would be. An example of this is the distinction between scribble-wavy and scribble-letterlike. We suspected that this was an important distinction since children learn to abstract subtle featural patterns of letters, phonemes, and other linguistic units. In this case, we decided to err on the side of overspecifying these subcategories rather than lumping data together and perhaps missing important patterns. Second, while we had begun to suspect that the forms of rereading might be highly similar to the patterns of emergent storybook reading (Sulzby, 1985a), we were not certain that we would find a direct modeling between the two. We knew that some distinctions that can be detected in storybook reading are hard to detect with written stories that tend to be brief; thus we did not divide oral and written monologues into subcategories, and we treated aspectual and strategic reading as one subcategory. Altogether, we were able to keep our checklist brief, and, we hoped, usable for both classroom teachers and researchers.

We found that the "Forms of Writing and Rereading" checklist captured most of the patterns. Because our data were limited to kindergartners, however, we could be underestimating the importance of some categories, such as letterlike units. We do not yet have an idea of the frequency with which this category occurs. We do have evidence from home studies (Sulzby, unpublished data) and from Ferreiro's (1986) work, that "pseudo letters" or "letterlike units," which are nonletters but have many letterlike features, appear in the development of younger children and continue to reappear as late as age six. Letterlike units are not to be confused, however, with poorly executed letters. They tend to appear well *after* a child knows, can produce, and can name a fair number of letters.

Another category that we may have underestimated, particularly in the group sessions, is copying from environmental print. We could detect when many of the children copied items on display in the room. But two other situations may have occurred and been undetected. In one, children who used random or patterned letter strings may have copied parts of these strings. In the second, children who appeared to have produced a conventional or an invented spelling may instead have copied from not-so-obvious environmental print. We were as careful as we could be, but we suspect we missed some cases.

Copying is important for at least two reasons. First, we have found developmental patterns in children's ability to copy from models in the classroom. Second, from Sulzby's (1983) case studies, we know that some children do a great deal of exploration of letter forms, and letter names, and what-gets-copied when they copy from models. We need to know more about how copying functions (see, in particular, the descriptions of Clay, 1975) and to keep in mind that the child may be using copying for a composition different from the original author's.

The patterns of rereading appear to model almost directly the patterns of emergent storybook reading (Sulzby, 1985a); some changes must be made, however, to account for the differences in the two text types (storybook vs. child-produced writing). It is not clear whether written monologue needs to be divided into three subcategories, as in the Sulzby storybook scheme, but there are at least two subcategories: the oral and written mix that is parallel to "reading and storytelling mixed," and the written monologue that currently parallels both "reading similar-to-original story" and "reading verbatim-like story." Since the reading behaviors of over-generalization and self-correction that separate these two in storybook reading would be almost impossible to detect using the procedures for group data collection, we must depend upon the individual sessions, with their repeated readings, to address this question.

A final example of the parallels between the storybook system and the writing and rereading system is in the aspectual/strategic category, another combination of two storybook categories. The relative brevity of the children's stories in contrast with published storybooks makes it almost impossible to separate these two.

Naming letters is at least one form of rereading handwritten stories that does not appear in storybook reading. Although theoretically it could appear as a form of aspectual storybook reading, so far we have not observed it. However, we placed it between written monologue and aspectual/strategic reading on the checklist for that reason and for the obvious reason that it shows that the child is attending to the print on the page.

Two Surprises: Scribbling and Invented Spelling. Scribbling is a much more ubiquitous and tenaciously used form of writing than we had expected, lasting through the school year for some children. Sulzby (1983, 1986; Sulzby & Teale, 1985) discovered that it appeared in the writings of children who also used other so-called high-level writing systems, such as invented spelling. The figures in this section illustrate the range of variation of scribble in our data. Figures 2.1 and 2.2 come from children who composed predominantly with scrib-

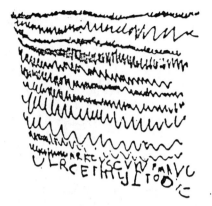

FIGURE 2.1 Predominant Writing Form: Scribble-Wavy

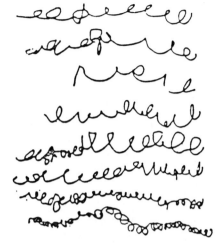

FIGURE 2.2 Predominant Writing Form: Scribble-Letterlike

ble. The first example combines scribble-wavy with letter strings. The second shows the variations of form called scribble-letterlike.

The distinction between wavy and letterlike scribble may need a third distinction. As we devised our operational definition, the issue of differentiation versus nondifferentiation became the dividing feature. That is, if the waves or loops were fairly consistent and formed in the same direction, we coded the scribble as wavy, but if there were obvious variations that did not appear to be due to motor control and if, for example, the child reversed the direction of loops a number of times, we coded it as letterlike. Yet there is a great difference between the rudimentary forms of differentiation and scribble in which clear features of cursive writing appear.

We discovered patterns in scribble heretofore found in invented spelling. Sulzby (1981, 1985b) reported that children begin to explore spacing between words in invented spelling and to show these spaces with hyphens, darkened blocks, column display, large dots, and so on. Similarly, we found children who insert underlinings, hyphens, long vertical lines, and dots in scribble (see Figures 2.3–2.5).

Another interesting characteristic of scribble is that it may be used with composing language and that the same scribble may be reread with the same speech over time (see Figure 2.6). Composing to scribble is often tied to the behavior of tracking the scribble and making finger, voice, and scribble end simultaneously. Some children have been observed to reread the same scribble and to recite the same

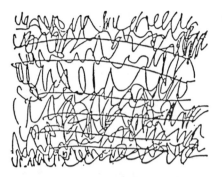

FIGURE 2.3 Scribble (with Underlinings Often Found to Indicate Boundaries) Used by Child Who Had Previously Written with Invented Spelling

FIGURE 2.4 Scribble with Vertical Lines Indicating an Awareness of Boundaries, Along with Letter Strings

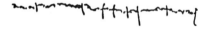

FIGURE 2.5 Scribble with Hyphens Indicating an Awareness of Boundaries

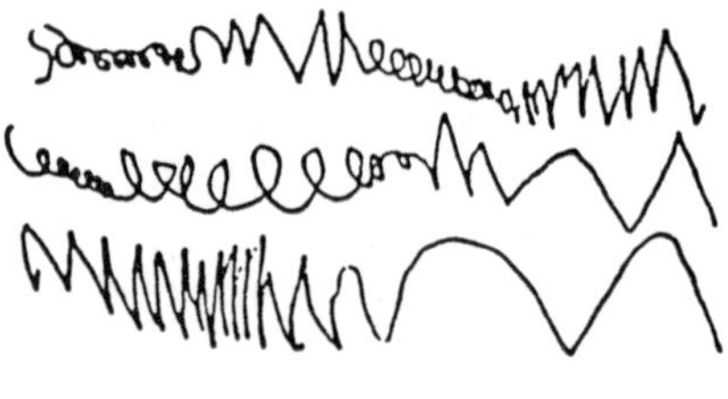

FIGURE 2.6 Scribble-Letterlike Used with Accompanying "Composing Language" and Subsequent Stable Rereading

words for the same portions of the scribble. (One child, not part of the study, who was videotaped for a television broadcast, reread the same scribble four times in this manner at the behest of the television crew, who did not know this behavior was unusual.)

It appears that there may be a developmental pattern, beginning with not matching the scribble to the amount of speech and not tracking the scribble, to beginning to try to coordinate scribble and speech through such methods as saying more words or elongating a final word or words, to accurately gauging the amount of both, and finally to matching scribble and speech by composing and remembering the composed speech for rereading. We have seen all these patterns; whether they fall into a direct line of development within the same child and across groups of children is a question yet to be addressed sufficiently. We certainly know this pattern does not exist alone but is intertwined with the use of other writing systems.

Invented spelling appears far later in most children than we had expected; it is also less ubiquitous and more complex than we had expected.[4] That is, it is for story writing. Our findings of task differences (Barnhart, 1986; Barnhart & Sulzby, 1984, 1986; Sulzby, 1981, 1983) have convinced us that most five-year-olds produce invented spelling for isolated words or brief phrases; however, they use invented spelling less often and later in age for longer pieces of composition.

Syllabic writing, according to Ferreiro (e.g., Ferreiro & Gomez Palacio, 1982; Ferreiro & Teberosky, 1982) can appear either as letters that represent the first phoneme of each syllable or as letters that represent each syllable but without direct phonemic mapping. For example, using the first method, "He wanted a bicycle" would be written as HWTABSK; using the second method, it might be written as MNMNDLM. In the current study, we found no syllabic writing that did not map the actual sounds of the syllables, but that is probably due to the age and literacy experience of our U.S. students. (We have found children of this age who give syllabic explanations in response to the tasks used by Ferreiro; see Barnhart, 1986). For these story-writing samples, all the syllabic-writing samples were classified as part of invented spelling in which the letters were used to map the phonetic elements of the spoken word.

We have divided invented spelling into three subcategories: syllabic, intermediate, and full invented spelling. As explained above, syllabic invented spelling refers to the use of one letter per syllable. Full invented spelling uses one letter per phoneme, and intermediate is anything between those extremes. Syllabic and full invented spelling appear to have a good basis in other research and in theory about how children think. The subcategory of intermediate invented spelling lacks such a rationale. It appears that when vowels are used in syllables there is a shift in kind, but it is not clear that using more than one consonant per syllable is such a shift (because as BK vs. BKS or BKZ). We expect that our data will provide clues and that the intermediate subcategory can then become better defined.

Another finding of this study documents in larger numbers some of Sulzby's earlier observations. Although it would appear logical that a child who wrote in invented spelling would reread by tracking the print, that is not necessarily the case. In other words, if the child *encoded* phonetically, we had expected the child to *decode* phonetically. But a fairly large sample of children apparently did not do this when they first used invented spelling (see Kamberelis & Sulzby, 1987). Many children who began using invented spelling near the end of kindergarten and in first grade did not track the print when they reread it. Some began tracking the print for a few words and then stopped. Others, when asked to locate a given word (e.g., *bike* written as BK), would locate it in the entire written text, in larger parts of the text (not necessarily including BK), and/or would not locate it in the same place over repeated requests. The most surprising instance involved one child who had written for most of the year with invented spelling. She showed a disruption pattern concerning story stability with print not written phonetically (see Sulzby, 1982). If this child was not asked to point to the print, she looked toward the paper and recited the story stably, but when directed to point while rereading (hence, to track), she varied the wording so much that entire clauses were changed. She showed this pattern over two complete replications in the same session. Our task now is to discover more details about how children gradually make the connection between their writing and conventional rereading once they begin to use phonetic encoding.

We are looking for documentation of children who move into conventional writing and reading with little or no use of invented spelling. (We are aware that children's spellings may be called invented spelling well into the grades, but we are concerned with the onset of children's writing texts that others can read conventionally and of their ability to read their own texts conventionally.) At this point, we do not have strong expectations about what we will find. We suspect that we will not find a total absence of invented spelling but rather a strong preference or aversion to using it for composing connected discourse. One of the problems in research that depends upon language production, of course, is the impossibility of tracking all the experiences of young children. Here converging evidence from naturalistic observation, case studies, and more formal elicitations are needed.

CONCLUSIONS AND IMPLICATIONS FOR THE CLASSROOM

Overall, while there were surprises in children's writing development that require much pondering, the children we studied were advancing firmly toward conventional literacy both in reading and in writing.

At the end of the kindergarten year, we predicted that all the children would be writing multiclause, readable stories and rereading them conventionally by the end of first grade. Indeed, this prediction was fulfilled.

The patterns during kindergarten are intriguing and appear puzzling at first glance. On the one hand, we found that kindergartners appeared to use a preponderance of low-level writing forms at the beginning of kindergarten. These forms persisted and changed very slowly for most children over the year's time. The number of children using invented spelling by year's end was not overwhelming. On the other hand, we learned that, so far as writing is concerned, appearance is indeed deceiving. Although children held tenaciously to scribble as a form of writing, its relationship to rereading showed literacy growth.

Other important findings also reflect the complex relationship between forms of writing and rereading. The child's first use of invented spelling was found not to be a clear-cut sign of a shift to alphabetic reasoning and conventional reading. The forms of rereading from emergent forms of writing were found to parallel the emergent ways that children read from favorite storybooks (Sulzby, 1985a) to a greater degree than we had expected. Our overall conclusion is that the developmental patterns of writing and rereading are at least as complex as we had expected but that they reflect a logic that both researchers and teachers involved in this study could understand.

From these patterns, we derived a number of suggestions for teachers of kindergarten children. First, teachers should not expect all or even most children to use invented spelling in connected discourse, especially early in the year. Second, teachers should be aware that the appearance of invented spelling is not necessarily the apex of writing development or the direct precursor of conventional orthography. Third, teachers should not expect children who begin to use invented spelling to reread from it conventionally at first; that may take a while longer. Fourth, teachers should recognize that children who write using scribble, drawing, or letter strings may nonetheless be quite advanced in literacy development.

Kindergarten teachers who are considering encouraging their children to write and to read their own writing may wish to use the technique we used when first inviting children to write in the classroom. Teachers who have used this technique have found that their children write easily and confidently. These teachers then moved into teaching adaptations of their own or into those described by Martinez, Montgomery, Cates, Bercher, and Teale (1985)—having children write recipes, letters to pen pals, notes to parents or teachers, responses to literature, or even complaints to estranged lovers (see Chapter 8). These emergent literacy behaviors appear so freely across kindergarten classrooms of different kinds in the United States that we are convinced they represent natural development upon which classroom instruction needs to build.

N O T E S

[1] After planning a study involving two full implementation classes, two minimal implementation classes, and two "control" classes, we learned that the teachers in the so-called control groups were already using emergent literacy techniques, although they were not identifying them as such. Thus we moved to a descriptive design for comparing the five participating classrooms.

[2] We were convinced that refusals to write and to reread were the artifacts of methodology; indeed, all of our work seems to support this conclusion. (See also note 3.)

[3] This procedure was a formalization of one Sulzby had already used in over forty kindergarten classrooms. It had eliminated almost entirely the problem of refusals in those classrooms, as it did in this study and subsequent work as well. A videotape of the procedure is now being produced through a collaboration between the University of Michigan's Project CIEL (Computers in Early Literacy) and the North Central Regional Educational Laboratory.

[4] Our percentages of invented spelling are far lower than those reported informally by some sources. Sharon Ward, who teaches in an urban public school serving academically advanced children, reported that at the end of her first year of using emergent writing and reading techniques, approximately two-thirds of her children were using invented spelling. At the end of the second year, thirty of thirty-two children were writing multiclause stories in invented spelling. She noted that the emphasis in her classroom was always on writing to communicate and that children read their stories to their classmates. A key factor in the shift to invented spelling, however, came when she asked the children to write letters to Santa and elicited invented spelling from them in a group setting. Such a task, we speculate, builds on the list genre in which children tend to use invented spelling, as well as on another genre that uses well-rehearsed phrases (such as "Dear Santa," and "Love, Jeremy"). In other classrooms with more normal distributions but highly literate environments, like those reported by Martinez et al. (1985) and by Teale (personal communication, January 1987), the percentages of forms of writing are more in line with our report. We need research in various kinds of classrooms in order to understand the relationship between contexts and forms of writing and rereading.

R E F E R E N C E S

Barnhart, J. E. (1986). *Written language concepts and cognitive development in kindergarten children.* Unpublished doctoral dissertation, Northwestern University, Evanston, IL.

Barnhart, J. E., & Sulzby, E. (1984, December). *Children's concepts of written language in emergent reading and writing*. Paper presented at the annual meeting of the National Reading Conference, St. Petersburg, FL.

Barnhart, J. E., & Sulzby, E. (1986, April). *How Johnny can write: Children's uses of emergent writing systems*. Paper presented at the annual meeting of the American Educational Research Association, San Francisco.

Bissex, G. L. (1980). *GNYS AT WRK: A child learns to read and write*. Cambridge, MA: Harvard University Press.

Buhle, R. (1987). *A study of teachers' implementation of emergent literacy*. Unpublished master's thesis, Northwestern University, Evanston, IL.

Chomsky, C. (1970). Reading, writing, and phonology. *Harvard Educational Review, 40,* 284–309.

Clay, M. M. (1975). *What did I write?* Auckland, NZ: Heinemann Educational Books.

Dyson, A. H. (1982). The emergence of visible language: Interrelationships between drawing and early writing. *Visible Language, 16,* 360–381.

Dyson, A. H. (1984). Learning to write/learning to do school: Emergent writers' interpretations of school literacy tasks. *Research in the Teaching of English, 18,* 233–264.

Dyson, A. H. (1985). Individual differences in emerging writing. In M. Farr (Ed.), *Advances in writing research: Vol. 1. Children's early writing development* (pp. 59–125). Norwood, NJ: Ablex.

Ferreiro, E. (1978). What is written in a written sentence? A developmental answer. *Journal of Education, 160,* 25–39.

Ferreiro, E. (1984). The underlying logic of literacy development. In H. Goelman, A. Oberg, & F. Smith (Eds.), *Awakening to Literacy* (pp. 154–173). Exeter, NH: Heinemann Educational Books.

Ferreiro, E. (1986). The interplay between information and assimilation in beginning literacy. In W. H. Teale & E. Sulzby (Eds.), *Emergent literacy: Writing and reading* (pp. 15–49). Norwood, NJ: Ablex.

Ferreiro, E., & Gomez Palacio, M. (1982). *Analisis de las perturbaciones en el proceso aprendizaje de la lecto-escritura* [Analysis of perturbations in the process of literacy development] (5 vols.). Mexico City: Office of the Director General of Special Education.

Ferreiro, E., & Teberosky, A. (1982). *Literacy before schooling*. Exeter, NH: Heinemann Educational Books.

Gundlach, R. (1982). Children as writers: The beginnings of learning to write. In M. Nystrand (Ed.), *What writers know: The language process, and structure of written discourse* (pp. 129–147). New York: Academic Press.

Gundlach, R., McLane, J. B., Stott, F. M., & McNamee, G. D. (1985). In M. Farr (Ed.), *Advances in writing research: Vol. 1. Children's early writing development* (pp. 1–58). Norwood, NJ: Ablex.

Harste, J. C., Woodward, V. A., & Burke, C. L. (1984). *Language stories and literacy lessons*. Portsmouth, NH: Heinemann Educational Books.

Kamberelis, G., & Sulzby, E. (1987, December). *"Levels mixture" relationships between children's narrative compositions and their rereadings*. Paper presented at the annual meeting of the National Reading Conference, St. Petersburg, FL.

King, M. L., & Rentel, V. M. (1981). *How children learn to write: A longitudinal study* (Final report to the National Institute of Education). Columbus: Ohio State University.

Martinez, M., Montgomery, K., Cates, C., Bercher, J., & Teale, W. H. (1985). Children's writing in a kindergarten emergent literacy program. *Reading Education in Texas, 1,* 7–15.

Martinez, M., & Teale, W. H. (in press). The ins and outs of a kindergarten writing program. *The Reading Teacher.*

Martlew, M. (1986). The development of written language. In K. Durkin (Ed.), *Language development in the school years* (pp. 117–138). London: Croom Helm.

Mason, J., & Allen, J. B. (1986). A review of emergent literacy with implications for research and practice in reading. In E. Z. Rothkopf (Ed.), *Review of research in education* (Vol. 13). Washington, DC: American Educational Research Association.

Read, C. (1970). *Children's perceptions of the sound of English.* Unpublished doctoral dissertation, Harvard University, Cambridge, MA.

Read, C. (1975). *Children's categorizations of speech sounds in English.* Urbana, IL: National Council of Teachers of English.

Reuning, C. (1986). *Prosodic features of written language: An exploratory study.* Unpublished master's thesis, Northwestern University, Evanston, IL.

Scollon, R., & Scollon, S. B. K. (1981). *Narrative, literacy, and face in interethnic communication.* Norwood, NJ: Ablex.

Sulzby, E. (1981). *Kindergarteners begin to read their own compositions: Beginning readers' developing knowledges about written language* (Final report to the Research Foundation of the National Council of Teachers of English). Evanston, IL: Northwestern University.

Sulzby, E. (1982). Oral and written mode adaptations in stories by kindergarten children. *Journal of Reading Behavior, 14,* 51–59.

Sulzby, E. (1983). *Beginning readers' developing knowledges about written language* (Final report to the National Institute of Education). Evanston, IL: Northwestern University.

Sulzby, E. (1985a). Children's emergent reading of favorite storybooks: A developmental study. *Reading Research Quarterly, 20,* 458–481.

Sulzby, E. (1985b). Kindergarteners as writers and readers. In M. Farr (Ed.), *Advances in writing research: Vol. 1. Children's early writing development* (pp. 127–199). Norwood, NJ: Ablex.

Sulzby, E. (1986). Writing and reading: Signs of oral and written language organization in the young child. In W. H. Teale & E. Sulzby (Eds.), *Emergent literacy: Writing and reading* (pp. 50–89). Norwood, NJ: Ablex.

Sulzby, E., & Teale, W. H. (1985). Writing development in early childhood. *Educational Horizons, 64,* 8–12.

Wolf, D., & Gardner, H. (1981). On the structure of early symbolization. In R. L. Schiefelbusch (Ed.), *Early language: Acquisition and intervention.* Baltimore: University Park Press.

APPENDIX 2.1
Forms of Writing and Rereading Example List

Elizabeth Sulzby

Following is an example list of the primary forms of writing which we have observed kindergarten children using, along with forms of rereading which we have observed children using with these forms of writing. This example list and the checklist which accompanies it can be used both for research and classroom assessment; the discussion here is primarily addressed to classroom use.

As discussed elsewhere (Sulzby, 1985b), one can only judge the quality of the form of writing by comparing it with the rereading a child uses with it. So-called lower level forms can be used either as low level forms or as the means of performing a higher level task. For example, scribble can be used and the child may say, "I didn't write," or "That's my story," or "See, he loves to eat bones and one day he ran away so's nobody couldn't find him and that's all." Or, the child may reread a very formal story with the wording and intonation of written language, even tracing the scribble with the finger and making the scribble, finger, and voice end at the same points.

The examples are intended to accompany the "Forms of Writing and Rereading" checklist (see Table 2A.1) to be used in kindergarten classrooms during the 1985-86 school year. This form can be used to keep a record of children's progress in writing stories or other forms of connected discourse. (We have not tried it out with other genres such as list writing, letter writing, or direction writing. Notice that the child may write a list when you ask for a story; if so, check "other" and write a note explaining what the child did on the back of the checklist.)

The "Forms of Writing and Rereading" checklist lists the forms of writing before the forms of rereading. When you use it, you can judge the form of writing by looking at the child's page. Check as

---

This appendix is a data-analysis manual used in the project conducted in 1985–86. It reflects a few changes that were made early in data collection but does not contain a number of changes or considerations discussed in this chapter. In training new researchers to use the system, Sulzby has subsequently begun with videotape illustrating the categories of the Classification Scheme for Emergent Reading of Favorite Storybooks and then has moved to training with videotape or audiotape of children's writing and rereading. A revised analysis manual will be available shortly, reflecting changes made during the entire study. All references in this manual are listed in the chapter reference list.

52

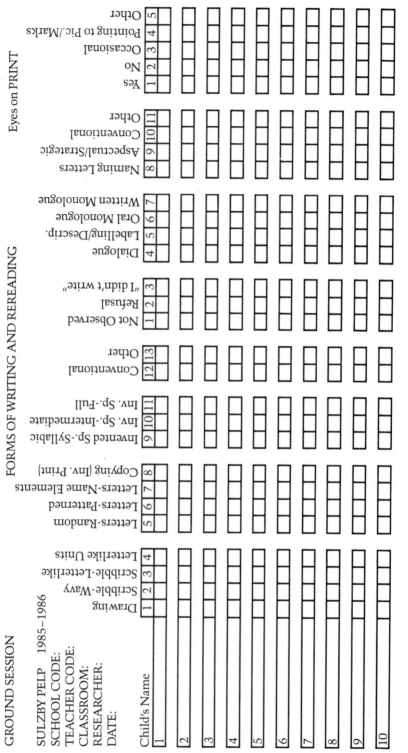

TABLE 2A.1 Forms of Writing and Rereading

many forms as the child uses. That is, the child may use some scribble, some drawing, some syllabic invented spelling, and some conventional writing. Check each one.

You will only be able to judge the rereading after the child has finished. Occasionally, a child uses more than one form; try to decide on one form and, if more than one is needed, explain on the line provided for comments. Similarly, you can only judge whether the child's eyes were on print, not on print, or occasionally on print after the child has completed the rereading. Always be certain to let the child terminate the rereading—when I [Sulzby] began using the form in classroom situations, I discovered I had a tendency to say, "Are you done?" rather than wait for the child's signal, perhaps because I was concerned about time.

In this list the rereading forms are listed first because you need to think about each of them as being possible responses with each of the following forms of writing. On the checklist, they are listed second.

Information categories in the top left-hand corner are primarily for the NU research team. We have assigned each teacher a code number. Use initials for the School and for the Researcher. Classroom means A.M. or P.M. or any special category such as bilingual.

List child's first name and, if possible, age in years and months down left-hand side. It's easiest to list them in the order in which they come up to read. Please note any absences.

FORMS OF REREADING

If you are a classroom teacher using this form for instructional purposes, you may want to hear only a few people read each day but may want to keep this checklist to record the forms of daily writing. Then at the end of a cycle, you could put together a composite of the class with a rereading for everyone.

1. Not observed. In some instances, you will not have heard the child reread. (This category refers to classroom teacher use, not research use.)
2. Refusal. Check this if the child says, "I can't," shakes head repeatedly, etc., after you give numerous encouragements and wait a long enough period of time to feel that s/he is not going to attempt to read. If you have checked refusal and the child reads later, check the form of the reading and write a brief note to explain the order.

3. "I didn't write." This response is important enough to indicate separately. Check this if the child says, "I didn't write," or the equivalent ("It doesn't say anything," "I didn't," "It's not anything").

4. Labelling/describing. Check this response if the child labels items (except naming letters) or describes items written or drawn. Examples of labelling include, "A sun," "My mom," "A dog," and describing is simply a fuller statement, "This is a sun," or "That's my daddy." This category is closely tied to dialogue but it is usually metalinguistic in nature with varying degrees of sophistication.

5. Dialogue. Check this if the child will only respond if you ask questions, so you have a question/answer response pattern. Or the child initiates a question/answer pattern by techniques such as, "Know what, my dad got me a drum set?" (Adult: "Really?") "Yeah, and it's got three drums and a triangle and I can play it." Also included here are one clause statements that do not fit the labelling/describing category.

6. Oral monologue. Check this if the child carries the full weight of responding and gives an orally-told story in the intonation and wording of oral language. The story may be about "it" and "he" and "they" without telling what or who these are. It may have sentences run together with "and" and "and then" and you may be in doubt about whether the child meant clauses to be separated or joined as compound sentences. The intonation will be entertaining and flowing, like that expected in oral storytelling. (There must be at least two sentences or full independent clauses to fit this category.)

7. Written monologue. Check this if the child recites a story that is worded like written language and sounds like written language in intonation. The child may begin with a title and will specify who the people are and what the things in the story are. The story may end with "the end." The intonation may be staccato-like: "Once-upon-a-time-I-saw-a-monkey." Or it may be both staccato and highly entertaining but sound like an expressive oral reading done by an accomplished reader. (You could close your eyes and almost think the child was reading from print.)

8. Naming letters. The child takes an important move toward attending to print when s/he "reads" by simply naming the letters s/he has written. Be sure to pause long enough to be certain that the child is not going to do more than simply name letters or is not going to ask you for assistance. If

s/he does that, the behavior may change to a higher or lower category.

9. Aspectual/strategic reading. I have taken these terms from children's storybook reading behavior but we have now seen a number of older kindergarteners and first graders use these behaviors. The child may sound out his/her own writing, or may simply read a few words and skip others. Or the child may recite the story while looking at print but not tracking accurately. The child is attending to print but not yet reading conventionally.

10. Conventional. The child is reading from print, conventionally. S/he will probably sound like the written monologue category but you will see his or her eyes on the print, note that s/he is tracking the print, and will notice evidence that s/he is understanding what is being read.

11. Other. Check this when the rereading does not fit the other categories. Also, write a brief description on the line beneath the child's name, on the back of the page, or elsewhere. The 10 items listed above appear to be the most frequent categories but they are not all-inclusive.

FORMS OF WRITING

Check all the categories that the child uses. There will typically be more categories of writing than of rereading. Mark a dark bar across the bottom of the box of the predominant writing form.

Please note that some of the categories are related: the two "scribble" categories; the three "letter" categories; and the three "invented spelling" categories. At times, you may not be able to distinguish between the closely-related categories. If so, then make a large X across all those related boxes (one that goes across both scribble boxes or one that goes over all three letter boxes). Make the distinction whenever possible and use the large X as a "last resort."

(Note: Samples gathered for research studies will be tape-recorded and rated by two judges, independently. Any difficulties in making distinctions under these conditions should be brought to my attention.)

1. Drawing. Check this form if the child draws one picture for the entire composition or embeds pictures within other forms of writing. Do not check this form if the child clearly states that the drawing is illustration and not writing. Instead, mark the box with a capital I for illustration. The example is one complete drawing used for an entire story (Barnhart & Sulzby, 1984).

EXAMPLE 2.1

2. Scribble-wavy. Scribble is a continuous (or continuous with breaks) form without the definition of letters. The scribble may be curvy or pointed in form but there will be no differentiation of shapes. See example (Sulzby & Teale, 1985).

EXAMPLE 2.2

3. Scribble-letter-like. This scribble is different from the wavy scribble because the child is using different forms within the scribble, and these forms have some of the features of letters. In the example shown (Sulzby, unpublished data), the child's scribble has forms that look like lower-case E's, or L's, it has M- or N-like forms, descenders as in a lower-

case G or Y. The relevant feature is differentiation of forms, in contrast with the undifferentiated character of scribble-wavy.

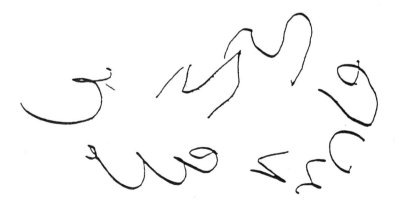

EXAMPLE 2.3

4. Letter–like units. These probably are closely related to letter-like scribbles, but they resemble manuscript letters (or, occasionally, separated cursive letters). The forms may resemble letters but they appear to be forms the child has created. Do not assign children's writing to this category, however, just because the child has formed real letters poorly. You may have evidence from the child's statements that s/he does not know what these "things" are. In the example shown, we did not have the child's statement about the letter-like forms, but two independent judges thought these were not letters but were letter-like forms. Elicit the child's explanation or labels whenever possible.

EXAMPLE 2.4

5. Letters-random. The child writes with letters that appear to have been generated at random. In the example shown, there was no evidence that the child made any letter-sound correspondences between the letters and his message. These patterns would not appear in the English writing system, at least for words which the child would likely be exposed to.

EXAMPLE 2.5

6 and 7. Letters-patterns and letters-name elements. The child writes with letters that show repeated patterns. Letters-patterns are actually the same form as letters-name elements but may include repeated letters (AAABBBCCCOPQMM) or patterns that approximate English spelling (MOVTIXREE-MOOT or DAbAGAWAWA). Example 2.6 shows elements repeated over and over.

EXAMPLE 2.6

Examples 2.7a and 2.7b shown below are actually "name elements" and "patterns" mixed. In example 2.7a, the AN and SU appeared to be elements from the child's last name, but the BO, RO, TO, and SO appeared to be repeated patterns. These patterns often are part of patterns of English spelling, but often they are repeated strings from the alphabet or other common strings. The brief part of example 2.7b shows the child's first name patterns in the first two units and strings from the alphabet at the end.

EXAMPLE 2.7a

EXAMPLE 2.7b

8. Copying. Here the child will copy from environmental print in the room, on articles of clothing or school supplies, or seen out the window. In the example below, the child copied from a tape-recorder and a crayon box and then "read" a story about a different topic.

$$SONrCrayoi?$$
$$\&INNEy\&SMITH$$

EXAMPLE 2.8

9. Invented spelling-syllabic. All invented spelling contains phonetic relationships between the sounds in the spoken words and the letters used to stand for those words. In syllabic invented spelling, the child uses only one letter per syllable, as shown in the example.

$$I\text{\$}WtRABW$$

```
I want to ride a big wheel.
```

EXAMPLE 2.9

10. Invented spelling-intermediate. Just as the title implies, we are using intermediate to contain all the invented spelling between syllabic and full. In the example shown, most of

the spelling is syllabic but the words pushed and myself are intermediate (it is encoded in full).

EXAMPLE 2.10

11. Invented spelling-full. In full invented spelling, there is a letter for all or almost all of the sounds in the spoken word. The example that follows is almost totally full invented spelling, although it has a few conventionally spelled words (such as, I'll and she).

EXAMPLE 2.11

12. Conventional. The child uses conventional ("correct"), or dictionary spelling. See the conventional spelling in Example 2.11. The following example shows a child who wrote a list of conventional words when asked to write a story. This child's writing would be marked as "conventional." If the child reread the "story" by reciting a story, the rereading would be marked in the appropriate box; but if the child read the list of words as, "at, cat, dog," then the rereading would be marked "other," since the rereading system is based upon the assumption of an attempt to create connected discourse.

EXAMPLE 2.12

13. Other. Mark this box if the child uses a writing system that does not fit the descriptions above. Always describe this system by writing a note on the back with the child's name or number. Some of the less frequent systems include using abbreviations, rebus writing, and inventing a set of new symbols (code). (For brevity, no examples are included.)

EYES ON PRINT

We have added this set of categories to expand our assessment of rereading. We could add numerous other categories, including use of the page space, directionality, spacing, etc., but the eyes on print category is particularly important. We have not, however, attempted to make these judgments extremely precise.

They cannot be retrieved, however, from the audiotapes or from the children's written products, so on-the-spot observation is necessary.

Mark yes if the child's eyes are on the printed page all of the rereading time; mark no if they are not on the page at all; and mark occasional if they are only occasionally on the page. You are not being asked to judge whether or not the child is actually tracking print, but you could add a note to that effect, if you wish. (If you marked aspectual/strategy dependent or conventional rereading, that means that the child was tracking print.)

We added the category pointing at pictures or marks for those instances in which the child is pointing and appears to be tracking but the print being tracked is drawing or non-linear units. (This would not be used for pointing at scribble.)

(Note: Not observed and refusals in rereading would imply that the eyes on print category could not be completed.)

3

MOVEMENT INTO WORD READING AND SPELLING

How Spelling Contributes to Reading

Linnea C. Ehri

The focus of this chapter is on theory and evidence regarding the relationship between reading and spelling skills and how these skills contribute to each other's development when they are intertwined in the curriculum. Writing draws learners' attention to sounds in words and to letters that might symbolize those sounds. This creates expectations about how spellings might be structured and makes learners more interested not only in the spellings of specific words but also in how the general spelling system works. Reading exposes learners to the conventional spellings of words and declares which of the various possibilities are "correct." It provides the input learners need to store the correct spellings of specific words in memory and also to figure out how the general system works. Thus reading directs writing toward more conventional forms, and writing enhances readers' interest in and grasp of the alphabetic structure of print.

Many preschool children are introduced to literacy through a variety of experiences. They watch adults reading signs and labels, they listen to stories read by adults and talk about the stories afterward, they learn to "pretend-read" the stories they have heard many times, they learn what print looks like even though they are not able to read what it says, they learn about letters by studying alphabet books and by watching "Sesame Street" on television, they scribble notes that resemble written language, they learn to write their names. Although young children may learn much about print and its functions, they may or may not become independent readers themselves during these early years (Mason & Allen, 1986).

Our research has focused on how young children move into independent word reading—that is, on how they become able to process print so they can read words without assistance from pictures and other contextual cues. Which early literacy experiences enable children to do this? What knowledge and skills does it take to begin reading independently? Are specific prerequisites needed? How does learning to write contribute to learning to read? These are some of the questions we have addressed in our research.

HOW WORD-READING SKILL DEVELOPS

It is important to understand how skill at reading words develops (Ehri, 1980; Rumelhart, 1977; Stanovich, 1980). Mature readers are thought to use two sources of information. The first is *lexical* knowledge. As a result of reading specific words repeatedly, information about spellings of these words is retained in memory and associated with their pronunciations and meanings. These words are then read by retrieving the associations from memory. With experience, this type of word reading becomes rapid and automatic, requiring little attention or effort (LaBerge & Samuels, 1974; Perfetti, 1985; Stanovich, 1980). The other source of information consists of *orthographic* knowledge—that is, knowledge of how the spelling system works, its rules and regularities, how spellings map phonemes and morphemes in speech, and so on (Chomsky, 1970; Venezky, 1970). This information enables readers to pronounce words and nonwords they have never seen before by using their knowledge of the system to transform spellings into pronunciations—for example, pronouncing the nonword *cibe* as /sayb/ (Venezky & Johnson, 1973). For many readers, this knowledge may be implicit rather than explicit. That is, they may have working knowledge of the system but may not be able to state what rules or regularities they apply.

Children become able to read words by using lexical knowledge before they acquire sufficient orthographic knowledge to read words by transforming letters into sounds (Ehri & Wilce, 1983). Researchers (Ehri & Wilce, 1985; Gough & Hillinger, 1980; Gough, Juel, & Roper/ Schneider, 1983; Mason, 1980) have distinguished three stages of lexical development. The earliest approach to reading words is *visual-cue reading*. Words are processed, like pictures, as strictly visual forms. The cues selected have nothing to do with sounds in the word. Children select some distinctive visual feature in or around the word, associate it with the word, and store this association in lexical memory. For example, the tail at the end of *dog* or the humps in the middle of *camel* might be selected. More often, however, the visual cues selected are only arbitrarily related to words—for example, two posts in the middle of *yellow*.

Readers have difficulty using visual cues to read many words reliably over time. Because the cues are arbitrarily related to words, they are easily forgotten, and because different words have similar visual cues, words are mixed up. Mason (1980) gave visual-cue readers practice reading a list of ten words. They learned to read only three or four of the words, they could not read the words when the case of the letters was altered, and they forgot most of the words after a fifteen-minute delay.

Masonheimer, Drum, and Ehri (1984) found that visual-cue readers do not pay much attention to the letters in words they can read. These researchers showed samples of environmental print (e.g., "Stop," "McDonald's") to preschoolers in order to select children who were experts at reading signs. They then removed logos and other nonalphabetic visual cues from the signs and showed them again to the children. This time the children were unable to read them, indicating that these expert sign readers were "reading the environment," rather than the print. The researchers next altered one of the letters in each label (e.g., "Pepsi" changed to "Xepsi" printed on its logo) and showed the labels to their experts. Most children failed to notice the print change even when they were asked whether there was a mistake in the sign and even when the original and altered signs were placed side by side. Masonheimer et al. (1984) have suggested that one reason young children do not process letters in environmental signs when they learn to read them is that logos and contextual cues are visually salient enough and reliable enough to preclude the need to notice letters in the signs. Another reason is that visual-cue readers may not know letters well enough.

Once children learn the shapes and names or sounds of alphabet letters, they are capable of advancing to the next stage of word reading. This stage, called *phonetic-cue reading*, entails reading words by forming and storing in memory associations between some of the letters seen in a word's spelling and some of the sounds heard in its pronunciation. The phonetic cues selected to form associations are drawn from readers' knowledge of both letter names and sounds. To illustrate, readers might learn to read the word *jail* by associating the names of the letters *j* and *l* with these sounds heard in the word. These associations are stored in memory and are retrieved to read the word the next time it is seen (Ehri & Wilce, 1985, 1987a). This is not visual-cue reading because it is the letter-sound unit, rather than just the visual letter itself, that provides the mnemonic link between spellings and pronunciations.

Phonetic-cue reading is more effective than visual-cue reading because the associations between spellings and pronunciations are systematic, rather than arbitrary, and thus are easier to remember. However, phonetic-cue reading has its problems. Only some, not all, letters in spellings are associated with sounds in pronunciations. The first letter or the first and final letters may be processed, creating the possibility that words with the same letter cues will be confused. Also, because phonetic-cue readers lack complete knowledge of the orthographic system, they cannot decode novel words and so are limited to reading only those words they have read before by retrieving them from memory.

The most mature stage of word reading, which Gough and Hillinger (1980) refer to as *cipher reading*, emerges when children acquire more complete knowledge of the orthographic system: how to segment pronunciations into phonemes, and which letters typically symbolize these phonemes. Cipher readers can apply their knowledge of the system to decode unfamiliar words. And they can store specific printed words in memory by forming associations between all the letters in spellings and the sounds in their pronunciations (Ehri & Wilce, 1987a). Achieving this stage is thought to require instruction and extensive experience in learning how letters correspond to sounds.

It is apparent that children begin paying attention to alphabetic cues in words at the phonetic-cue reading stage. Biemiller (1970), Chall (1983), and others have identified this as a very important initial step in enabling children to begin acquiring independent word-reading skill. Chall describes it as the time when readers become "glued to print." It is at this stage, when printed words become easier to distinguish and remember, that word reading becomes more reliable. At what point during development does phonetic-cue reading become possible? As soon as children become able to read a few words consistently out of context? Or only after children have learned to read thirty to forty words using visual cues?

A STUDY OF THE ONSET OF PHONETIC-CUE PROCESSING

We wanted to find out when young readers begin processing phonetic cues (Ehri & Wilce, 1985). We selected and classified kindergartners into three groups on the basis of their ability to read preprimer- and primer-level words on a forty-word list. Children who recognized one word or none were called *prereaders*, children who read from one to eleven words were called *novices*, and children who read eleven to thirty-six words were called *veterans*. We gave each child practice in reading two kinds of word spellings (See Table 3.1). One set consisted of simplified phonetic spellings in which the name of every letter contained a sound in the word's pronunciation (e.g., *JRF* to spell *giraffe*). The other set consisted of visually distinctive but nonphonetic spellings having no letters corresponding to sounds (e.g., *WBC* to spell *elephant*). Visual distinctiveness was achieved by using different letters across spellings and by varying the size and ascending positions of letters in spellings. The children were told the spoken word that corresponded to each spelling, and they were given several trials to learn the words. Incorrect readings were corrected.

We were interested in whether each of the three beginning-reader groups would find the visual spellings or the phonetic spellings easier to learn. We reasoned that if beginning readers use visual cues in learning to read their first thirty to forty words, then both novices and prereaders should learn the visual spellings more easily. However, if phonetic-cue reading is used at the outset to read even a few words, then novices, along with the veterans, should learn to read the phonetic spellings more easily. Results, presented in Figure 3.1, supported the latter hypothesis. Novices and veterans learned to read the phonetic spellings more easily than the visual spellings, whereas the prereaders learned to read the visual spellings more easily than the phonetic spellings. These differences were statistically significant. From these results, we concluded that phonetic-cue reading is possible at the outset, when children first begin reading words out of context, and that visual-cue reading characterizes how prereaders read words.

In this study, we also measured subjects' ability to identify the names and sounds of alphabet letters and found a big and statistically significant difference. Novices knew, on average, the names of 25 letters and the sounds of 20.6, whereas prereaders knew, on average, the names of only 20 letters and the sounds of 6.7. In other studies, we have observed that letter mastery distinguishes preschoolers who can read isolated words from those who cannot (Masonheimer et al., 1984). Knowing the names of letters is one of the best predictors of beginning reading achievement, better even than IQ (Chall, 1967; Ehri, 1983; Share et al., 1984). This may be because beginners must know the letters before they can shift from visual to phonetic-cue processing of words.

A STUDY OF THE EFFECT OF SPELLING ON WORD READING

If it is important for children to know phonetic cues in order to read words, how might this skill be strengthened? One way, of course, is to teach children letter names or sounds. Another possibility is to

TABLE 3.1 Phonetic and Visual Spellings Taught to Prereaders, Novices, and Veterans. Subjects were taught two sets, the set in the middle and either the set on the left or the set on the right. Each spelling was taught as a symbol for the word in parentheses. For example, *JRF* was the phonetic spelling that symbolized *giraffe*, and *WBC* the visual spelling that symbolized *elephant* for one group of subjects; for another group, *LFT* (phonetic spelling) symbolized *elephant* and *WBC* (visual spelling) symbolized *giraffe*.

Phonetic Spellings	Visual Spellings		Phonetic Spellings
LFT (elephant)	**WBC** (elephant)	(giraffe)	**JRF** (giraffe)
DIPR (diaper)	**XGST** (diaper)	(balloon)	**BLUN** (balloon)
KOM (comb)	**uHE** (comb)	(mask)	**MSK** (mask)
RM (arm)	**Fo** (arm)	(knee)	**NE** (knee)
PNSL (pencil)	**qDJK** (pencil)	(scissors)	**SZRS** (scissors)
HKN (chicken)	**YmLp** (chicken)		
	YMP (turtle)		**TRDL** (turtle)

FIGURE 3.1 Mean Number of Phonetic and Visual Spellings Identified Correctly in the Word-Learning Task of Prereaders, Novices, and Veteran Beginning Readers

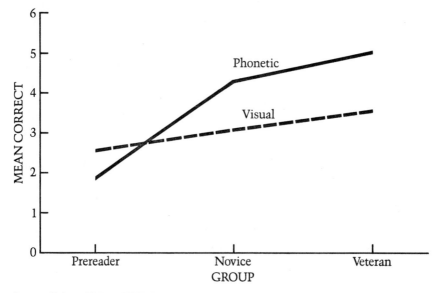

Source: Ehri and Wilce (1985). Reprinted by permission of *Reading Research Quarterly.*

give children practice in pairing letters with sounds, but more than knowledge of letter-sound relations is involved in phonetic-cue reading. Readers must also be able to detect sound segments in pronunciations of words so that letters in spellings can be associated with these sounds. One activity that develops both letter-sound knowledge and sound-segmentation skill is learning to spell. We decided to investigate whether training beginners to spell words phonetically would facilitate their ability to use phonetic cues to read words, and whether this training would be superior to letter-sound practice (Ehri & Wilce, 1987b).

The children selected for study were kindergartners who were able to read, on average, only four words on a preprimer list of twenty-two words, who knew nine of the ten letters to be used during training, but who could neither spell words with consonant clusters nor read any of the words to be taught in the word-learning task. Children were randomly assigned either to the experimental group who received training in phonetic spelling or to the control group who received letter-sound training. The experimental group was taught to use letter tiles to spell words and nonwords consisting of *cvs* (c stands for consonant, *v* for vowel), *vcs*, *cvcs*, *ccvs*, *ccvcs*, *vccs*, and *cvccs*. A total of ten sounds—six consonants and four long vowels—were practiced in spelling these words. Examples of the words are *na, el, sip, sto, stak, ens, tins,* each pronounced with a long vowel and spelled phonetically. The control group practiced matching the same ten letter tiles to their isolated sounds for many trials. After training, both groups of children were given a test in which they were told how to read a list of twelve similarly spelled words and were given seven trials to learn to read them. Examples of words taught are *sals* (sails), *sel* (seal), *slis* (slice), *sop* (soap), *ston* (stone). (Printed forms appear in italics, pronunciations in parentheses.) We wanted to see whether the subjects who received training in phonetic spelling would learn to read more of the words than control subjects. If so, this would indicate that such training facilitates phonetic-cue reading.

The results are presented in Figure 3.2. Clearly, children who received spelling training learned to read the words more effectively than those who had been trained in letter sounds. We also examined how children read the words. From Figure 3.2 it is evident that neither group learned to read most of the words. One reason was that the words were similarly spelled and hard to distinguish for subjects who were using only some of the letters to remember how to read the

FIGURE 3.2   Mean Number of Words Read Correctly Across Trials in the Word-Learning Task for Subjects Given Phonetic-Spelling Training and for Control Subjects Given Letter-Sound Training

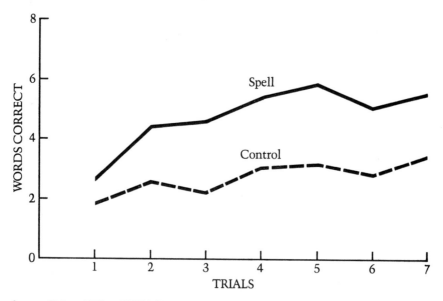

Source: Ehri and Wilce (1987b). Reprinted by permission of *Reading Research Quarterly.*

words. We calculated correlations between the extent of letter overlap shared by each word with the other words and the number of subjects reading each word correctly at least twice. Results revealed high negative values, particularly among spelling-trained subjects ($r = -.91$ for trained, $-.60$ for controls), indicating that words sharing more letters with other words were harder to learn to read. Additional evidence that subjects were using partial phonetic cues to read words came from analyzing their misreadings. The proportion of letters that were given plausible pronunciations was significantly higher among spelling-trained subjects than among control subjects (66 percent versus 49 percent), indicating that trained subjects were processing more phonetic cues.

One advantage provided by spelling training was that it enabled subjects to segment pronunciations into their phonetic constituents. This ability was evident on a posttest in which trained subjects divided more nonsense words correctly into sounds than did control subjects. Segmentation differences favoring experimentals were especially large on consonant clusters (e.g., *st-, sl-, sn-, -ts, -ls, -ns*), which are known to be hard for novice readers to divide into sound (Treiman, 1985). In the word-learning task, trained subjects also learned to read more words with consonant clusters than controls did.

From this study, we concluded that learning to spell contributed to beginners' ability to read words because it enabled children to process phonetic cues in the words. Phonetic-cue processing was probably helped by the training in phonetic-segmentation that children received as part of spelling instruction. The advantage we observed was not due to superior letter-sound knowledge, because both groups practiced letter-sound relations. It was also not a result of superior skill in sounding out and blending words. Experimental subjects did not use this strategy more successfully than control subjects to read words because they were not very good at it; spelling training does not teach blending skill.

Other studies also provide evidence that reading and spelling are highly correlated. In samples of first graders, the correlations ranged from .68 to .86 (Morris & Perney, 1984; Roper/Schneider, 1983). In second graders, the correlation was .66, and in fifth graders, it was .60 (Shanahan, 1984). Chomsky (1979) showed how learning to write can precede and facilitate learning to read. Our findings thus corroborate and extend earlier findings.

In drawing conclusions, we should point out that we designed our study to examine processes that are important in learning to read and spell, not to identify specific methods of teaching those processes. Although we used a highly structured task that included using nonsense syllables to teach children to spell, we are not suggesting that this is necessarily the way to handle phonetic-spelling instruction in class-rooms. Which methods are most effective has still to be determined. Our guess is that methods that not only teach children how to make their spellings more phonetic but also engage them in meaningful writing activities will turn out to be the most effective, as well as the most motivating.

We believe our results carry implications for instruction. They suggest that learning to spell phonetically at the outset can help a child learn to read. However, we recognize that there may be problems in implementing this suggestion. Because English words are typically not spelled completely phonetically, children who practice writing real words will misspell the words. In addition, when novices first begin generating spellings of words, their inventions will necessarily deviate substantially from correct forms because they are at an early, immature stage of spelling development. In fact, misspellings may predominate for a prolonged period before children can easily remember the correct spellings of words. Teachers of primary grades may be reluctant to allow their students to misspell words because they fear errors will persist and the children will develop into poor spellers. An alternative approach is to have beginners rote memorize correct spellings of words. However, because English spellings are variable and not strictly regular, beginners' knowledge of the spelling *system* may not develop from this sort of practice. Juel and Roper/Schneider (1985) found that children who learned decoding rules but then practiced reading words that did not conform to the letter-sound relations with which they were familiar did not learn to apply a decoding strategy in reading words. The same may be true in learning to spell.

HOW SPELLING SKILL DEVELOPS:
A CASE STUDY

To assess whether teachers' concerns about allowing students to misspell are legitimate, it is important to examine how people generate spellings of words and how spelling skill develops. People are thought to draw from two sources of information in spelling words: information about specific words stored in memory, and knowledge of how the general spelling system works (Ehri, 1986; Jorm, 1983; Simon, 1976; Simon & Simon, 1973). Spellers acquire both sources of information from their reading and from their spelling experience. They remember which letters symbolize sounds in the conventional spellings of specific words, as well as visual properties of words, such as length. Spellers also learn which letters typically symbolize particular sounds across many words, how to segment pronunciations into sound units, typical positions of letters in words, and so forth. When spelling a word, they first look in memory for specific information about the word. If it is not there or only partially there, then they use their general knowledge to invent a spelling or to supplement the recalled spelling.

It takes several years for children to develop spelling proficiency. Not only must they learn how the general system works; they must also store spellings of many specific words in memory. The spellings listed in Table 3.2 illustrate the course of spelling development. They were produced by a boy of average reading and spelling ability during first and second grades. At the time of the first test, he could read only a few words in isolation. By the fifth and final test, he was reading words at grade level. The spelling test of twenty words was given five times during the two-year period by the classroom teacher, who never taught these words directly to the students. When they wrote,

TABLE 3.2 Spelling Test of Twenty Words Dictated to One Student Five Times over a Two-year Period. Correct Spellings are Underlined.

Words	Test 1 (Grade 1.3)	Test 2 (Grade 1.6)	Test 3 (Grade 1.9)	Test 4 (Grade 2.3)	Test 5 (Grade 2.8)
rag	l	RG	rag	rag	rag
buzz	BP	BZ	Boz	buz	buzz
lid	E	LD	lad	lid	lid
six	6	SS	sis	siks	six
game		GEM	gam	gars	game
nice	SAT	Nis	nis	nis	nice
doctor	DA	DOD	did	doktdr	doctor
view	Y	vyou	vo	vu	view
yellow		yellw	yao	yellow	yellow
kiss	C	kits	kis	kiss	kis
camp	MP	CAP	cap	kap	camp
zero	O	ZW	zio	ziro	zero
hill		Hill	ole	hil	hill
tack	P	TAK	tac	tac	tack
five	5	FAV	fi	five	five
pickle	PO	PL	pal	pikl	pikel
muffin	KO	MN	mufn	mufin	muffen
wife	l	yuf	wif	wif	wife
job		JB	jig	job	job
quick	Ka	KWK	cwy	kwic	quice

children in this classroom were encouraged to invent spellings. They encountered correct forms of words mainly in their readings.

Table 3.2 shows that the number of correctly spelled words (underlined in the table) that the boy produced increased from the first to the fifth test, slowly at first and then dramatically at the end: zero, one, one, six, and sixteen words correct, respectively. In addition, although in the first three tests the boy spelled few words correctly, the quality of his spellings changed markedly during this time, from forms that bore little resemblance to the words to forms that symbolized a number of sounds in the words. This progression indicates that much happens to spelling ability early in the process, before children develop much skill at spelling words correctly. In fact, consistently correct spellings may be fairly late to develop, as they were with this child.

Researchers have examined the kinds of spellings young children produce when they do not know the correct spellings of the words (Ehri, 1986; Gentry, 1982; Henderson, 1981; Morris & Perney, 1984). These spelling inventions have suggested four stages of development in knowledge about the orthographic system. Although each of these stages denotes a discrete period of development, the boundaries of one stage may overlap with those of the next. At the earliest stage, called *precommunicative,* children produce scribbles, strings of randomly selected letters, or numbers to represent words or sentences. At this stage, children may know only a few letters and may not differentiate them from numbers, and when they select letters for words, it is not because the letters correspond to sounds. The first test in Table 3.2 shows a few precommunicative spellings—for example, *P* (for *tack*) and *KO* (for *muffin*). This stage may begin very early when preschoolers begin noticing what written language looks like and where to find it; it parallels the visual-cue stage of word reading.

The next stage, called *semiphonetic,* begins when children learn the names or sounds of letters and use this knowledge to select letters for their spellings. At the onset, only one or two of the letters may correspond to sounds. However, as children gain more experience with print, they become able to detect and spell more sounds in words. In the first test in Table 3.2, 40 percent of the spellings produced were semiphonetic, and most included only one letter corresponding to a sound. In the second and third tests, all the spellings contained letters symbolizing sounds; most included two such letters. Examples of semiphonetic spellings are *BP* (for *buzz*) and *PL* (for *pickle*). Letter names may be the basis for selecting letters—for example, *y* (named *wie*) used to spell *wife* as *yuf*, and, as Read (1971) reported, *h* (named *aich*) used to spell *chicken* as *hkn*. This stage parallels the phonetic-cue-reading stage at which children use partial letter-sound cues to read words.

Although children's letter choices may violate spelling conventions, they are nevertheless logical and indicate that learners are attempting to use what they know about letters to figure out how the spelling system works. Nonconventional choices, such as *y* for *w* and *h* for *ch*, typically appear early in development but subsequently disappear as learners discover that the conventional system works another way. Note in Table 3.2 that *yuf* changes to *wif* at the next test period.

At the semiphonetic stage, children may know very few correct spellings of words. In Table 3.2, no words were spelled conventionally during the first test, and only one word was spelled correctly during the second and third tests. As indicated by the correct spelling of *hill* in the second test and its incorrect spelling in the next two tests, memory for correct spellings may be unstable during this stage.

Third is the *phonetic* stage, which occurs when children become able to produce spellings that contain letters for all the sounds in words. In the second and third tests in Table 3.2, 10 percent to 25 percent of the spellings are phonetic, but phonetic spellings do not predominate until the fourth test, where they account for 91 percent of the total. One of the most important acquisitions that distinguishes the phonetic stage from the semiphonetic stage is the ability to spell vowels. In Table 3.2, vowel accuracy rose from 40 percent in the second test to 100 percent accuracy in the fourth test.

During the phonetic stage, children begin to believe that every sound they detect in a pronunciation requires a letter in the spelling. In stretching out pronunciations to spell words, children may even find extra sounds not symbolized in conventional spellings but detectable in pronunciations—for example, DOKTDR (for *doctor*). However, the ability to detect the preconsonantal nasal in such words as *camp*, *bend*, and *sink* is late to develop, because the nasal is not articulated separately but instead overlays the vowel (Read, 1971).

Acquiring the idea that words consist of a sequence of phonemes is a very important insight for the development of both reading and spelling skill. In fact, phonemic awareness is one of the best predictors of how well children learn to read (Bryant & Bradley, 1985; Juel, Griffith, & Gough, 1986; Share et al., 1984). According to our theory, phonemic awareness is the capability that enables children to analyze and to store complete spellings of words in memory (Ehri, 1980, 1984).

It may be that children who know how to spell words phonetically have a much easier time remembering the correct spellings of English words than children who do not. Some evidence for the relationship between phonetic-spelling ability and memory for correct spellings is apparent in Table 3.2. It was not until the final test that this child was able to spell the majority of the words (80 percent) correctly. In the preceding test, only 30 percent of his words were correct. Interestingly, the number of his correct spellings surged only after his ability to spell words phonetically matured (in the fourth test). This suggests that children may need to learn how the orthographic system works phonetically before they can store the correct spellings of very many English words in memory. Because different letters may symbolize the same sounds in English words (e.g., the *s* and *c* in *sit* and *city*) and because all the letters may or may not symbolize sounds, knowing the phonetic system may enhance memory for letters that are instances of regularities and may reduce the number of letters that need to be remembered as variations or deviations. For example, it may be easier to remember that *hill* has two *l*'s, that *listen* has a silent *t*, and that *city* is spelled with *c* rather than *s* if the learner knows the system and can recognize how the other letters in the word symbolize sounds. The correct spelling of *hill* in the second test and its subsequent misspellings is another indication that memory for spellings may be unstable if the phonetic system has not been mastered.

Another interesting observation in Table 3.2 is that most of the misspellings were not repeated from one test to the next. In fact, 90 percent changed. The few that did not change were phonetic spellings (*wif, tac, nis*) that were correct by the final test period. These results indicate that, contrary to the beliefs of some teachers, children may not remember their misspellings—that misspellings may not linger in memory or delay the acquisition of correct spellings. Because children's knowledge of the system is developing, their inventions would be expected not to remain the same but to change, reflecting the growth that has occurred in their systematic knowledge.

In a study that examined whether producing misspellings at the outset of learning delays learning the correct spellings of words (Ehri, Gibbs, & Underwood, in press), children and college students were taught the correct spellings of a set of made-up words. Before they studied the correct spellings, half the subjects were directed to invent their own spellings, most of which were incorrect. Results showed that spelling errors had no deleterious effects on learning correct forms. Both groups learned correct spellings with equal ease.

The final stage of spelling development is called the *morphemic* stage because spellers begin recognizing and using word-based spelling patterns when these are seen as more appropriate than phonetic spelling—for example, spelling past-tense verbs consistently with -*ed* rather than according to their sounds (*woched* rather than *wocht* for *watched*). This stage is thought to emerge after children learn the conventional spellings of several specific words and begin recognizing spelling patterns that recur across words. None of the misspellings in Table 3.2 exhibits morphemic-stage characteristics.

According to our stage theory of spelling development, it is natural for beginning readers and spellers to misspell words. Learning about the English orthographic system requires time and experience. Allowing children to practice what they know about the system by inventing spellings of words appears not to inhibit development but, rather, to enhance progress in learning to spell and read; this may be particularly true if children receive instruction in how to generate phonetic spellings, as our research has indicated. In sum, more research is needed to substantiate our portrayal of spelling development and its relationship to reading. Some of our conclusions are based on preliminary data. However, our characterization is plausible and consistent with the evidence to date.

CONCLUSION

We believe that spelling contributes to the development of reading and likewise that reading contributes to spelling development when the two are intertwined in school curricula. Writing draws learners' attention to sounds in words and to letters that might symbolize those sounds; this creates expectations about how spellings might be structured and makes learners more interested in the spellings of specific words, as well as in how the general spelling system works. Reading exposes learners to the conventional spellings of words and indicates which of the various possibilities are "correct." Reading provides the input learners need to store the correct spellings of specific words in memory and also to figure out how the general system works. Thus reading directs writing toward more conventional forms, and writing enhances readers' interest in and grasp of the alphabetic structure of print.

R E F E R E N C E S

Biemiller, A. (1970). The development of the use of graphic and contextual information as children learn to read. *Reading Research Quarterly, 6,* 75–96.

Bryant, P., & Bradley, L. (1985). *Children's reading problems.* Oxford: Blackwell.

Chall, J. S. (1967). *Learning to read: The great debate.* New York: McGraw-Hill.

Chall, J. S. (1983). *Stages of reading development.* New York: McGraw-Hill.

Chomsky, C. (1970). Reading, writing and phonology. *Harvard Educational Review, 40,* 287–309.

Chomsky, C. (1979). Approaching reading through invented spelling. In L. B. Resnick & P. A. Weaver (Eds.), *Theory and practice of early reading* (Vol. 2, pp. 43–65). Hillsdale, NJ: Erlbaum.

Ehri, L. C. (1980). The development of orthographic images. In U. Frith (Ed.), *Cognitive processes in spelling* (pp. 311–338). London: Academic Press.

Ehri, L. C. (1983). Summaries and a critique of five studies related to letter-name knowledge and learning to read. In L. Gentile, M. Kamil, & J. Blanchard (Eds.), *Reading research revisited* (pp. 131–153). Columbus, OH: Merrill.

Ehri, L. C. (1984). How orthography alters spoken language competencies in children learning to read and spell. In J. Downing & R. Valtin (Eds.), *Language awareness and learning to read* (pp. 119–147). New York: Springer Verlag.

Ehri, L. C. (1986). Sources of difficulty in learning to spell and read words. In M. L. Wolraich & D. Routh (Eds.), *Advances in developmental and behavioral pediatrics* (pp. 121–195). Greenwich, CT: JAI Press.

Ehri, L. C., Gibbs, A., & Underwood, T. (in press). Influence of errors in learning the spellings of English words. *Contemporary Educational Psychology*.

Ehri, L. C., & Wilce, L. S. (1983). Development of word identification speed in skilled and less skilled beginning readers. *Journal of Educational Psychology, 75*, 3–18.

Ehri, L. C., & Wilce, L. S. (1985). Movement into reading: Is the first stage of printed word learning visual or phonetic? *Reading Research Quarterly, 20*, 163–179.

Ehri, L. C., & Wilce, L. S. (1987a). Cipher versus cue reading: An experiment in decoding acquisition. *Journal of Educational Psychology, 79*, 3–13.

Ehri, L. C., & Wilce, L. S. (1987b). Does learning to spell help beginners learn to read words? *Reading Research Quarterly, 22*, 47–65.

Gentry, J. R. (1982). An analysis of developmental spelling in GNYS AT WRK. *The Reading Teacher, 36*, 192–200.

Gough, P. B., & Hillinger, M. L. (1980). Learning to read: An unnatrual act. *Bulletin of the Orton Society, 30*, 180–196.

Gough, P. B., Juel, C., & Roper/Schneider, D. (1983). Code and cipher: A two-stage conception of initial reading acquisition. In J. A. Niles & L. A. Harris (Eds.), *Searches for meaning in reading/language processing and instruction: Thirty-second yearbook of the National Reading Conference* (pp. 207–211). Rochester, NY: National Reading Conference.

Henderson, E. H. (1981). *Learning to read and spell.* DeKalb: Northern Illinois University Press.

Jorm, A. F. (1983). *The psychology of reading and spelling disabilities.* London: Routledge & Kegan Paul.

Juel, C., Griffith, P. L., & Gough, P. B. (1986). Acquisition of literacy: A longitudinal study of children in first and second grade. *Journal of Educational Psychology, 78*, 243–255.

Juel, C., & Roper/Schneider, D. (1985). The influence of basal readers on first grade reading. *Reading Research Quarterly, 20*, 134–152.

LaBerge, D., & Samuels, S. J. (1974). Toward a theory of automatic information processing in reading. *Cognitive Psychology, 6*, 293–323.

Mason, J. (1980). When *do* children begin to read: An exploration of four-year-old children's letter and word reading competencies. *Reading Research Quarterly, 15*, 203–227.

Mason, J., & Allen, J. (1986). A review of emergent literacy with implications for research and practice in reading. In R. Rothkopf (Ed.), *Review of research in education* (pp. 3–47). Washington, D.C.: American Educational Research Association.

Masonheimer, P. E., Drum, P. A., & Ehri, L. C. (1984). Does environmental print identification lead children into word reading? *Journal of Reading Behavior, 16,* 257–271.

Morris, D., & Perney, J. (1984). Developmental spelling as a predictor of first-grade reading achievement. *The Elementary School Journal, 84,* 441–457.

Perfetti, C. A. (1985). *Reading ability.* New York: Oxford University Press.

Read, C. (1971). Preschool children's knowledge of English phonology. *Harvard Educational Review, 41,* 1–34.

Roper/Schneider, D. (1983, December). *Spelling as an independent skill and in its relationship to reading.* Paper presented at annual meeting of the National Reading Conference, Austin, TX.

Rumelhart, D. E. (1977). Toward an interactive model of reading. In S. Dornic (Ed.), *Attention and performance* (Vol. 6). Hillsdale, NJ: Erlbaum.

Shanahan, T. (1984). Nature of the reading-writing relation: An exploratory multivariate analysis. *Journal of Educational Psychology, 76,* 466–477.

Share, D. L., Jorm, A. F., Maclean, R., & Matthews, R. (1984). Sources of individual differences in reading acquisition. *Journal of Educational Psychology, 76,* 1309–1324.

Simon, D. P. (1976). Spelling—a task analysis. *Instructional Science, 5,* 277–302.

Simon, D. P., & Simon, H. A. (1973). Alternative uses of phonemic information in spelling. *American Educational Research Journal, 43,* 115–137.

Stanovich, K. E. (1980). Toward an interactive-compensatory model of individual differences in the development of reading fluency. *Reading Research Quarterly, 16,* 32–71.

Tierney, R., Caplan, R., Ehri, L., Healy, M. K., & Hurdlow, M. (in press). Writing and reading working together. In A. Haas Dyson (Ed.), *Writing and reading: Collaboration in the classroom?* Urbana, IL: National Council of Teachers of English.

Treiman, R. (1985). The development of reading skills. In T. Carr (Ed.), *Language, cognition, and reading development* (pp. 5–18). San Francisco: Jossey-Bass.

Venezky, R. L. (1970). *The structure of English orthography.* The Hague: Mouton.

Venezky, R. L., & Johnson, D. (1973). Development of two letter-sound patterns in grades one through three. *Journal of Educational Psychology, 64,* 109–115.

4

CONNECTIONS IN LEARNING TO WRITE AND READ

A Study of Children's Development through Kindergarten and First Grade

Lee Dobson

Research into emergent literacy shows that young children learn a good deal about writing and reading before they attend school. Teachers can build on this knowledge in an integrated instructional program. But just how reading and writing are intertwined in the learning process has not been clearly defined. To trace children's development through kindergarten and first grade in an environment conducive to language learning, we asked children to read and write in any way they could. We identified the common strategies of eighteen children and compared their use of these strategies across tasks. Our findings showed that children initially explore the mechanics of written language in their writing and in their reading of their own writing. They develop composing strategies within the context of storybook reading. In other words, writing and reading support each other, with a transfer of strategies occurring in both directions.

Reading and writing are two aspects of the same language system. We would therefore expect them to be mutually supportive in literacy learning. Yet the vast majority of researchers have focused on reading and the effectiveness of the various methods used to teach it in isolation from writing. Some researchers (e.g., Read, 1971) have investigated preschoolers' developing knowledge of phonology as indicated by their early writing, and others have described the writing process and how it develops (Graves, 1983). But research that traces the concurrent development of writing and reading, examines the relationships between them, and considers their relative contributions to literacy learning is rare, especially in the context of school learning. Such information is important for researchers and educators alike. Without it, there will not be a complete picture of reading and writing acquisition or of literacy learning in general.

Teachers have traditionally taught reading first, but some teachers and researchers are suggesting that children find it easier to write first, with children spelling in any way they can (Chomsky, 1979; Clay, 1975; Hurst et al., 1984). An interesting facet of this approach is that the young writers are readers also, for they read their own writing (Aulls, 1975; Dobson, 1986). How do writing and the reading of one's own writing affect the acquisition of reading? Conversely, how does reading affect writing? Educators need such information from integrated studies before they can make informed decisions about curricula. They need to recognize the strategies involved in reading and writing and the ways these strategies interact in the course of development. They also need to reflect on the teacher's role in an integrated reading and writing program. Knowledge about children's growth as readers and writers will enable teachers to create the kind of environment that promotes literacy learning.

This chapter, which describes a study of children's growth as writers and readers over their first two years at school, addresses some of these concerns. The study involved observations of writing and reading strategies used at the same points in time and considered connections in their development. Reading strategies were observed in two contexts: children's reading of their own writing, and their reading of storybooks. Because the definitions of writing and reading extended to include all writinglike and readinglike events, even children's earliest responses were noted.

BACKGROUND AND METHOD

Teachers who reflect on their pupils' work are naturally led into research because their constant question is, "What and how are my pupils learning?" They are also uniquely equipped to conduct their own investigations, for they have constant access to the same children over time and a measure of control over the teaching and learning

TABLE 4.1 Principles for Nurturing Literacy

1. Provide a warm social setting
2. Immerse learners in a literate environment
3. Accept and encourage successive approximations of literacy
4. Expect self-selection of materials and of topics
5. Respond to intended meaning as the absolute priority
6. Emphasize the process rather than the product
7. Expect hypothesis-testing and self-correction
8. Expect a developmental progression along the learning continuum
9. Evaluate individually and longitudinally

Source: Hurst (1985).

environment. Our research began when as resource-room teachers in an inner-city school where a number of children were learning English as a second language, we decided to put recent theoretical formulations to the test. Co-teacher Marietta Hurst (1982) searched the literature for key elements that foster language learning and listed them as environmental principles (see Table 4.1). With these in mind, we set up a classroom environment in which we expected children to communicate as readers and writers in any way they could. The progress of reluctant readers (Dobson, 1985) and of first-grade writers (Dobson, 1986) indicated the effectiveness of the environment, and it supported current views of writing development (Gentry, 1982; Temple, Nathan, & Burris, 1982). Our preliminary studies also stimulated questions about connections between learning to write and learning to read.

Our next step was to undertake a series of planned observations and interactions with children in a writing and reading context. We decided on systematic, bimonthly sampling sessions from the beginning of kindergarten to the end of first grade—a total of twenty-six sessions. In each sampling session, we asked children to draw a picture, to write about it, and to read their work when they were through. We also asked them to choose and to read a storybook from a preselected group of three. The storybooks, unknown to the children, were from the *Get Ready* and *Ready Set Go* series (Melser, 1980). Each book is eight pages long and contains structural patterns of language based on rhythm, rhyme, and/or repetition. On one occasion, we presented a book the children knew: *Brown Bear, Brown Bear* (Martin, 1970).

The sampling sessions took place in the resource room in the same kind of nurturing environment that characterized our preliminary studies. To narrow our observations and reactions, we constructed checklists of characteristics that seemed to act as signposts to children's development (Clay, 1982). Our findings indicated how children learn to write and read when communication of meaning is the central focus (Dobson & Hurst, 1986).

FINDINGS

An analysis of eighteen children's progress in reading and writing over a two-year period suggested continuous rather than stagelike development, with new strategies gradually becoming integrated into existing patterns (as in Mason & Allen, 1986). The effect was cumulative, but there were also shifts of priority and focus. For example, readers initially used illustrations as a basis for their construction of text; they later favored the print, but picture interpretation continued to play a strategic role, supplementing and sometimes prompting their print-related strategies.

Learners acquire certain insights as they come to use written language in a conventional way. Thus it is possible to recognize levels of understanding, with each level reflecting learner growth in awareness. This study examined children's writing and reading strategies at the following five levels of understanding. Each level reflects a more advanced state of print awareness in a progression toward the conventional.

Level 1: The child understands that the contents of books are meaningful and can be read as such.

Level 2: The child understands that spoken text matches the written text (time-space match).

Level 3: The child is aware that the alphabetic principle is used to match speech and print, thus producing a stable wording.

Level 4: The child knows that words appear on a page as units of print, separated by space.

Level 5: The child understands that morphemes (word, base, or affix) have a constant spelling but can be combined to form new units of meaning.

Parallel to these insights of print awareness were developments in children's knowledge of stories, including story structure and composing strategies. Children's compositions also revealed a developing repertoire of booklike language.

The understanding of all but five children was at level 1 at the beginning of the study; the initial understanding of these five was at level 2. This is not to suggest that level 1 represents the beginning of literacy development. All the children's earliest responses indicated some knowledge of literacy, which they could use to approximate the behavior of writers and readers.

Level 1

At level 1 children used many of the same strategies when responding to reading and writing tasks. They followed conventional book-handling procedures except for page sequence; here the right-hand page often claimed their first attention. When reading their own writing or the storybooks, they applied their knowledge of meaning and grammar to the accompanying pictures and constructed a possible text. They paid little attention to their own representations of writing (scribblelike or printlike) or the printed text, but they touched the appropriate parts of the pictures as they spoke.

The children's early and extensive use of names suggested that they already had a well-established naming strategy. Zelko read his writing by naming the people in his drawing: "That's me. That's my friend. That's my mom. That's my dad." And on the same day he read a storybook by naming the animals pictured in the illustrations: "Fish in the water. And a butterfly. Cat go in the house." The tendency to name was apparent in both reading contexts, but the storybook response involved more complex language structures and concepts. It suggested location ("in the water") and movement ("go in the house"). Such elaborations appeared first in children's storybook reading, and the most likely explanation involves the quality and quantity of the illustrations. It was several months before Zelko used similar constructions when reading his own writing.

The examination of children's writing revealed more about their print-related strategies. They wrote scribblelike and/or letterlike and/or numberlike symbols, and they sometimes identified them. They also commented on how and why they were writing as they did. One child, for example, pointed to a number he had printed and incorporated it in his message, saying, "That's the ghost's ten dollars." And Janie explained, "I just wanted the *A*'s to follow that *O*."

Such comments revealed that children were thinking about strategies of both transcription and composition and knew a number of metalinguistic terms. At this level such information was seldom available from their storybook reading. Writing focused attention on print, and it therefore seemed that print-related strategies were developing in this area first.

Level 2

The children's first attempts to match written text and spoken words occurred in the context of their own writing. On Januay 9 Zelko initiated the strategy of pointing to his writing as if it corresponded to his reading, even though he had not written any words. When reading a storybook on this same date, he continued to point to the illustrations. On March 7, two months later, he adopted a similar finger-tracking strategy when reading a storybook.

When reading his own writing on April 19, Zelko indicated a unit-to-unit match between the words in his message and his printed letters. When reading a storybook that same day, he finger-tracked the print so that the beginning and end of his spoken sentence coincided with the print. Both strategies indicate an awareness of the necessary time-space match between speech and print, but the unit-to-unit strategy is the more sophisticated.

Leslie's initial reading of a storybook indicated that he knew quite a bit about the task. Example 4.1 shows him trying to use letter names, knowledge of a particular story, and picture cues. But he could not integrate these sources of information to produce a meaningful reading. Upon reaching the last page, he settled on the illustrations as a guide to text invention.

Leslie's initial writing sample contained the correct spelling of his name and other letters and numbers. When he read his own work, he commented on the message and his transcription. He pointed to his own name while reading *me:*

> See! I wrote on the lines. I wrote *me* in the chalk drawings. Those chalk drawings can be very funny. There's a squirrel in there. Look at the funny *L*. [He had printed a lower-case *l*.]

Leslie explained his message and its representation, but he did not integrate these two aspects to produce a conventional piece of work. His reflections on his own thinking and language indicated an awareness of print (see Chapter 10) and of strategies for its use.

Some children at level 2 read storybooks by repeating sentence patterns across successive pages, while others adopted a storylike framework. Their language was also becoming more booklike (see Chapter 2). In general, the compositional aspect of their storybook reading was more elaborate and complex than their reading of their own writing.

Level 3

Children gradually refined their writing strategies to incorporate more features of the print until they used letters to represent sounds of speech. To reach this level, they needed to know the form of some letters and their identification by name, as well as the match between speech and print.

EXAMPLE 4.1 Leslie's Reading of a Storybook

Reading		Text
Leslie:	I know that one is *G*. And that's the first name of Graham. I have Leslie Graham.	Go, Go, Go.
Researcher:	Say how it goes. Say what is in your head.	
Leslie:	I'm trying to think. Let me see—what that fox is doing. I'll try to think what that fox is doing so then I'll know.	
Researcher:	Tell me what's in your mind.	
Leslie:	You know what all I can get in my mind is?	
Researcher:	What is that?	
Leslie:	Only the words.	
Researcher:	What are the words?	
Leslie:	Let me see. Can I turn the page? [He pauses.] I'm not very good at thinking.	I fly.
Researcher:	I think you are.	
Leslie:	A bit good. All I can think about is a cat and the owl in the pea green boat.	swim.
Researcher:	Let's keep going.	
Leslie:	Now I should start. [Turns three pages.] Hey! *X O X* [identifying print on a vat].	
Researcher:	What are you thinking now?	I jump
Leslie:	I have no idea [pause].	and
	Now let me see what the words are.	I ride.
	"Stop hopping Mama." And Mama's saying, "I can't stop hopping.	
	We have to meet Daddy, remember?"	
Researcher:	So you did have a good thought after all.	
Leslie:	Only on the past page.	

At level 3 children purposely attempted to translate speech into print. They were now articulating a message as they wrote and representing its sounds as they perceived them (Read, 1971). Writers using such a strategy need to plan the wording as they write or even before they write. While the children's previous representations looked somewhat like writing, the meaning actually resided in their pictures, and the wording therefore varied with each rereading. Now that they were transcribing words into print, the message was governed by the written text and thus remained stable.

Significant signposts to Zelko's development occurred as follows. A month after making his first attempt to track print, he wrote *ABCDE* and said, "[Those are] the ABC's." For some months he explored these strategies of tracking and naming letters, but he did not seem to attempt a precise message. After ten months at this level, on November 20 of the first-grade year, he produced a message that indicated a new level of development. He printed *RABO HOS* and read it as "rainbow house." Four months later he made his first attempt to read the print in a storybook word by word; this new strategy was characteristic of level 4. Overall, the alphabetic strategy appeared in the children's writing and their reading of that writing three to nine months before it appeared in storybook reading.

Shirley's behavior at the start of kindergarten placed her at level 2. At that time she printed some letters and tracked and named letters in storybooks. She began moving into level 3 with a story called "Mighty Mouse," which she wrote on May 1. She indicated two matches initially (*M* for *mouse* and *S* for *saved*), but as she read she reached for a pencil to represent another word (*mouse*). She corrected the omission with an *M* and then retrieved her original wording on two successive readings.

Once Shirley began to match letters and sounds, she continued to do so. Successive samples of her writing in the fall of first grade indicate rapid progress:

1. *TWATN* [There was a tornado.]
2. *TW—AMSLD*]There was a magical land.]
3. *TR WZ A BTA FL HS* [There was a beautiful house.]
4. *TR WZA BTAFL PESTD* [There was a beautiful present.]

Lines 1 and 2 show Shirley's awareness of the need to represent each word (or perhaps each syllable), and, typically, she chose the initial consonant (Gentry, 1982; Read, 1971). The dashlike mark on line 2 seems to indicate a separation between two elements in her sentence. She did not comment on this strategy, but two other boys who used a similar strategy did explain it. According to Dirk, such marks "connect—you know, they divide up the —so they don't go into each other." Alan explained, "They go together, but it keeps it away from each other."

Was the mark meant as a dash or a hyphen? The children's explanations suggest both functions. At this level, before they began using spacing, other children used periods, colons, and slash marks to indicate separation between phrases and words. One reason may be the need to fill space (Temple et al., 1982), but another may be the wish to indicate connections.

Two weeks after writing line 2, Shirley produced line 3. Here she represented the sounds of all the consonants and separated syllables with space. Two weeks later, when she wrote line 4, she recognized *beautiful* as a word unit and spaced it accordingly. She also represented the short vowel *e* in *present*. These strategic changes are typical of level 4.

When Shirley wrote "Mighty Mouse" on May 1, she was not using her knowledge of the alphabetic principle in her reading of storybooks. On the same date she chose to read a harder book. She began with an intent look at the word "silly" on the title page. "*S?*" she asked, and paused. Then she began to invent a text compatible with the illustrations. At times she tracked the print, but her reading was not governed by its features.

At level 3 children used quite different strategies in the two reading contexts. When they read their own writing, they had the support of knowing the content and the wording; they needed only a minimal number of graphophonic cues to retrieve the messages as written. The unfamiliar storybooks did not offer this kind of support, nor did the children have enough knowledge of the graphophonic system to make a meaningful reading on their own. Thus they continued to use the illustrations to construct a possible text.

In two instances the context of storybook reading did provide some support for word identification. The first occurred when children used the name sound of the first consonant of a word as the principal clue to locating it. Leslie's initial use of this strategy to read the line "Put some cheese on it" resulted in the following self-correction (his asides are bracketed):

One day Jenny and Thomas went out.
[Oh, God. Nothing starts with a *J*.]
My best is Swiss cheese.
[Ah, it starts with a *c*—Swiss.]

Leslie found the initial consonant *c* in the text and matched it with the *s* in Swiss in his second reading. Such a strategy combined with picture cues can result in word identification, but it will not reveal the wording of an entire story.

In the second situation children were offered the storybook *Brown Bear, Brown Bear*. Because they had some knowledge of this book's content and wording, they could use their knowledge of initial consonant sounds to confirm the match between spoken words and their corresponding units in print. Leslie's question—"Am I supposed to just do this, just turn the page?"—seemed to indicate that he understood the possibility of initiating a new strategy. When told that he was supposed to read the text, he proceeded to dip in and out of the print for the first six pages (two or three lines each). He achieved a number of word-unit matches, some of which were word-perfect. On the seventh page he began by saying, "What do" (pointing to *blue horse*), stopped, corrected to "blue horse," and then proceeded to stay with the print for four more pages. As he read, he heavily emphasized the word units, reading accurately except for one recurring phrase: *looking at me.* But it was laborious, for he said, "I just turn a few pages—so it won't be so long, right?" After skipping four pages, he gradually read more rapidly, solving his problem with *looking at me* by using one part of the refrain a second time.

At earlier levels, longer and more elaborated stories had seemed to signal progress. But once the children began trying to match sounds and letters in writing, they were more successful when they reduced the length and complexity of their compositions. The examples of Shirley's writing, previously listed, are similar in structure and content but show her working on aspects of transcription. Other children struggled along for some time without making such adjustments, and it took them longer to refine their strategies toward the conventional.

Level 4

Children gradually refined their writing strategies, making more conventional letter-sound associations, spelling more words as visual units, and representing more of the surface sounds in words. They also began to use spaces to demarcate word boundaries. The appearance of spacing was critical, for it signaled an awareness of the word as a unit in language (Henderson & Beers, 1980), as well as a strategic change from representing sounds to representing words. Figure 4.1 shows an example of Dirk's writing at level 4.

On the day Shirley wrote line 3 ("There was a beautiful house"), she suddenly introduced a new storybook reading strategy. She followed the print word by word and identified 66 percent of the words in the book as written (twenty-five out of thirty-eight words). She lost the meaning on only two occasions, and at those times her errors were syntactically appropriate. She seemed to identify many words at sight, but she also sounded out an unfamiliar word. She used graphophonic and picture cues to make three self-corrections. Two weeks later she read 85 percent of the words in her storybook as written.

Once the children could identify a number of words, they used semantic, syntactic, graphophonic, and picture cues to predict the rest. Their reading of storybooks was at first a bit choppy, as they carefully attempted to match each spoken and printed word. Sometimes they focused so heavily on the print they temporarily lost sight of the meaning, but their comments, hesitations, and self-corrections indicated that meaning was still the central focus. Dirk, for example, realized that his reading of "Go home" as "Go him" didn't make sense. In

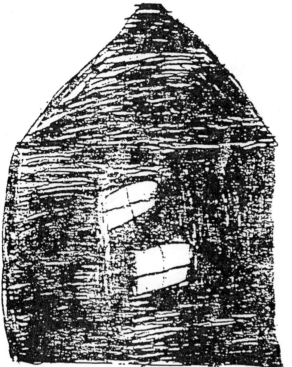

A KCID

SOD

A rAD

AND

PEC

HWS

FIGURE 4.1 "A kid saw(d) a red and pink house."

solving the problem by omitting the word *home*, he noted that he
had maintained the meaning of the text. He was equally doubtful
about his substitutions of "chickens" for "hens," but he seemed satisfied when he realized it sounded all right.

Level 5

Several strategic trends emerged across children's reading and writing.
One was a progression from sounding-out strategies to strategies involving the recognition and representation of words as units of meaning
(see Chapter 3). Spelling had become so conventional that words could
be deciphered without the assistance of the writer. Punctuation marks
appeared in some children's writing, although not necessarily in conventional places (see Figure 4.2). When asked how he knew to "do"
periods, Jay replied, "Mrs. S. told us to put those"; when asked how

FIGURE 4.2   "The captain of the boat."

he knew where to put them, his answer was, "After my writing I have to put a period."

Only a few months before Serge reached level 5, he had been working to make letter-sound associations. Now his fluent reading and confident remarks reflected an ability to recognize word units at sight. When asked after a storybook reading if he had read the book before, he replied, "No, I just know the words." His writing included a rendition of the favorite story, *Jack and the Beanstalk* (see Figure 4.3).

Children's increasing control over aspects of transcription enabled them to focus more intensely on matters of composition. Their writing showed more attention to storybook language and structure. It now stood on its own without the context of a drawing. Some children reversed the previous order of drawing and writing; they wrote first and then illustrated their written story. In addition to writing journal pieces and retelling stories, children wrote original stories like Shirley's, shown in Figure 4.4.

FIGURE 4.3 "Jack climbed on the beanstalk but on the way he saw a giant."

Children's fluent reading enabled them to concentrate on comprehension, and they seldom failed to make sense of a piece. Whereas they had previously looked to drawings or book illustrations for the meaning, now they looked to the print and the context of the story. The children used meaning and syntax as cues for prediction, and one child's response indicated her awareness of a rhyming pattern.

DISCUSSION

Our findings not only highlight the mutually supportive and complementary nature of the development of children's reading and writing;

It Was fun To
See The little
Mos BecoS

Snecing Be HoiNd
The Cat and
The Dog was To

The Mos
was

aprl6)1985

FIGURE 4.4 "It was fun to see the little mouse because the mouse was sneaking behind the cat and the dog was too."

they also reveal certain differences in the way strategies develop across the two tasks. For example, children tried out and refined their print-related strategies in their own writing and the reading of that writing, and they only later applied these strategies to the print in storybooks. However, children composed richer and more complex messages in response to storybooks than they did in their own writing, which suggests that story telling (i.e., composition) initially develops in the storybook context.

Print-Related Strategies

The first major finding concerned the initial development of print-related strategies in writing and the reading of it. At level 1, children attempted representations of writing, including printlike symbols and their own names. They did not refer to them as they read, however. A major advance occurred when children began to match time spent reading their messages with the amount of writing. They used at least four different strategies to achieve a time-space match:

1. They slowed down or speeded up their finger-tracking according to the amount of print available and the length of their story.
2. They tracked the lines of print several times until the message ended.
3. They added extra letters to accommodate a longer story.
4. They matched a printed letter to a single spoken word or syllable, omitting or adding letters as necessary.

They still looked to their drawings as the source of meaning, but they were also taking account of their written representations. It was some time before they used similar strategies when responding to storybooks.

At level 3 children applied the alphabetic strategy in writing and in reading that writing. Children initiated this strategy in their own work three to nine months before they applied it to the words in unfamiliar storybooks. They generally began with a letter-name strategy applied to initial sounds in words and set down as a letter string (Read, 1971). The message (in Figure 4.5) is typical. Such a phonetically based strategy is very functional for writers because it enables them to choose words that best convey their message.

Children used the contextual support of a known meaning and wording when they read their own writing. Somewhat similar supports were present when they read the familiar storybook *Brown Bear, Brown*

FIGURE 4.5 "I saw a little girl walking down at night."

Bear. In this case their knowledge of story and language provided a scaffolding for the use of strategies that had not yet matured, and they succeeded in a way that was otherwise beyond them. Some researchers (e.g., Doake, 1979; Holdaway, 1979) have elaborated on the benefit of repeated readings for children's growth as readers.

Writing and reading have different requirements, and these requirements make it necessary for learners to attend to different aspects of written language. The need to represent writing directs writers' attention to print—to the selection of letter forms, the organization of a page, and other mechanical details involved in transcription. Because writers control the print, they seek out and pay attention to information purposeful to its production.

Children who construct their own written representations need to make decisions about form and content, and these decisions both precede writing and accompany it. It is therefore not surprising to find explanations about thinking and language occurring earlier and more often in the context of children's own writing than in their reading of unfamiliar storybooks. Such comments suggest that children try out the mechanical aspects of the written language system, including its vocabulary, in that situation.

When the children finally incorporated a graphophonic strategy into their repertoire for reading unfamiliar storybooks, they did not focus so heavily on the print that they lost the meaning. They moved from a strategy of text construction directly to the integration of graphic and contextual clues.

Why did this change in children's storybook-reading strategies occur so suddenly and completely? One reason may be the considerable experience the children had had as readers of their own written t˜xts. They were writing almost daily in their classrooms and reading their own work to themselves and also to their teachers (as documented in Dobson, 1986) u.jing conventional reading strategies. As their spellings became more conventional, their own printing began to resemʰle the print in storybooks. And what they could identify in one context, they could identify in another. Once they realized they could apply their reading strategies to decipher print in storybooks, they were proficient enough to read with meaning as a central focus. Kendall, Lajeunesse, Chmilar, Shapson, and Shapson (1987) found that English-speaking children who were receiving intensive training in reading French texts used a similar transfer of strategies when they read English texts.

The strategic change in the children's reading of storybooks coincided with more conventional writing, including spelling representations of short vowels, visual approximation, and spacing of words. Initially, print-related strategies developed in the context of writing, but now the direction of influence altered in favor of storybook reading. By the end of first grade, the most advanced group of children were reading text as written, and that text was usually more complex in language and content than their own writing.

Composing Strategies

The second major finding was that children initially develop composing strategies in the context of storybook reading. This finding seems to go against the conventional wisdom that associates composition with writing. But in this study, the children were asked to respond to storybooks before they had adopted conventional print strategies. This circumstance seemed to direct their attention to the illustrations, which they used to construct a plausible text. As readers of storybooks, their control lay in text invention, and they thus developed strategies in this area first.

The children's initial problem was to figure out the illustrations. They began by reacting to each picture as a discrete unit, naming or labeling the pictured objects. Soon, however, they were trying to relate one picture to the next, and eventually they came to construct stories that extended across the pages of the storybooks. The successive pictures in the books seemed to encourage this trend, but the children were not above changing the order of the pages to suit their own idea of an appropriate story. On one occasion Dirk read a few pages and then decided to alter the format to fit his preferred interpretation. The book was about pigs and houses, and the first illustration showed a house made of bricks. He turned to the end of the book and began reading toward the beginning. He was thus able to retell the story of *The Three Pigs* and end with the pigs all safe in the brick house.

Storybook illustrations seem to stimulate detailed descriptions and explanations, and this additional content requires more complex language structures. Over time, the children increasingly used storylike structures and booklike language (Sulzby, 1985). They did not attempt to write stories that continued from page to page until they reached an advanced level of transcription. In fact, children reduced the length and complexity of their compositions when they first put the alphabetic principle to use. Once they had worked out strategies for transcription in writing, they were then free to focus on composing strategies. Only some children had reached this level by the end of the study.

CONCLUSION

The developmental view of literacy learning on which this study was based suggests that learning occurs through successive refinements (Bissex, 1981). We therefore did not expect conventional representations at the start but looked beyond the children's representations in evaluating children's progress and in reflecting on the appropriateness and effectiveness of teaching practices.

Our approach to sampling and analyzing children's knowledge of literacy and its growth was influenced mainly by studies of emergent literacy that have examined preschool knowledge and development (e.g., Teale & Sulzby, 1986). Our results indicate that this approach is also appropriate for investigations of the progress of primary school children, for the pattern of development is similar.

The findings of this study support the hypothesis that reading and writing are mutually supportive and connected at each step to learners' knowledge of the system of written language and how it works. The patterns of growth indicate the advantage of integrated models of writing and reading instruction that focus on content and form. The findings also provide a basis for speculation about how the exercise of writing affects progress in reading, and vice versa.

The research took place as a regular part of the school program and as such was carried out in the context of a normal school routine with the central features of teacher-pupil and pupil-pupil relationships intact. Although the study was observational in tone, the environment was carefully constructed in accordance with Hurst's (1985) principles. This environment, which was also a basis for classroom practices, had a positive influence on children's growth (Dobson & Hurst, 1986).

The subjects represented a cross section of pupils in an inner-city school and included a number of children who were learning English as a second language. Home and community environments were therefore probably not prime factors in the children's achievement; other children in more favored circumstances should make the same kind of progress at least as easily. It was the similarities in the children's development that were striking and that were therefore the focus of this report.

Throughout the study, the children showed a willingness and desire to communicate in written language. They indicated their awareness of the functional aspects of reading and writing before they adopted conventional forms (Halliday, 1975). All signs indicated that their decisions were deliberate and intellectual in nature, although they may not have been conscious of all the ramifications. Even though the routine remained the same over the two years of the study, the children retained their enthusiasm and remained eager to participate and to explain their participation. In fact, as Snow (1983) has suggested, the regularity of the routine itself may have been a factor in growth.

The investigation showed that children can engage in written language from an early age and through its use learn about its features. Their reading and writing contained a series of revelations about the content of their world, the level of their intellectual activity, and how they were bringing their knowledge and their intelligence to bear on the task of learning a written language. Although they began at different levels, developed at varying rates, and responded in various ways, they progressed in a similar fashion. Taken together, the children's reading and writing convey a cohesive and complementary picture of literacy development.

R E F E R E N C E S

Aulls, M. (1975). Relating reading comprehension and writing competency. *Language Arts, 52,* 808–812.

Bissex, G. L. (1981). Growing writers in the classroom. *Language Arts, 58,* 785–791.

Chomsky, C. (1979). Approaching reading through invented spelling. In L. Resnick & P. Weaver (Eds.), *Theory and practice of early reading* (Vol. 2, pp. 43–64). Hillsdale, NJ: Erlbaum.

Clay, M. M. (1975). *What did I write?* Auckland, NZ: Heinemann Educational Books.

Clay, M. M. (1982). Learning and teaching writing: A developmental perspective. *Language Arts, 59,* 65–70.

Doake, D. B. (1979, April). *Book experience and emergent reading behavior.* Paper presented at the Preconvention Institute, annual convention of the International Reading Association, Atlanta.

Dobson, L. N. (1985). Learn to read by writing: A practical program for reluctant readers. *Teaching Exceptional Children, 18,* 30–36.

Dobson, L. N. (1986). Emergent writers in a grade one classroom. *Reading-Canada-Lecture, 4,* 149–157.

Dobson, L. N., & Hurst, M. E. (1986). *How do young children learn to read and write when meaning is the major focus?* (Report No. 86). Vancouver: Educational Research Institute of British Columbia.

Gentry, R. L. (1982). An analysis of developmental spelling in GNYS AT WORK. *The Reading Teacher, 36,* 192–200.

Graves, D. H. (1983). *Writing: Teachers and children at work.* Exeter, NH: Heinemann Educational Books.

Halliday, M. (1975). *Learning how to mean.* London: Arnold.

Henderson, E. H., & Beers, J. W. (Eds.). (1980). *Developmental and cognitive aspects of learning to spell.* Newark, DE: International Reading Association.

Holdaway, D. (1979). *The foundations of literacy.* Sydney: Ashton Scholastic.

Hurst, M. E. (1982). *The influence of evolving theory and practice on teaching emergent readers and writers.* Unpublished master's thesis, Language Educational Resources Centre, University of British Columbia, Vancouver.

Hurst, M. E. (1985). *Principles which nurture literacy.* Unpublished manuscript.

Hurst, M. E., Dobson, L. N., Chow, M., Nucich, J. E., Stickley, L., & Smith, G. (1984). *A program to foster literacy: Early steps in learning to write.* Vancouver: British Columbia Teacher's Federation Lesson Aids. (ERIC Document Reproduction Service No. ED 244 511)

Kendall, J., Lajeunesse, G., Chmilar, P., Shapson, L., & Shapson, S. (1987). English reading skills of French immersion students in kindergarten and grades one and two. *Reading Research Quarterly, 22,* 135–159.

Martin, B. (1970). *Brown bear, brown bear.* New York: Holt, Rinehart, and Winston.

Mason, J., & Allen, J. (1986, April). *A review of emergent literacy with implications for research and practice in reading.* Unpublished manuscript.

Melser, J. (1980). *Story-box readers.* Lexington, MA: Ginn.

Read, C. (1971). Preschool children's knowledge of English phonology. *Harvard Educational Review, 41,* 1–34.

Snow, C. (1983). Literacy and language: Relationships during the preschool years. *Harvard Educational Review, 53,* 165–189.

Sulzby, E. (1985). Children's emergent reading of favorite storybooks: A developmental study. *Reading Research Quarterly, 20,* 458–481.

Teale, W. H., & Sulzby, E. (Eds). (1986). *Emergent literacy: Writing and reading.* Norwood, NJ: Ablex.

Temple, C. A., Nathan, R. G., & Burris, N. A. (1982). *The beginnings of writing.* Boston: Allyn & Bacon.

5

READING AND WRITING ATTEMPTS BY KINDERGARTNERS AFTER BOOK READING BY TEACHERS

Jana M. Mason, Carol L. Peterman, Barbara M. Powell, and Bonnie M. Kerr

We explored two questions about reading and writing connections: (1) How does the reading of books to kindergarten children affect their reading, writing, and text recall? (2) Does the type of book read to children make a difference? Six kindergarten teachers read three types of books—a narrative, an expository text, and a picture-phrase book—to their students. Directly after the reading, eight to ten children from each classroom were tested individually on their ability to write, read, and remember the book they had just heard. The type of book read to the children affected the content of their writing, their responses to probe questions, and their ability to read selected pages. Performance with the picture-phrase book was better on all measures than performance with the other two books. Children's reading was moderately correlated with their writing, but probe recall of texts was not correlated with either reading or writing.

Young children benefit from home and school experiences that feature talking and writing about their own language. According to Harste, Woodward, and Burke (1984) and Allen and associates (see Chapter 6), children need to attend to important language features in informal ways in order to understand and learn about written language. Informal activities, including those organized by the teacher and those children choose themselves, may enable children to learn and to progress at their own rate, as well as to predict and to test hypotheses about how written language differs from their own oral language. In this chapter we suggest that learning about written language occurs when teachers read books to students, talk to them about the book contents, and arrange for them to try reading and writing about what they have heard.

We know that oral language is organized differently from written language and serves different functions (see Perena, 1984). We also know that written texts differ substantially. Consider, for example, how differently a newspaper, a novel, and a science textbook are organized and how all these differ from a conversation between two people. Although the same words could appear in each one, the organization of sentences and paragraphs would certainly be dissimilar. There is no doubt that to become good readers and writers, children need to notice how they can use their oral language to form written language and that they must then learn the varying ways that written texts are organized.

Assumptions about the process of learning to read, together with the nature of adult-child interactions in storybook reading, indicate that children refine their understanding of language when adults read to them. It is indeed fortunate that many parents and teachers read to young children, for this presumably helps them form a bridge from oral to written language and allows them to begin analyzing the distinguishing features of written language.

We believe that reading books to children allows them to focus on the material they are hearing and simultaneously to relate it to their own experiences. When they discuss the text with the adult, they can predict and summarize story events, become critical about the topic by questioning and elaborating on their own understanding of the contents, and test possible generalizations of ideas presented in the text. The role of the adult in book-reading sessions follows Vygotsky's (1979) notion of helping the child learn within a zone in which the child is a novice; the adult supports and guides the child and at the same time gradually relinquishes responsibility:

> At first the novice participates more or less as a spectator responsible for very little of the actual work. But as she becomes more experienced and capable of performing at a higher level, the expert guides her to increasingly more competent performance. The teacher and student come to share the cognitive work load equally. Finally, the adult fades herself out, as it were, leaving the student

to take over, and the adult teacher to assume the role of a sympathetic coach. [Reeve, Palincsar, & Brown, 1985, p. 16]

By applying these concepts to book reading, teachers may be able to gradually shift the responsibility of understanding and interpreting written language to their young students. The role shift might take place in the following ways:

1. Modeling text comprehension through expressive oral reading and discussion of story characters' feelings and actions.
2. Demonstrating how things work and how they are related to concepts presented in informational texts.
3. Showing comprehension strategies through discussions with students about what a particular word or phrase means.
4. Diagnosing students' comprehension difficulties during the book reading by stopping to ask questions and to interpret or expand on the text and on their answers.
5. Assigning students more responsibility for text interpretation by encouraging comments and questions about the text, by having them read parts of the text, by arranging for them to act out important story incidents, and by setting aside time for them to write or draw pictures about interesting story events.

How much evidence do we have that children are read to in these elaborate ways and that the approaches help them form constructs about written language? Research shows a relationship between parents' reading to their children and children's later reading achievement. According to Snow (1983), parents provide literate, "decontextualized language" features in their story reading. These features include acquainting children with an impersonal author, a distant setting, characters with varying points of view, and forms of written language. Studying her son's early language acquisition, Snow found the routine of book reading ideal for learning language. Because the story events are the same each time the book is read and can be used for discussion, the child can gradually take on more and more of the adult role in the reading situation. The child has the chance to learn the rules for reading and to acquire knowledge of the features of written language.

Corroboration of the value of parental reading to children comes from Wells (1982, 1986), who made a retrospective accounting of the academic achievement of seven-year-olds in reading, math, and vocabulary. In interviews with parents when the children were five (i.e., before school entry) and when they were seven, Wells gathered information on home influences during the first two years of school. Variables significantly correlated with reading attainment at age seven were parental interest and help with school work, child oral-language production, child knowledge of and interest in literacy, and time spent listening to stories read aloud. Wells concluded that book reading between parents and children was a primary factor in children's later reading achievement.

The evidence that reading books to children in school makes a difference requires further investigation, in part because large-scale correlational studies have found that such book reading is not related to progress in reading (Meyer, Linn, & Hastings, 1988; Rosenshine & Stevens, 1984). However, experimental studies have found that reading books to students does help them in their reading. Feitelson, Kita, and Goldstein (1986) reported two studies in which reading to kindergartners and first graders speeded their progress in learning to read. In one study, kindergarten teachers who read to their students four times a week for four months found that the children were better able to understand, recall, and tell stories. In the other study, first-grade children whose teachers had read to them had higher scores on word reading and reading comprehension. In an experimental study that followed Headstart children through kindergarten, McCormick and Mason (1986) found that reading little books (Mason & McCormick, 1984a) to children at school, mailing the books home to the children during the Headstart year, and then mailing the books home during kindergarten without school previewing had a long-lasting effect on children's later reading.

Further evidence that reading to children in school is beneficial comes from a descriptive study (Peterman, Mason, & Dunning, 1985), two experimental studies (Peterman, Dunning, Eckerty, & Mason, 1987), and a doctoral dissertation (Peterman, 1987). These studies involved microanalyses of ongoing teacher-student discussions during book-reading sessions. The quality of this talk was judged and compared with students' recall of stories and their ability to read portions of them. The descriptive study showed that some kinds of discussion helped students when they tried to read selected pages from the story, and the other three studies indicated that the quality of the teacher-student story discussion affected students' story recall.

How might young children be encouraged to *write* in ways that would help them learn about the features of written language? Sulzby (1985) found that children from homes where literacy was supported knew how to form some, if not all, the letters of the alphabet. They knew how writing should appear on paper and that it conveys meaning. They appeared to use "this awareness to indicate what should get read in storybooks, although when they tried to read those books themselves, most of the children did not keep their eyes on print" (Sulzby,

1985, p. 192). Sulzby also found that when these children were asked to write stories, they tended to use a form of writing that differed from conventional orthography. They were aware of the effort needed to write a story, and they usually reverted to pretend-writing or to a much abbreviated form of writing. Their writing forms included drawing, scribbling, letterlike forms, strings of well-learned elements, and invented spelling, as well as conventional spelling.

Several investigators have examined the effect of writing on reading achievement. Chomsky (1972) described invented spelling in first grade as valuable because it allows children to see how letters represent sounds in words, and it thus aids decoding. According to Clark (1976) and Durkin (1966), children who begin to write before they go to school are more likely later to be better readers. Clay suggested that writing "plays a significant part in the early reading progress" (1975, p. 70) by providing "synthetic experience where letters are built into words which make up sentences . . . [because] when a child writes she has to know the sound-symbol relationship inherent in reading" (1982, p. 208). Clay found that writing was particularly effective in helping children organize and figure out the features of written language if they were also being taught a number of different strategies for analyzing words. Finally, she noted that having children share their stories with classmates provided a framework within which to write and a purpose for writing.

RESEARCH METHOD

One aspect of research on reading to children and their writing and reading attempts that has been virtually ignored is the effect of reading different types of books to children. We decided to investigate the effects on kindergarten children when teachers read different kinds of books to them. We chose three kinds of texts: a narrative (a story that contained fictional characters who confronted and solved a problem), an expository text (a science text about what shadows are, how they are formed, and why they are useful), and a little book (a six-page, illustrated set of statements that focused on the familiar event of getting ready for bed and that contained a small number of words on each page).

Our purpose was to understand the extent to which a book type affects children's ability to recall, write about, and read the text that their teacher has just read to them. In addition, because each child was asked to read, write, and recall information from three different books, we had enough data from each child to measure the extent to which reading and writing about a book are related to one another and to story recall.

Six teachers were involved in this study. Five of them worked at schools in a small midwestern city, and one taught in a rural area. One of the schools was in a working-class neighborhood, but because it was a magnet school with a full-day kindergarten program, its population included a number of bused-in, middle-class students. The remaining city schools were in middle-class neighborhoods and had half-day kindergarten programs. These experienced teachers agreed to participate in the study so that we could learn how their story-reading techniques affected children's recall of text and their ability to read and write portions of it.

All 139 children in the six classrooms participated in storybook-reading sessions. Because we could not test this large number individually, we asked each teacher to choose 10 average achievers for testing. Of these 60 children, 8 missed some of the reading sessions, and so the analyses were based on 52 children's test responses to three book-reading sessions.

The six teachers agreed to read three books to their whole classes in their usual manner as we videotaped each reading. They read the books on three successive days during the spring semester. The narrative was *Strega Nona* (DePaola, 1975); the expository text was *Shadows: Here, There, and Everywhere* (Goor & Goor, 1981); and the little book was *Time for Bed* (Mason & McCormick, 1984b). We placed the video camera in the classroom before each book reading, and it remained stationary throughout the lesson. The camera was focused primarily on the teacher, with the children partially visible.

Immediately after the story was read, we took the preselected children from the classroom, one by one, to tell us about the book they had just heard. Every child agreed to come and talk to us. First, they were given a blank piece of paper and a choice of pencil or crayon and asked to write anything they could remember from the book they had just heard. They were encouraged to write something even if they did not know how to spell correctly and to tell us what they had written. We then asked questions about the book content. Finally we showed children several pages from the book read that day: four pages from the narrative text (forty-six words), four pages from the expository text (thirty words), or the entire six-page text of the little book (nineteen words). We asked them to read as much of each page as they could. If they could not read, we asked them to pretend-read the pages.

The entire testing took from five to ten minutes per child, depending on the amount of time each child spent in writing or trying to sound out words. Reactions of the children to the test situation varied from intense concentration on every aspect of each task by some children to mild disinterest on the part of others, but in only one case did a child refuse to do any of the writing or answer any of the questions. When asked to do the writing task, many children said at first that they could not write or spell, but when we explained they could pretend that they were writing, most of them made some attempt. Their attempts included pictures, a few letters with no recognizable relation to one another, and even complete sentences. Reactions to book questions varied from "I don't know" by a few children to almost complete retellings of the book by others; most gave brief answers. On the reading task, some children attempted to sound out each word on the page, some pretended to read, and others used the accompanying picture as a reference for retelling the part of the story depicted by the picture.

When the data had been collected, we had seventeen pages of information from each of fifty-two children and few guidelines about how to score or interpret them. Since our goal was to learn in what ways children's reading and writing responses were similar and different across readings of different books, we needed to develop scoring systems that would allow comparisons, even though the texts differed substantially in length and complexity.

Our method of measuring the quality of children's ability to write is a modified version of Sulzby's scale (Chapter 2). An 11-point scale was formed (see Table 5.1) and evaluated for interrater reliability (96 percent). One rule that simplified the scoring was to assign the highest possible value when children produced more than one type of writing. For example, one child, Kendra, whose writing for *Shadows: Here, There, and Everywhere* included a picture (level 1), words unrelated to the book (level 0) and *SDE* for *shadows* (level 5), earned a score of

TABLE 5.1 Ranking of Children's Writing Attempts

0. No response or response unrelated to task
1. Picture
2. Nonpicture; scribble
3. Single letterlike forms
4. Multiple letters, either not wordlike or copied
5. Wordlike forms, containing prominent consonants, usually initial ones, and with more than half of all letter pairs in the invented spelling being possible English combinations
6. Isolated word(s) with good attempt at spelling: (i.e., with the word's having more than half its phonemes)
7. Single sentence or phrase
8. Unrelated multiple sentences or phrases
9. Event-related sentences or phrases
10. Story-related sentences

TABLE 5.2 Ranking of Children's Talk about Their Writing

1. Does not talk about the writing
2. Describes the writing but does not relate it to the book
3. Describes a single idea about the book
4. Describes several ideas about the book but does not connect the ideas
5. Connects several book ideas using event sequence, part/whole, cause/effect, or statement/example
6. Tells a story about the book using the written product

5. Our assumption, also used by Allen (Chapter 6), in assigning a score representing children's highest-level response when they wrote several things was that it was a fair way to describe their writing ability. When a child's responses were unrelated to the text (e.g., child's name or favorite words, such as *cat*) and the child produced no other writing, we assigned a score of zero; our rationale here was that we had expressly asked the children to write something about the book.

Although our writing scale rated children's movement toward the construction of conventional words and sentences, it disregarded differences in the children's talk about what they had written. For this reason we developed a scale that focused on the quality of their talk about their writing (reliability of scoring was 89 percent). A 6-point scale described levels of sophistication of their talk (see Table 5.2). Because the children's talk was scored independently of their writing ability, they could secure a high score on the talk even if their writing had consisted of a picture. An example of how this scale worked is that Kendra was given a score of 4 on her talk about her written response to the little book because her comments were relevant to the text but did not describe the text sequence. She simply described what she wrote, saying, "Time for bed, sleep tight. Can I write 'Get a hug?' Get a hug."

In an unpublished report, Kerr determined another way of analyzing the writing attempts. She distinguished the content of the writing by categorizing the topic or content of each sample. Six categories were identified (see Table 5.3). On the little book, Kendra wrote about

TABLE 5.3 Categories Describing Content of Children's Writing

Test concept: abstract, general text idea
Text object: specific, relatively concrete item from book
Text event: an action in the book
Text character: person in the book
Text setting: a place where the story or events take place
Other: writing does not mean anything or is unrelated to the book (e.g., child's name, "Mom," or "I love you")

two events ("time for bed" and "get a hug") and one concept ("sleep tight").

To score children's attempts to read the book pages, which included the accompanying pictures, two scores were constructed. The first score counted the number of words read correctly. For each correctly reported word, the child received one point, even if he or she looked only at pictures and not at the printed words. This raw score rewarded children who read the text, as well as those who "pretend-read" it, if they referred to the content using words that appeared on the page. A proportional score was computed by dividing the child's raw score by the number of words appearing on the pages.

The second score evaluated the quality of the reading in terms of use of conventional reading strategies, thus ranking children's movement toward a mature reading approach. This scale (see Table 5.4) extended Sulzby's scale (1985) with research based on our current work. Reliability of scoring was 95 percent.

Kendra read the text of the little book text remarkably well, earning a raw score of 14 words correct out of a possible 19, or a .74 proportional score. Since she was attending to more than 50 percent but less than 75 percent of the print, she received a rank of 8 on her movement toward conventional reading strategies.

In scoring children's text recall, we conservatively interpreted their answers to our questions about the content of each book. All answers that mentioned portions of the text were separated into idea units. Each idea unit received one point. These were summed across the several answers to obtain an overall raw score. Then, because the narrative contained eighty-nine idea units, the expository text con-

TABLE 5.4 Ranking of Children's Reading Attempts

1. Repeats one word or phrase throughout
2. Labels each picture with single labels
3. Embellishes on the labels, describing pictures as isolated events
4. Forms primitive story using oral languagelike phrases and picture information
5. Forms story with written languagelike phrases; repeats some phrases from the book
6. Attempts to use print by picking known words on the page, but attempt results in disconnected ideas
7. Tries to integrate by filling in with made-up words or mumbles unknown words, but reads fewer than half the words correctly
8. Has moderate success at reading, with 50 percent to 74 percent of words read correctly
9. Almost succeeds at reading, with 75 percent to 84 percent of words read correctly
10. Is successful at reading and integrating book ideas, with 85 percent to 100 percent of words read correctly

tained fifty, and the little book contained only five, a proportional score (the child's raw score divided by the number of text idea units) was also computed. In her recall of the little book, Kendra received one point for "brushes her teeth" and one point for "reads a story"; her proportional score was 2/5, or .40.

RESEARCH RESULTS

Substantial differences were found in children's responses to the three books. To put these differences in a classroom context, we analyzed the teacher-student talk from the videotaped book-reading sessions (Mason, Peterman, & Kerr, in press). The analyses revealed that the teachers provided quite different information for the three books. Teachers typically introduced the narrative with comments about the title, author, and setting, and as they read, they asked many questions about vocabulary, characters, and interpretation of events. Their closing remarks dealt with the resolution of the story. With the expository text, teachers explained and demonstrated text concepts before and during the reading, and arranged follow-up activities that extended some of the book concepts. Also during the reading they had children look at and label the illustrations as a way of helping them understand the text ideas. Teachers typically introduced the little book by asking children to relate their own experiences to the text content (getting ready for bed) and encouraged them to look at the print as they read. After the reading some teachers allowed children to read with them, and others had children discuss or act out the events.

We expected that children would read, write, and recall different aspects of the books they had just heard. In other words, as Sulzby, Barnhart, and Hieshima discuss in Chapter 2, we did not expect to find uniform scores for each child. Instead, we expected that the ease or difficulty of the book itself, as well as differences in the way the teacher presented the book, would affect the level and completeness of children's responses.

Proportional scores confirmed that children remembered the little book more completely than either the narrative or exposition. They recalled an average of .80 of the ideas in the little book but only between .12 and .14 of the ideas in the other two books. Not unexpectedly, raw scores were highest for the narrative; children recalled twice as many idea units for the narrative as for the expository text, and nearly twice as many idea units for the expository as for the little book. Table 5.5 presents the average values of children's recall, reading, writing, and talk about their writing.

TABLE 5.5 Average Values of Children's Recall, Reading, Writing, and Talk about Their Writing

	Narrative	Exposition	Little Book
Recall, raw score	12.15	6.01	3.98
Recall, proportional score	.14	.12	.80
Word reading, raw score	11.92	9.08	15.27
Word reading, proportional score	.26	.30	.80
Word reading, level	5.10	4.73	8.90
Writing attempt	3.92	4.21	4.37
Talk about writing	3.21	2.73	3.08

Both raw and proportional scores indicated that the little book was easier for children to read than the other two books. Children had .80 of the words correct with the little book, .26 with the narrative, and .30 with the exposition. These differences are not surprising, since the teachers pointed out the print as they read the little book and encouraged children to read portions of it but did not use these tactics as they read the other two books. The reading-strategy score corroborated this finding. Children achieved a higher ranking on their reading of the little book than on the other two books. With the little book, children were likely to be moderately or nearly successful at attending to and identifying words. With the other two texts, they were more likely to make up stories using languagelike phrases, both oral and written, and to rely on the pictures rather than on the print. Thus, when asked to read a book with few words, large print, useful pictures, and a familiar experience, children were able to stretch toward conventional reading in the testing situation.

When we examined the children's forms of writing and their talk about what they had written, we found unexpectedly small differences across the text types. All three texts generated quite similar results. The typical response on the writing attempts was to write letters rather than words. The typical response when talking about the writing was to label a single idea about the book. A content analysis of the writing attempts did, however, show other differences across book types (see Table 5.6). Children were most likely to focus on events and characters when talking about the narrative, to present concepts for the expository text, and to identify events in the little book.

Correlations among the measures helped determine the relationships between children's reading and writing attempts. We analyzed whether children who obtained high reading scores also obtained high writing scores and whether low scores were similarly correlated. The analyses were carried out separately for each book; Tables 5.7–5.9 summarize the results. We found that the two reading measures—

TABLE 5.6   Content of Children's Writing Attempts

	Narrative		Exposition		Little Book	
	Frequency	*%*	*Frequency*	*%*	*Frequency*	*%*
Text concept	14	14	54	62	15	15
Text object or name	16	16	4	5	15	15
Text event	32	31	2	2	42	41
Text character	23	22	0	0	0	0
Text setting	0	0	0	0	0	0
Other	17	17	27	31	30	29
Total	102		87		102	

Note: Totals do not equal one writing sample per child because some children wrote more than one item and other children wrote none.

TABLE 5.7   Correlations of Reading, Writing, and Recall Scores for the Narrative Text

	Writing Attempt	*Writing Talk*	*Word Reading, Raw Score*	*Word Reading, Level*
Writing talk	.65	—	—	—
Word reading, raw score	.47	.41	—	—
Word reading, level	.47	.44	.84	—
Recall, raw score	.18	.33	.17	.27

TABLE 5.8   Correlations of Reading, Writing, and Recall Scores for the Expository Text

	Writing Attempt	*Writing Talk*	*Word Reading, Raw Score*	*Word Reading, Level*
Writing talk	.62	—	—	—
Word reading, raw score	.55	.46	—	—
Word reading, level	.49	.43	.86	—
Recall, raw score	.05	.26	.14	.22

TABLE 5.9   Correlations of Reading, Writing, and Recall Scores for the Little Book

	Writing Attempt	*Writing Talk*	*Word Reading, Raw Score*	*Word Reading, Level*
Writing talk	.68	—	—	—
Word reading, raw score	.33	.07	—	—
Word reading, level	.30	.06	.89	—
Recall, raw score	.10	.14	.15	.16

raw score and level—were highly correlated and that the two writing measures—writing attempt and writing talk (i.e., talk about writing)—were moderately correlated. The reading measures were nearly interchangeable measures of reading, and the two writing measures provided overlapping but somewhat different information about children's writing. Reading and writing were moderately well related for the narrative and expository text (Tables 5.7 and 5.8), with correlation values in the middle range (.41 to .55). Correlations for the little book (Table 5.9) were lower (.06 to .33), indicating that word reading here was poorly related to writing attempts and not at all related to writing talk. As is also indicated in Tables 5.7–5.9, neither reading nor writing was related to recall.

INTERPRETATION OF RESULTS

Children were strongly affected by the type of book their teacher read to them. When they heard a narrative or an expository text, they recalled proportionally much less, read fewer words, and used less effective reading strategies than when they heard a little book. Yet their writing attempts and levels of talk were similar across the three book types. What might account for these findings?

The expository and narrative texts are similar to one another and different from the little book in many ways: length, print form, text complexity, content familiarity, and usefulness of illustrations (for word recognition). In a sense, children were flooded with print and given too few clues even to attempt reading the narrative or exposition. That was not the case with the little book, for those words were easily seen, limited in number, and connected to pictures in ways that served as reminders for children when they were tested.

Differences in book type were strengthened by the teachers' reading approaches. They set up good listening activities for the narrative, interesting picture- and object-viewing experiences around the expository text, and print-reading attempts for the little book. They all read the books to their students, but they added activities and discussion topics that changed the listening experiences.

These large differences in reading were mirrored in the children's recall of each book type. They remembered proportionally larger amounts of the little book than of the other two books. The actual amount recalled was greatest for the narrative and then for the expository text, but this can be explained in part by the amount of text that was available to recall and in part by the differences in the number of questions asked about the books.

What is surprising, then, is that the writing levels did not change with book type. Neither dissimilar book-reading sessions nor unlike book forms affected children's writing attempts or talk. Only the content of their writing changed. Why? The possibility we offer is that writing attempts and talk about that writing are less affected by teachers' book reading than are reading attempts when children are just becoming literate. At that time, writing may affect reading, but reading and book listening do not affect writing. This possibility is carefully presented and supported by Dobson (see Chapter 4). She found that at early reading levels, writing activity helps improve reading, while at higher reading levels, reading and (we add) book listening help improve writing. The children in this study were at Dobson's earlier levels, and so their writing was not affected by listening to books.

Our finding of moderate correlations between reading and writing for the narrative and expository books supports the proposition that reading and writing abilities are related and that they emerge together or, as Dobson showed, that writing ability emerges before reading ability. Low correlations between reading and writing for the little book indicate that the simple text changed the children's reading performance but not their writing performance. As the little book made only reading, not writing, much easier, the true relationship between reading and writing was obscured. The low correlations between recall and reading and recall and writing cannot be explained by this study. They could mean that children learning to read and write do not necessarily recall the ideas from the book they just heard, or they could mean that we have a poor measure of children's memory of the book. We would like to believe that book recall is relatively independent of reading and writing at this age—that is, that young children begin to figure out letters, sounds, and words and to write them down without necessarily being able to understand and remember the stories they have heard. Further research is needed to evaluate this possibility.

INSTRUCTIONAL IMPLICATIONS

This study suggests that the kinds of books kindergarten teachers read to their students can affect students' recall, their attempts to read, and the content of their writing, but not their writing forms or talk. A predictable book, or one with simple text and clarifying pictures, can aid children's attempts to read, and a narrative can improve their recall, when teachers employ some of the Vygotskian book-reading approaches described at the beginning of this chapter. These approaches, which the six teachers in this study tailored to each text, are summarized as follows:

When reading a narrative, teachers can focus on the story problem and the series of events that lead to its resolution. They can relate the story content to children's knowledge about similar situations and encourage children to make predictions about subsequent story events. After reading the narrative, they can help children summarize the important story ideas and arrange follow-up activities, such as writing, drawing, and acting out story events. When reading an expository text, they can help children build knowledge of the major text concepts and any associated new terms. They can help children focus on the key ideas through demonstration and visual props, highlighting relationships among the ideas and clarifying the value of the concepts for children. When reading a little book—a book that features a briefly told, simply illustrated, familiar event—they can place the book pages in clear view, read them more than once, and encourage participation in the reading. They can extend the book's ideas by encouraging children to relate text events to their own background knowledge. Follow-up activities can involve discussion, retelling, rereading, or writing by extending the story line or by constructing new, student-designed little books.

Kindergarten teachers can extend book reading with opportunities to talk, act, read, write, and draw. Such activities help children focus on written texts, and because the activities and responses vary with the type of book, children will be involved in exploring differences in written texts.

REFERENCES

Chomsky, C. (1972). Stages in language development and reading exposure. *Harvard Educational Review, 42,* 1–33.

Clark, M. (1976). *Young fluent readers: What can they teach us?* Portsmouth, NH: Heinemann Educational Books.

Clay M. M. (1975). *What did I write?* Auckland, NZ: Heinemann Educational Books.

Clay, M. M. (1982). *Observing young readers: Selected papers.* London: Heinemann Educational Books.

DePaola, T. (1975). *Strega Nona.* Englewood Cliff, NJ: Prentice-Hall.

Durkin, D. (1966). *Children who read early: Two longitudinal studies.* New York: Teachers College Press.

Feitelson, D., Kita, D., & Goldstein, Z. (1986). Effects of listening to series stories on first grader's comprehension and use of language. *Research in the Teaching of English, 20,* 339–356.

Goor, R., & Goor, N. (1981). *Shadows: Here, there, and everywhere* (1st ed.). New York: Crowell.

Harste, J. C., Woodward, V. A., Burke, C. L. (1984). *Language stories and literacy lessons.* Portsmouth, NH: Heinemann Educational Books.

Mason, J., & McCormick, C. (1984a). *Little books for early readers*. Champaign, IL: Pint-sized Prints.

Mason, J., & McCormick, C. (1984b). *Time for bed*. Champaign, IL: Pint-sized Prints.

Mason, J., Peterman, C., & Kerr, B. M. (in press). Reading to kindergarten children. In D. Strickland & L. Morrow (Eds.), *Emerging literacy: Young children learn to read and write*. Newark, DE: IRA Publications.

McCormick, C., & Mason, J. (1986). *Use of little books at home: A minimal intervention strategy for fostering early reading*. (Tech. Rep. No. 388). Urbana: University of Illinois, Center for the Study of Reading.

Meyer, L. A., Linn, R. L., & Hastings, C. N. (1988). *Teachers' reading to students correlates negatively with students' achievement in reading: Why might this be?* Manuscript submitted for publication.

Perena, K. (1984). *Children's writing and reading: Analyzing classroom language*. New York: Blackwell.

Peterman, C. (1987). *The effects of storyreading procedures collaboratively designed by teacher and researcher on kindergarteners' literacy learning*. Unpublished doctoral dissertation, University of Illinois, Champaign-Urbana.

Peterman, C. L., Dunning, D., Eckerty, C., & Mason J. (1987). *The effects of storyreading procedures collaboratively designed by teacher and researcher on kindergarteners' literacy learning*. Paper presented at the annual meeting of the American Educational Research Association, Washington, DC.

Peterman, C. L., Mason, J., & Dunning, D. (1985). *The storybook reading event: How a teacher's presentation affects kindergarten children's attempts to read*. Paper presented at the annual meeting of the National Reading Conference, San Diego, CA.

Reeve, R., Palincsar, A., & Brown, A. (1985). *Everyday and academic thinking: Implications for learning and problem solving* (Tech. Rep. No. 349). Urbana: University of Illinois, Center for the Study of Reading.

Rosenshine, B., & Stevens, R. (1984). Classroom instruction in reading. In P. D. Pearson (Ed.). *Handbook in reading research* (pp. 745–798). New York: Longman.

Snow, C. (1983). Literacy and language: Relationships during the preschool years. *Harvard Educational Review, 53*, 165–189.

Sulzby, E. (1985). Kindergarteners as writers and readers. In M. Farr (Ed.), *Advances in writing research: Vol. 1. Children's early writing development* (pp. 127–199). Norwood, NJ: Ablex.

Vygotsky, L. (1979). *Mind in society: The development of higher psychological processes*. Cambridge, MA: Harvard University Press.

Wells, G. (1982). Story reading and the development of symbolic skills. *Australian Journal of Reading, 5*, 142–152.

Wells, G. (1986). *The meaning makers: Children learning language and using language to learn*. Portsmouth, NH: Heinemann Educational Books.

6

READING AND WRITING DEVELOPMENT IN WHOLE LANGUAGE KINDERGARTENS

JoBeth Allen with Wanda Clark, Muriel Cook, Peggy Crane, Irmie Fallon, Laura Hoffman, Kathy S. Jennings, and Martha A. Sours

Seven kindergarten teacher/researchers and a university teacher/researcher studied kindergarten children's development as writers and readers. Each quarter, teachers recorded all the writing behaviors they had observed in their students. At the beginning and end of the year, they assessed students' ability to recognize letters, sounds, words, and connected text. Children were found to grow as writers, regardless of the reading and writing behaviors they brought to school. The patterns of growth were quite individual, although a common theme was that children incorporated new writing behaviors without abandoning their old ones. The study indicates how literacy can emerge in kindergartens that espouse a whole language program.

Jun Kim, who spoke both Korean and English, drew many detailed pictures his first few months of school, but he rarely added any type of print. By the end of the year, he was making long lists of perfectly copied words, which he systematically gathered from around the room. Allie, from a highly literate home, dictated stories to her teacher and scribbled her own stories at the beginning of the year. By May, she was sounding out the words she needed for her writing. Lawrence, who came to school with little previous interaction with print, fell in love with books. He imitated and invented texts through scribble writing, mock letters, and dictation. He did not give up these varied methods of expression, but by the end of the year he had added letter inventories and mock words and had occasionally attempted to write the sounds he heard in words.

These children and the other 180 whom we studied during their kindergarten year might appear to be from disparate classrooms: one where the teacher encouraged copying to learn about words, one where the teacher used dictation as a lead into reading and writing, and one in which the teacher emphasized literature as the connection to literacy. In fact, all seven kindergarten teachers in the study ascribed to the same basic philosophy of literacy development: a whole language philosophy grounded in the belief that children who have daily opportunities to interact with a variety of print sources for a variety of real purposes, and who are supported by peers and a knowledgeable teacher, become more literate. Because of their philosophy, the teachers were able to build on individual interests and strengths.

The teachers taught writing as a process, integrated the language arts, surrounded the children with real books, (including child-authored texts), and made songs, rhymes, and chants an integral part of the literacy environments they created. Then, because they wanted to know more about how what they did affected how their children learned, the teachers studied themselves and the children.

These seven teachers were part of a group of twenty-five elementary-school teachers who had asked me to lead a year-long study of literacy development in whole language classrooms in the school district of Manhattan-Ogden, Kansas. We met each week to discuss common readings and to share observations, problems, and insights from our implementation efforts. I asked that all the teachers study some aspect of whole language instruction in their classrooms (Allen, 1988); in turn, I agreed to serve as an additional teacher, a classroom observer, and/or a co-researcher.

The teachers were eager to explore and to document a number of reading, writing, teaching, and learning issues in their rooms. Two key issues emerged early in our weekly meetings. First, we wanted to know how kindergarten teachers implement a whole language philosophy when teaching writing. Because the guidelines in our writing program were from Graves (1983) and his book begins with the first grade, we wanted to document what the writing process looks like in kindergarten. How much time would we devote? Where would we find the time? What kind of assistance and how much assistance would we provide our young readers and writers? What place would our district's curricular materials find in our whole language classrooms? How would we be able to integrate reading, talking, thinking, writing, and listening in a true whole language approach—that is, one in which language is used for meaningful purposes, in natural forms? Would each teacher be different, as in the methodology studies of first-grade reading (Bond & Dykstra, 1967)? Would there be common elements across teachers?

The second issue was what and how the children were learning. Farr (1985) provided a framework for several of our questions: *literacy learning is similar to other language learning, literacy growth is developmental,* and we should expect *great individual variation in literacy development,* especially across contexts. Each of these tenets merits some discussion.

We have learned from children to view language holistically rather than in discrete categories of talking, reading, and writing. A holistic view of literacy leads us to questions about the relationship of reading and writing behaviors in the kindergarten learner. Ferreiro (1984) and Ferreiro and Teberosky (1982) documented some concepts young children have about reading and writing—concepts that are related to children's own writing and to adult-written tasks in an experimental setting. However, we wanted to look at children in a supported literacy environment, to document what happens over the course of a year, rather than in cross-sectional teacher-task situations. Other researchers have looked at specific connections between learning to read and write. Morris and Perney (1984) found the level of invented spelling to be highly predictive of first-grade reading achievement as measured by word recognition. On the other hand, Bussis, Chittenden, Amarel, and Klausner (1985, p. 107) found "little connection between the children's reading and the mechanical aspects of writing" in the first- and second-grade students they studied over a two-year period. Although the classrooms in both these studies were similar to our whole language classroom, neither study dealt with kindergarten children with such writing behaviors as scribble writing, drawing, mock letters, and so on. We decided to investigate questions the teachers felt parents and administrators would ask, more traditional questions about the alphabet, sounds, words, and texts in relation to the writing forms we were observing.

Although teachers and researchers tend to agree that writing growth is developmental, various attempts at describing writing growth have yet to provide a clear answer to whether there is a uniform progression of writing behaviors. Ferreiro and Teberosky (1982) found five writing levels, ranging from reproduction of writing features (scribbling, mock letters) to alphabetic writing (phonemic spelling). Temple, Nathan, and Burris (1982) found developmental writing levels closely paralleling Ferreiro and Teberosky's, which they called prephonemic, early phonemic, phonemic, transitional, and conventional. On the other hand, Clay (1975), Dyson (1985), Harste, Woodward, and Burke (1984), and Sulzby (1985) found no uniform pattern of development; instead, they identified increasingly diverse and sophisticated writing behaviors based on abiding principles. What would we find when studying a large number of kindergartners over the course of a whole year? Would children move from one writing behavior to a more sophisticated one, abandoning the earlier form? Would they accumulate new behaviors, using a variety by the end of the year? Would they take similar paths to more conventional writing?

Questions about writing growth took us directly to questions about individual variation. Because this was a classroom research study, we had no interest in controlling for variation of social variables. We chose to study all the children in each classroom, maintaining a wide variety of social, ethnic, language, and experiential backgrounds. Our classrooms included children with various learning abilities, including those for whom English was a second or foreign language. However, we did intentionally limit the situational context for writing. The teachers emphasized writing for expression and communication, to be shared with peers. Children wrote within this context regularly, with sharing an integral part of the process. We felt that our classrooms were based on the best model of literacy learning available and that we would be able to describe emergent writing in a school setting that re-created the most facilitative home environments. What we wanted to discover was how do kindergarten-entry reading and writing behaviors, the result of previous literacy experiences, affect development? How can both individual variation and a pattern of writing growth be characteristic of young children (Dyson, 1985; Sulzby, 1985)? We felt that with seven classrooms and 183 children, we would be able to shed more light on this relationship than had previous studies that dealt with smaller numbers.

METHOD

Of the many questions generated in our meetings early in the year, this chapter deals with the following:

1. How do different kindergarten teachers who are implementing a whole language philosophy structure literate environments and interact with emergent readers and writers?
2. What is the relationship between reading and writing development in kindergarten, based on entry knowledge of various aspects of reading and writing?

3. How do children develop as writers in whole language kindergartens?

Participants

Three of the kindergarten teachers had used a whole language teaching philosophy the year before the study; four were developing whole language classrooms for the first time. Three teachers recorded both morning and afternoon sessions of kindergarten (N = 46, 46, 23); four recorded only half days (N = 20, 13, 17, 18). We had a total of 183 children to follow through the whole year. At two schools especially, the turnover rate was quite high (over 60 percent in one case), keeping the number of full-year students low. No children were excluded from the study. There were children with identified or suspected learning problems, language delays of up to two-and-a-half years, children who were repeating kindergarten, and those with probable emotional strains stemming from stressful home situations. In addition, English was a foreign or second language for about 10 percent of the children.

Data-Gathering Procedures

Classroom Context. To determine how the teachers translated their stated philosophies about literacy learning, I asked them to respond quarterly to a questionnaire about their writing instruction and support (see Figure 6.1). The teachers responded to the questionnaire by noting the nature of typical writing periods and their philosophy regarding dictation, "overwriting" the child's invented message with conventional writing, and handwriting, or correct letter formation. They also described other aspects of the writing process, including instruction, conferences, and sharing. At the end of the year, teachers detailed additional aspects of their literacy programs, including instruction in letter names and sounds, integration of reading with other learning, and the role literature played in their rooms (see Figure 6.2). In addition to meeting weekly with the teachers, and receiving their quarterly written reports, I was often invited to participate in classroom writing workshops, conferences, and sharing times. Since I did not enter any classroom unless invited, I did not conduct systematic observations.

Writing. At the end of each quarter, teachers filled out a form called *"Types of Writing Produced"* (TWP) for each student (see Figure 6.3). Teachers marked every category in which they saw activity. They based their evaluations on daily interactions with their students during

Teacher

Date

Writing Practices

Typical writing period (1   2   3   4   5   times weekly)

Instructions to children during writing period

Your role during writing period

Comments on topic choice

    talking/writing

    conferences

    publishing

    other

Assistance Philosophy

Do you offer to take dictation? How do you offer? Under what circumstances?

Do you offer to overwrite? How do you offer? Under what circumstances?

If you do not offer to take dictation or to overwrite, how do you respond when a child asks for one of these services?

How are you documenting offers and requests for dictation and overwriting?

What trends are you seeing in these two areas at this point in the year?

Handwriting

What is your approach/philosophy to correct letter formation?

FIGURE 6.1   Writing Instruction and Support: Quarterly Questionnaire

Teacher

Date

How would you describe your reading instruction in terms of the following:

Approach

Supplementary materials

Phonics instruction

Alphabet instruction

Integration with other learning

Time spent each day

Library, other books used

Learning sight words (including colors, numbers, etc.)

FIGURE 6.2   Reading Instruction: End-of-Year Questionnaire

Name ______________________ Date ______________________

Category	Frequency: Some	Often	Always	Comments
Pictures only				
Scribbles				
Mock letters				
Own name				
Recurring sign				
(music, pattern)				
Letter inventory				
Word inventory				
Repeated word: mock or read				
Free copy (from print in room)				
Copy from model on own paper				
Dictated: words				
sentences				
stories				
Writes from teacher spelling				
Invented spelling: beginning				
. . . + ending				
. . . + middle				
. . . + vowels				
Labels on pictures				
Syllabic principle: prephonemic				
phonemic				
Sentences				
Stories				

On back, jot notes on the following:

1. Chronological description of several examples of writing, noting trends (attach copies).
2. Dictation and overwriting requests or your response to offers.
3. Child's attitude toward writing.
4. Summary of progress.

FIGURE 6.3 Types of Writing Produced

writing, as well as on the writing products accumulated in their folders. Teachers also used the TWP to inform parents of their children's progress at conference times.

In devising the TWP we drew on our own observations, as well as on our readings (Clay, 1975; Ferreiro & Teberosky, 1982; Sulzby, 1985; Temple et al., 1982; and others). Our analysis and discussion in this chapter include fourteen of the writing behaviors listed in the TWP: *pictures only* (drawing with no writing), *scribbles* (intended as writing, not drawing), *mock letters* (letterlike forms—Clay's flexibility principle), *recurring sign* and *repeated word: mock or real* (Clay's recurring principle), *letter inventory* and *word inventory* (lists of memorized or copied letters or words—Clay's inventory principle), *free copy* and *copy from model on own paper* (Clay's copy principle), *writes from teacher spelling* (when teacher responded to a request to spell a word), and four levels of *invented spelling*. The levels of invented spelling, based on the research of Graves (1983), Henderson and Beers (1980), Morris and Perney (1984), and Temple et al. (1982), are shown in the following list, along with how the word *kitten* might be written at each level:

Beginning	K
+ Ending	KN
+ Middle	KTN
+ Vowels	KETN, KITN, KITTN

Reading. We assessed each child on recognition of upper- and lower-case letters, environmental-print word lists (names of colors, numbers, and classmates), the reading of connected text (out of a pre-primer from the district's basal series), and sound-to-letter analysis. For the latter, teachers asked children to identify pictures of objects and to tell what letter the word began with. This assessment was done in September and again in May.

Analysis

Classroom Context. All teachers' questionnaires were examined for common elements each quarter, as well as for trends across quarters.

Writing. Numerical weights were assigned to the frequency of each behavior: 1 (some), 2 (often), and 3 (always). A zero was assigned to categories not marked. The writing behaviors were examined for what the students did most frequently each quarter, as well as for the "highest" (most sophisticated) writing behavior the student attempted. The following seven categories, similar to types of writing observed by Sulzby (1985), were used to determine and compare writing sophistication:

Category	Writing Behavior
Drawing	Pictures only
Prealphabetic	Scribbles, mock letters, and/or recurring sign
Prephonemic	Letter inventory, word inventory, repeated word, free copy, copy from model on own paper, and/or writes from teacher spelling
Phonemic 1	Invented spelling (IS): beginning
Phonemic 2	IS: beginning + ending
Phonemic 3	IS: beginning + ending + middle
Phonemic 4	IS: beginning + ending + middle + vowels

Reading. Data from the reading pretest (September) and posttest (May) were tabulated and compared for the number of letters, words, and sounds children knew and for whether they could read the level 3 preprimer with 90 percent accuracy. This information was cross-tabulated in order to group children according to reading knowledge. On the pretest, most children (160) fell into one of nine categories of varying letter, sound, and word knowledge; only one child fell into a tenth category (used for end-of-year comparisons), which included the ability to read connected text. Table 6.1 shows the number of children in each reading category at the beginning and end of the year. Reading gain was determined by pretest and posttest comparisons of these categories, but categories 3 and 4 were combined, as were 6 and 7 (since there was no clear hierarchy within these pairs). Cutoffs were used to group the data within each skill into "don't know" (recognition of ten or fewer letters, no word or sound recognition, no conventional text reading), "learning" (middle-range values), and "know" (high values).

Reading-Writing Relationships. Spearman correlations were used to determine whether children's kindergarten-entry knowledge of letters, sounds, and words correlated with the progress they made in writing or whether their initial writing behaviors correlated with gains in reading knowledge. Comparisons were made between all reading-related behaviors (pretest and posttest) and all writing behaviors (each quarter) to determine how specific reading knowledge and writing knowledge might be related.

TABLE 6.1 Distribution of Kindergartners in Reading Categories

Category	Description	No. in Sept.[a]	No. in May[b]
1	Does not yet know alphabet, words, or sounds	35	2
2	Is learning alphabet but does not know words or sounds	31	1
3	Is learning alphabet and sounds, but does not know words	9	0
4	Is learning alphabet and words but does not know sounds	18	8
5	Is learning alphabet, words, and sounds	12	7
6	Knows alphabet and is learning sounds but not words	10	1
7	Knows alphabet and is learning words but not sounds	13	6
8	Knows alphabet and is learning sounds and words	20	37
9	Knows alphabet, words, and sounds	12	57
10	Knows alphabet, words, and sounds and can read connected text, preprimer level 3	1	27

[a] There were 22 children who did not fall into one of these categories at the beginning of the year.

[b] There were 37 children who did not fall into one of these categories at the end of the year.

FINDINGS AND DISCUSSION

Classroom Context

Our whole language kindergartens did have important elements in common, as well as individual differences. All teachers found thirty minutes to be about the right amount of time for the specified writing period, but the number of times writing was included in the curriculum varied from two to five times a week, depending on the teacher and the week. Kathy Jennings noted, "In the beginning I tried writing three times a week, whenever time permitted. At that time writing was the first thing to be cut if we ran short of time. Once I worked it into the daily schedule, the kids came to enjoy and expect writing times." All teachers reported that during the year, more and more writing was done at other times (e.g., during art, phonics, social studies), and especially during "free time."

All teachers encouraged and taught children to choose their own topics, although they often suggested that children write about topics they were studying. They found three "bandwagon" themes: superheroes, rainbows, and friend books. Several teachers noted that toward the end of the year, children began writing more collaborative texts, such as Joey, Ted, and Nick's eight-page book entitled "E.T.": "ETANDI FRIENDS E.T. SADTOHISFRNDUWANTTO PLAY HWTBHO TheEND" (translation: "E.T. and I [are] friends. E.T. said to his friend, 'You want to play?' He went back home. The End").

In some rooms, children worked in teacher-organized writing groups; in others, grouping was a casual, student-determined process. Children worked at writing tables or on the floor. Teachers encouraged the children to talk about what they were writing and to say the words and sounds they were using in their writing. Most conferences were initially informal, "roving" chats, focusing on talking about the picture the child had drawn, with the teacher taking dictation if the child requested it. The procedure varied somewhat, depending on the teacher's philosophy about the role of dictation in emergent literacy. As the year progressed, conferences became longer and more structured with growing emphasis on independence and risk taking, including finding words in books and on walls, getting help from peers, and attempting invented spelling.

Sharing was an integral and key element of the writing program; however, the format and focus varied from room to room. One teacher emphasized good listening skills and responding in a way that "helps, not hurts." Another teacher encouraged sharing in small groups whenever a child wanted to read, whether the teacher was part of the group or not. Another worked very specifically on the quality of questions the listeners asked and the quality of answers the author provided. Some classes did their sharing in small groups, others with the whole class. In some, children shared library books, as well as their own writing. Wanda Clark noted that the quality of share time improved greatly when she included the sharing of library books.

Publishing, when it occurred at all, was very informal in these classrooms. The teachers noted that sharing seemed much more important to the children than publishing. The publishing that did take place usually involved only folding and stapling, which the children learned to do themselves. Occasionally, the teachers put students' work together to make a class book; this occurred most often when the writing was related to topics of study. Published books went into the class library, home to share with families, or to related centers (e.g., the science center).

Perhaps the most important trend we saw across classes was increased student independence in using reading and writing strategies. Teachers encouraged students to listen for sounds in words, to seek help from each other, and to use the entire room (walls, books, etc.) as a writing resource. Teachers who had been offering to take dictation phased out their offers for many students about midyear; instead, they would collaborate with a child who requested dictation, asking the child to tell what sounds she or he heard, to find a word in the room, or to write a name from memory. Teachers also noted that while from the start of the year they had been "nudging" individual children to write words, sentences, or stories (those children who had made attempts in these areas), about midyear they began having some group lessons for the whole class at the beginning of the writing period on hearing and writing sounds in words.

I was invited to do such a lesson in two classrooms one day. It was shortly after the Challenger disaster. I told the children that it was on my mind and that I had decided to write about the one thing I wanted to tell them the most. We had a group discussion on how I should write, "I am very sad." In Muriel Cook's class, the children agreed I should write "i am f sad," which they had me change to "i m fr sad" after we reread it. In Laura Hoffman's class, the children had me write, "I'm vre sad," after much discussion of "very." Then one child volunteered to try his hand at the board, writing "etbldp" as he repeated several times, "It blowed up."

We did not see immediate or dramatic effects of such group lessons, nor were we looking for them. Children who were not attempting phonemic writing did not suddenly try it. In fact, most children's immediate response to our lessons was to copy the model sentences off the board—something we never would have asked them to do. Then they resumed their chosen mode for the day. But we did, over time, find more and more children making phonemic attempts, as discussed in the next section.

Where did the teachers find the time to incorporate writing into their half-day programs? They reported much less use of "readiness" materials and a more integrated presentation of reading and writing throughout the day. Some of the formal writing period came from "free time"; also, children increasingly chose to write during free time. In addition, teachers reported fewer "craft" projects and more reading and writing related to areas of study. Although teachers reduced their use of worksheets and copying exercises, most of them continued to teach letters and sounds (usually a letter a week, then a sound a week). In contrast to their teaching practices in previous years, they placed more emphasis on sounds in the context of words, especially in rhymes and songs, and they had children do much more writing in conjunction with letter and sound study. These writing sessions often became group invented-spelling times.

The biggest change in the reading program was that reading also involved writing. Teachers emphasized reading and writing connections as children shared their own writing, sounded out words during writing and reading, and looked words up in their favorite books. Teachers included reading and writing in the study of other content. Most teachers did not teach any "sight words" directly, although they sometimes helped children learn such a word if they used it often in their writing.

We have reported some common characteristics of our whole language kindergartens, but many differences also existed. In some rooms, there was a major emphasis on literature; in others, on oral language development. Some rooms were organized around learning centers. What we found encouraging about this diversity was that no teacher felt she had given up anything important to her (learning centers, nursery-rhyme units, alphabet instruction) in order to implement her developing whole language philosophy. Teachers modified only portions of the curriculum with which they had been dissatisfied.

Writing Development

The preliminary analysis of the writing data supports the observation of Dyson (1985), Sulzby (1985), and others that there is a general sequence of development in young children's writing but with great individual differences. Most children were writing more conventionally by the end of the year, according to the seven categories ranked as increasingly conventional, but their paths and rates were quite diverse. A conservative interpretation of writing growth from first quarter to fourth, with growth defined as movement "up" the seven writing categories, is that 84 percent of the children showed growth, or movement in a positive direction. Of those who did not show growth, 2.5 percent were at the top level throughout the study, 5 percent seemed to regress, and 8.5 percent seemed to make no progress.

Interestingly, the majority of those who seemed to make no progress stayed in the third category (prephonemic), which is by far the most diverse and which may very well conceal developmental change. For example, one might expect *letter inventory* to precede *word inventory, free copy* was increasingly encouraged by the teachers, and *writes from teacher spelling* was usually discouraged. As Table 6.2 shows, prephonemic was the only category without a consistent, clear pattern. The incidence of *pictures only* (the first category) remained high, all aspects of the second category (*scribbles, mock letters, recurring sign*) dropped dramatically, and each level of *invented spelling* increased dramatically. Growth in the third category may therefore have occurred but may not have been measured. Furthermore, growth in some categories may be characterized by frequency changes and additions to one's

TABLE 6.2 Weighted Scores of Individual Writing Behaviors

		Quarter			
Writing Category	*Writing Behavior*	*1*	*2*	*3*	*4*
Drawing	Pictures only	298	282	241	227
Prealphabetic	Scribbles	134	90	43	35
	Mock letters	98	77	42	12
	Recurring sign	18	12	12	8
Prephonemic	Letter inventory	78	74	61	61
	Word inventory	34	35	70	53
	Repeated word	47	48	37	50
	Free copy	61	78	90	108
	Copy from model	25	40	35	17
	Writes from teacher spelling	24	28	42	38
Phonemic 1	Invented spelling: Beginning	34	65	148	229
Phonemic 2	. . . + Ending	36	56	117	183
Phonemic 3	. . . + Middle	24	32	74	139
Phonemic 4	. . . + Vowels	19	17	45	106

Note: Score for each writing category =
1 × frequency of "some";
2 × frequency of "often";
3 × frequency of "always."

writing repertoire, neither of which would be picked up by these gross measures.

For example, Tanya was one of eleven children who stayed in the prephonemic category throughout the year. However, her individual record sheet and accumulated writing samples clearly indicated that she did indeed become more literate. At the beginning of the year, Tanya could not write her name, knew only five letter names, and no letter sounds or words. By the end of October, she was producing the following types of writing some of the time: pictures only, scribbles, mock letters, recurring sign, a few letters in a letter inventory, and repeated mock words. She also dictated occasionally. Although Tanya was frequently absent, her teacher described her as a child who loved school and who engaged in all activities enthusiastically. "She has written on reams of paper," the teacher noted at the end of the year. She also had learned her upper- and lower-case letters, the written names of most of the children in the class, and several other words posted around the room. She still was not making sound-symbol correspondences either in reading or writing, but her writing profile revealed growth in frequency of various types of writing and additions to her writing repertoire. She was writing not only her first name but also her middle and last names, as well as using most of the letters of the alphabet in her letter inventories, writing word inventories, copying from environmental print, and asking the teacher to spell words for her.

The group data showed quarter-by-quarter increases in the number of children who attempted phonemic spelling, as well as in the sophistication of the children's spelling. Growth across classes can be seen by examining the distribution of 183 students according to the highest category of writing they attempted. Table 6.3 shows that while prephonemic activity was highest during the first and second quarters, some children were at that time attempting phonemic writing. The prephonemic category, a large and diverse one, remained high during the second and third quarters, but by the third quarter there were more children attempting various levels of phonemic spelling (98) than prephonemic (56). By the fourth quarter, one third of the children were attempting to use consonants and vowels throughout the words they spelled; 72 percent were using some level of invented spelling at least some of the time.

It is important to note that in contrast to Ferreiro and Teberosky's (1982) findings, our findings showed that these writing categories were *not* exclusive. Ferreiro and Teberosky explained movement to increasingly higher writing levels as necessary when children become dissatisfied with the failure of their hypotheses to match new insights about written language; for example, when the syllabic hypothesis comes into conflict with the previously held hypothesis about minimum number of letters, children move to the alphabetic hypothesis. Instead, and in agreement with Sulzby (1985), we found a more cumulative pattern of development; children in our study continued to use several categories of writing, even as they added more conventional categories to their repertoires. Writing development is thus not a stair-stepped

TABLE 6.3 Distribution of Students in Highest Category in Which Writing Activity Occurred

Writing Category	Quarter			
	1	2	3	4
Drawing	35	23	14	10
Prealphabetic	47	28	15	5
Prephonemic	68	85	56	36
Phonemic 1	8	9	21	24
Phonemic 2	10	15	27	29
Phonemic 3	5	12	21	18
Phonemic 4	10	11	29	61
(Totals for Phonemic levels 1–4)	(33)	(47)	(98)	(132)

sequence. Rather, children become more flexible in their use of an increasing number of literacy strategies.

To get at the nonexclusive nature of the writing behaviors more systematically, we looked at the fourteen writing behaviors discussed in this chapter, as well as at the seven writing categories in which we grouped the behaviors. We learned that the majority of children did not abandon previous writing behaviors altogether but did, in fact, add new ones to their repertoires. One way of making sense of the frequency counts is to examine how many children were exhibiting three or more types of writing. Looking at this arbitrary figure over four quarters, we found a steady percentage increase: 57 percent in the first quarter, 65 percent in the second, 70 percent in the third, and 80 percent by the end of the year.

The categorical analysis is also important, because if our categories do represent something akin to new hypothesis—new insights about creating text—we need to know whether children abandon one category to move to the next or whether they *add* categories to their writing repertoires. We found the latter to be the case. The number of children operating in three or more categories nearly doubled by the end of the year, moving quarter by quarter from 38 percent to 44 percent to 58 percent to 73 percent. Furthermore, only 10 percent of the children were operating in fewer categories at the end of the year than at the start. So children did not abandon prealphabetic behaviors, for example, when they began exhibiting prephonemic strategies.

In addition to increasing their repertoires of writing behaviors with increasingly conventional kinds of writing, children showed the individual variability that Sulzby (1985) and Dyson (1985) described, and which Farr (1985) included as a major tenet of language development. There were a great many patterns of development across the four quarters. When we examined the numerical patterns of the highest category attempted by quarters, we found 124 different paths. For example, the following children moved from the prealphabetic category in the first quarter to the second phonemic level by the fourth quarter, but their paths were quite different.

Child	Quarter 1	Quarter 2	Quarter 3	Quarter 4
A	Scribbles	Pictures only	Phonemic 2	Phonemic 2
B	Scribbles	Scribbles	Scribbles	Phonemic 2
C	Scribbles	Writes from teacher spelling	Phonemic 4	Phonemic 2

We have learned from this study that most children in whole language kindergartens progress as writers; only 5 percent of those studied seemed to regress. These findings are consistent with what Dyson calls "progress toward the conventional model" (1985, p. 64) and with Sulzby's "evidence of patterns of development emerging toward conventional performance" (1985, p. 195). They are also consistent with a loose hierarchy of writing development, rather than Ferreiro and Teberosky's (1982) strict hierarchy.

Several questions remain. We suspect that the prephonemic category is too broad, for reasons discussed earlier. There should be some way of accounting for movement within a category, to show that children who appeared to stay at one level throughout the year were perhaps adding to their repertoires by producing other types of writing and/or were applying the writing behaviors in increasingly sophisticated situations (e.g., stories). Reexamination of individual data sheets may answer some of these questions; others will require further research.

The definition of conventionality poses another question. The argument could be made that when sound-symbol encoding becomes more of a priority, other conventions may temporarily lose their salience. Linear, cursivelike scribble writing covering a sheet to resemble a letter is certainly more conventional in form than DGMILVUPAUL (Dear Grandma I Love You Paul). If we consider quality of message (Dyson, 1985) or quality of composition (Graves, 1982), then drawings and elaborated dictations are often superior to invented spellings and word inventories.

It is helpful at this point to remember that movement toward phonemic conventionality was not exclusive—that even though children attempted "higher" levels with more frequency as the year progressed, they did not abandon earlier forms altogether. In fact, drawing without any accompanying writing remained extremely high all year, even when most of the children were using at least some letters to represent words. The need to express themselves and to communicate may have been fulfilled both by their drawing and by the extensive sharing of all types of writing, while the need to approximate conventionality provided the impetus for growth in sound-symbol representation. Thus it seems that children act on sustaining principles (Clay, 1975) that will continue to guide them as writers *and* concurrently progress developmentally toward conventional writing.

The sequence of writing development we have described, one of several possible sequences (Sulzby, 1985), must also be considered in the context of the great individual variation found in the present study and described in many recent studies of emergent literacy (Dyson, 1985; Graves, 1982; Harste et al., 1984). What we were able to document on a larger scale was that even children who begin and end at the same approximate places take very different paths in their writing development.

What does this combination of growth and individual variation mean at the classroom level for children as different as Allie and Lawrence? Allie came to kindergarten knowing forty-five upper- and lower-case letters, twenty-one words, and three consonant sound-symbol correspondences. During the first quarter, she produced many dictated stories, many scribble stories, and one letter inventory, and she often included music in her stories. As her teacher noted, "She seems to find security in writing the repeated patterns of [musical] notes for her stories." For example, Allie dictated on October 4, "Two girls were lost in the woods. They were trying to find their way home so they made up a land of love. The heart land returned the girls to home [hum here]. They saw their house that was rainbow colors. Their mom and dad said they could go and visit the heart land."

As the year progressed, Allie dictated less and sounded out her own words more. She stopped scribble writing at midyear. Her teacher reported that by the third quarter Allie had "begun to try invented spelling for ambitious words—still needs some continuing encouragement." By the fourth quarter, she was writing many sentences and some stories. She often left out "little" words but noted orally that she was doing so ("I'll skip 'the' "). For example, she wrote "KraRLS" ("Carissa [and me] were looking [at my] dolls") to caption a photo of herself and Carissa in the house corner. On shorter works, she tended to include more letters, as in "I YtBotng" ("I went boating"). Allie's teacher also noted that by the end of the year, Allie and her mother were often writing at home in the same manner Allie wrote at school, lending support to Allie's emerging sense of words and sounds.

Lawrence came to kindergarten having had little interaction with print. His mother wrote on a second- or third-grade level, according to the teacher's estimate. His grammatical patterns showed language immaturity, although he was highly verbal and an entertaining storyteller. He recognized only two letters, no sounds, and no words; his early writing consisted mainly of pictures, scribbles, mock letters, and dictation.

Lawrence's teacher, Laura Hoffman, recognized specific reading and writing connections in Lawrence's development. Early in the year, when Lawrence produced mostly scribbles and mock letters, she noted, "Lawrence asked me to read *B* and assorted mock letters—satisfied with garbled words." When the teacher listened to one of his stories, he invariably shouted, "Write it, write it!" He was an enthusiastic audience for other writers; he once retold a story Jed had shared, adding a reason for Jed to be sad. His teacher reported, "Lawrence loves the stories I read to the class. He is very often (nearly always) the first person to pick up a book after I've read it, hanging back from the next activity until I discover him. If he finds the book I'm going to read on my chair, he will look through it and then give away what is going to happen! He also finds books on my desk (a hands-off place) he wants me to read. He truly loves books."

By the end of the year, Lawrence was still drawing, scribbling, using mock letters, and dictating whenever he could get someone to write for him. However, he was scribbling and using mock letters less frequently. He stopped using the recurring sign after the first quarter. He added letter inventories, repeated mock words, and labels to his repertoire. In her last report, Laura Hoffman noted that he knew forty-two upper- and lower-case letters, twelve of eighteen sounds, and twelve of twenty-three words around the classroom (mostly classmates' names), and that "he will do some invented spelling [beginning and ending sounds] with a lot of help from me or another student." For example, in labeling a photograph of himself and classmates on the playground, he agreed to write "picture" ("PR") if his teacher would write "We were taking a picture." He continued his active engagement with books.

For Allie, school was an extension of her literate home environment; for Lawrence, school was an introduction to the joys of literacy. Their whole language teachers had provided the supportive literacy environments that produce real language learners.

Reading-Writing Relationships

Using gross measures of writing growth and reading growth from the beginning to the end of the year, we looked at correlations between specific writing and reading behaviors in September and overall growth. We were interested in how entry behaviors and knowledge might be associated with the child's rate of literacy development.

We found no significant correlations between the writing growth of children and the reading knowledge they brought to kindergarten in letter identification, word reading, sound-symbol production, or text reading. Similarly, there were no significant correlations between the reading growth of children and the writing behaviors they exhibited at the beginning of the school year. This is indeed a significant finding. It means that children are not limited in their ability to grow as writers by the alphabet, sound, or word knowledge they bring to school. Nor is their acquisition of these reading-related behaviors limited by their level of writing sophistication upon entering kindergarten.

This finding is contrary to Ferreiro and Teberosky's finding (1982) that "lower-class" children who entered first grade with limited literacy made little or no progress. In our study, entry level did not determine exit level; most children made progress regardless of where they started in either reading or writing. Although our children were in kindergarten rather than first grade, both our study and Ferreiro and Teberosky's described initial instruction. We believe it was the instruction in these kindergartens—instruction that supported the continued exploration and "invention" of language—that was the crucial difference. Our hypothesis supports Ferreiro and Teberosky's contention that it is the mismatch between instruction and children's concepts about literacy that stymies development.

Next we examined a complete array of correlations between reading pretest and posttest categories (alphabet, words, sounds, text reading) and all fourteen writing behaviors. Ten of the fourteen writing behaviors showed low correlations throughout the year. However, the four phonemic writing categories were correlated with reading knowledge, and the values had increased by the fourth quarter (see Table 6.4). Correlations between letter, sound, and word knowledge at the end of the year and the use of letters in spelling beginning, ending, and middle sounds were particularly strong.

Correlations between reading posttests, and writing followed a somewhat predictable pattern; that is, correlations were highest when

TABLE 6.4 Reading and Writing Correlations

	Phonemic Writing Levels, by Quarter															
Reading Pretests	Phonemic 1				Phonemic 2				Phonemic 3				Phonemic 4			
	1	2	3	4	1	2	3	4	1	2	3	4	1	2	3	4
Alphabet	.26	.37	.43	.57	.27	.42	.46	.53	.28	.35	.38	.43	.24	.27	.35	.37
Words	.43	.34	.32	.38	.37	.40	.37	.40	.30	.35	.31	.39	.29	.34	.37	.38
Sounds	.37	.43	.46	.53	.38	.49	.50	.48	.32	.38	.37	.53	.30	.30	.35	.44

	Phonemic Writing Levels, by Quarter															
Reading Posttests	Phonemic 1				Phonemic 2				Phonemic 3				Phonemic 4			
	1	2	3	4	1	2	3	4	1	2	3	4	1	2	3	4
Alphabet	.23	.25	.32	.40	.18	.24	.32	.39	.17	.21	.27	.34	.14	.15	.20	.28
Words	.36	.44	.45	.58	.32	.45	.46	.52	.28	.37	.39	.49	.27	.28	.34	.43
Sounds	.26	.40	.50	.63	.23	.41	.51	.62	.25	.35	.38	.54	.24	.26	.34	.47
Text	.35	.23	.33	.32	.32	.34	.41	.31	.29	.38	.40	.41	.24	.29	.39	.34

Note: All correlations are based on 183 children; correlations over .25 are significant at $p < .001$.

the testing times were closest to each other (at the end of the year). What was contrary to prediction, and thus more interesting, is that correlations between reading pretests and writing also increased over the four quarters. We would have expected correlations to be higher in the first quarter, because of the proximity of testing. This finding may mean that entry reading measures did have some predictive value for children's use of invented spelling. Children improved their ability to make connections between sounds and letters in words they were reading as they learned to represent words on paper.

Although there appear to be some differences among correlations involving sounds, letters, and words, we cannot make meaningful comparisons because of the correlations among these variables: alphabet with words, $r = .45$; alphabet with sounds, $r = .56$; and words with sounds, $r = .65$. In view of the distributions of reading knowledge exhibited on the pretest (shown in Table 6.1), we did not think it would be meaningful or accurate to aggregate these scores. We therefore chose to include the correlations as they occurred and to interpret broad trends, rather than specific differences.

What we have learned from these comparisons of reading and writing behaviors from the beginning to the end of the kindergarten year is that children entering school with some knowledge of the alphabet and/or letter-sound correspondence are more likely to be using that knowledge to compose with invented spelling by the end of the year. We also know that entry reading and writing behaviors do not limit literacy development.

In interpreting these findings in light of the whole language classrooms in which they occurred, we might conclude that such an instructional philosophy helps each child develop fully, regardless of initial strengths, and that it promotes the vital connection between reading and writing, since conventional measures of these abilities showed increasing correlations. Conversely, one might argue that this growing correlation is a natural maturational phenomenon. Actually, the second interpretation is consistent with the first. As we have argued, the teachers' philosophy supported the continued emergence of literacy, built on what each child understood about literacy. Instruction supported emergent literacy development (Teale & Sulzby, 1986).

The findings about reading-writing relationships in this study are limited by the measures of reading, as well as by the method of inquiry. We addressed our interest in traditional reading measures and writing growth but are left dissatisfied. We did not have effective, comprehensive measures of reading. We looked at writing as a whole, in a natural context throughout the year, but we measured reading only in parts, with not enough of the parts represented and not enough context to focus the picture. We are still searching for methods to study larger groups of children in school settings where reading (e.g., levels of storybook reading, strategies for decoding, reading to continue a writing piece) and writing (both the development of sustaining principles and growth toward conventionality) must surely be intertwined.

IMPLICATIONS FOR RESEARCH AND TEACHING

The first implication we derived from this study is that more teachers as researchers are needed in the field of emergent literacy. We began with questions that really interested and concerned teachers. Teachers not only formulated the questions for inquiry; they also constructed the data-gathering techniques and instruments. We met regularly to exchange findings, to talk about individuals and whole classes, to speculate on writing development and reading-writing relationships. We converted a need to know more about how children develop and a desire to explain that development to others (especially parents) into a collaborative research project.

Second, we need research that describes large, representative populations, as well as research that describes a few children in great detail. Studies of individual children and specific classrooms have given us a firm knowledge base for both teaching and inquiry. We urge others to include, as we did, children who come to school hungry, who speak little or no English, who live in emotional and physical conflict, and others whom our *system* might be "at risk" for failing to teach. In addition to studying whole groups, we need to find out more about children who do not show clear progress, especially about children— like the 5 percent in our study—who appear to regress.

Third, we need more research in classrooms in which the instructional program is organized on the basis of new research, classrooms that are responding to what we are learning about how children learn and how they can be taught. The theory has informed practice; now practice needs to inform theory. In our study, the instructional philosophy was consistent with what we believed to be the best possible learning conditions for literacy development. The teachers attempted to foster literacy in school the way it is fostered in homes where literacy develops without formal instruction. We extended Thomas's (1985) observations about learning to read at home to learning to write at school; according to Thomas (p. 473), such learning is the result of "the time, the social interaction, the clarification of linguistic/literacy factors, and the systematic approach to print engaged in by . . . parents [which] would be called exemplary teaching if done in the classroom." Studies in whole language classrooms provide a feasible continuum for studying emergent literacy; more research needs to be done in classrooms like these.

Fourth, we need more research that describes what children do in natural settings (in this case, the classroom) over time, as well as research that reports how children respond to certain tasks. Uniform tasks provide valuable information about what children can do; coupled with interviews, such research provides a window on literacy development. But we must continue to balance this information with accurate descriptions of what children actually do on a day-to-day basis, without experimenters' questions or conditions.

How can a better understanding of children's growth as writers inform our teaching? First, it helps define a zone of proximal development, areas in which growth is most likely to occur. Kindergarten teachers should not expect all children to write long stories with invented spellings (see Sulzby, Barnhart, and Hieshima's discussion in Chapter 2), nor should they expect children to "progress" away from drawing pictures with no attempts at print. They should expect that once children start to hear beginning sounds, they will soon be ready to listen for ending sounds, and then middle and vowel sounds. A problem for many teachers moving from a skills-oriented teaching philosophy to a process-oriented one is how to help children learn without preempting the learning process. When asked how a teacher knows when to intervene, when to "push," Graves told a group of whole language teachers that he intervenes more and more as he gets to know young writers. "Then I watch like a hawk to see if they understand, and if they don't, I try a little later in the year and watch again" (Allen, 1986). The information in our study should help teachers decide what to observe in children's literate behaviors and how to organize successful, relevant intervention. Expecting wide individual differences, both in writing development and in reading-writing relationships, does more than comfort "failed" instruction. It forces teachers to replace any predetermined curricula with daily interaction around what each child is doing. Graves (1982) describes this process as drawing the curriculum out of each child. Teachers should note that it was in the areas where our teachers encouraged independence (free copy, invented spelling) that students showed the most consistent growth (see Table 6.2).

Our study should assure teachers that the majority of their students will make progress in writing without required copying, handwriting exercises, or other tasks of dubious value. When given the opportunity, children provide their own practice (Clay, 1975). They list words they know, make pages of symbols that increasingly approach conventional form, copy print from their own papers and from print throughout the room, borrow each others name tags to include them in their stories, and ask—at the exact moment they need to know—"How do you make a *j*?"

Kindergarten teachers can also build on the correlations we found between alphabet, word, and sound knowledge and invented spelling. Teachers in our study talked a great deal about connections between reading and writing, and they made these connections explicit. It may be especially noteworthy that letter-sound instruction turned into reading-writing instruction in these classrooms. If teachers can convince the administrators who purchase separate workbooks for phonics, "readiness," and handwriting to put the money into the real tools of reading and writing (paper, pencils, books, typewriters), children will develop integrated views of reading and writing, views that should enable growth in both areas (Graves & Hansen, 1983; Smith, 1983).

Finally, teachers can rejoice that the knowledge children bring to school about reading and writing does not limit their literacy learning. All children have an equal opportunity to grow if teachers respond to what they can do and facilitate what they attempt.

R E F E R E N C E S

Allen, J. (1986). A 1500 mile teaching conference. *Kansas Journal of Reading*, 2, 22–28.

Allen, J., Combs, J., Hendricks, M., Nash, P., & Wilson, S. (1988). Studying change: Teachers who become researchers. *Language Arts*, 65, 379–387.

Bond, G. L., & Dykstra, R. (1967). The cooperative research program in first-grade reading instruction. *Reading Research Quarterly*, 2, 5–142.

Bussis, A., Chittenden, C., Amarel, M., & Klausner, E. (1985). *Inquiry into meaning: An investigation of learning to read*. Hillsdale, NJ: Erlbaum.

Clay, M. M. (1975). *What did I write?* Auckland, NZ: Heinemann Educational Books.

Dyson, A. H. (1985). Individual differences in emerging writing. In M. Farr (Ed.), *Advances in writing research: Vol. 1. Children's early writing development* (pp. 59–125). Norwood, NJ: Ablex.

Farr, M. (Ed.) (1985). *Advances in writing research: Vol. 1. Children's early writing development*. Norwood, NJ: Ablex.

Ferreiro E. (1984). The underlying logic of literacy development. In H. Goelman, A. Oberg, & F. Smith (Eds.), *Awakening to literacy* (pp. 154–173). Exeter, NH: Heinemann Educational Books.

Ferreiro, E., & Teberosky, A. (1982). *Literacy before schooling*. Exeter, NH: Heinemann Educational Books.

Graves, D. H. (1982). *A case study of observing the development of primary children's composing, spelling, and motor behavior during the writing process*. Final report to the National Institute of Education (NIE-G-78-0174).

Graves, D. H. (1983). *Writing: Children and teachers at work.* Exeter, NH: Heinemann Educational Books.

Graves, D. H., & Hansen, J. (1983). The author's chair. *Language Arts, 60,* 176–183.

Harste, J. C., Woodward, V. A., & Burke, C. L. (1984). *Language stories and literacy lessons.* Portsmouth, NH: Heinemann Educational Books.

Henderson, E. H., & Beers, J. (1980). *Developmental and cognitive aspects of learning to spell.* Newark, DE: International Reading Association.

Morris, D., & Perney, J. (1984). Developmental spelling as a predictor of first-grade reading achievement. *Elementary School Journal, 84,* 441–457.

Smith, F. (1983). Reading like a writer. *Language Arts, 60,* 558–567.

Sulzby, E. (1985). Kindergarteners as writers and readers. In M. Farr (Ed.), *Advances in writing research: Vol. 1. Children's early writing development* (pp. 127–199). Norwood NJ: Ablex.

Teale, W. H., & Sulzby, E. (1986). *Emergent literacy: Writing and reading.* Norwood, NJ: Ablex.

Temple, C., Nathan, R., & Burris, N. (1982). *The beginnings of writing.* Boston: Allyn & Bacon.

Thomas, K. (1985). Early reading as a social interaction process. *Language Arts, 62,* 469–475.

PART TWO

Establishing a Classroom Context for Reading and Writing Development

Introduction by Sandra Murphy

The past twenty years have seen significant changes in the fields of reading and writing research—in our conceptions of reading and writing, in the kinds of research questions asked, and in the kinds of implications drawn for teaching and learning. Because numerous theoretical models of the reading process have been generated, views of the nature of this process have changed substantially, shifting from a focus on retrieval of information from text to a focus on the active, *constructive* role of the reader in an interactive, recursive process. An explosion of research on the writing process during the 1970s and 1980s has brought about a new understanding of the complexity of the writing process, identifying and distinguishing between the kinds of strategies employed by expert and novice writers.

In recent years, new strands of research have been added in both fields—strands that focus on the social contexts in which reading and writing occur. In the field of reading, concern for the social dimension has focused largely on the contexts of instruction, a strand of research that Duffy (1982) has labeled the new "looking-in-classrooms" research. In the field of writing, researchers have also begun to look closely at social contexts—homes, classrooms, and workplaces—in which people learn to write in interaction with teachers and peers (Freedman, Dyson, Flower, & Chafe, 1987).

As promising as these advances in research on literacy are, unproductive schisms have arisen. Studies of writing are disconnected from studies of reading; few studies have actually focused on the links between reading and writing; additionally, studies of social contexts often exclude consideration of cognitive processes. If research is to move on and be conducive to the improvement of teaching, the disparate threads of our research in both reading and writing will have to be interwoven. We need to pay more attention to the connections between writing and reading, to the ways symbolic worlds are embedded in social worlds, and to the connections between the powerful forces of language, cognition, and context.

From research and our own experience as readers, writers, and teachers, we know that social contexts are intricately interwoven with the development of writing and reading. Interpretation—by the reader of the text and by the writer of the writing task—is influenced by both cognition and social context. Purpose and situation influence both the process and the outcome—both the reader's understanding and the writer's product. In different populations, at different ages, in different situations, the transactions between readers and texts can take radically different forms.

The beauty, as well as the significance, of Louise Rosenblatt's contribution to this volume is that she gives us, in Chapter 7, a theory—indeed a *language*—for talking about this richly tangled web. Rosenblatt's theory interweaves three threads of reading and writing research: *process, product,* and *social context.* In her view, writing and reading, like all human activities, can be seen as "transactions in which the individual and the social, cultural, and natural elements" reciprocally participate. Although she places writing and reading squarely in a social context, it is not done at the expense of the role of the individual or the text. For example, she defines reading as an "event," a transaction involving a particular reader and a particular configuration of marks on a page, and occurring at a particular time in a particular context. The individual, the text, and the context carry equal weight in her definition.

Rosenblatt argues eloquently against viewing language as an autonomous system, in the sense that meaning resides in the text alone, but she balances that stance with recognition that generally accepted meanings and methods of conveying them are an integral part of what children must learn in order to communicate with others. She also places instruction in a social context, pointing out that learning to write is not simply skill acquisition; it also involves learning that there are a multitude of written discourse communities, each with its own rules and expectations.

Many of Rosenblatt's insights have important implications for instruction. For example, she cautions us against oversimplification of reading and writing processes, against seeing any of the complex activities of the writing process—such as planning, revising, and editing—as fixed stages. This insight seems particularly important given the new wave of enthusiasm for teaching the writing process.

Rosenblatt also offers us important insights into the conjoining of reading and writing processes and the unique character of two kinds of reading that are special to the writer. One of these, the reading a writer does to test what has been written against an evolving purpose, argues against the idea that writing is something one does after all the planning has been done. Rosenblatt's concept of this kind of authorial reading captures the simultaneity of the planning and discovery that go on during composing, and it has profound implications for instruction. In our enthusiasm for teaching "process," we should be careful not to ignore the complexities of the reading and writing processes or to legislate a specific sequence of "stages."

Rosenblatt's second kind of authorial reading, the kind that occurs when a writer reads the text through the eyes of a potential reader, is also important, especially so because it is perhaps one of the most difficult types of reading for children—and adults, for that matter—to master. We need to explore ways to foster the development of this ability to "read through the eyes of others." Both kinds of authorial reading, intimately intertwined as they are in the writing process, offer rich topics for further research. Such research promises new insights into the relationships between reading and writing, as well as potential for improvements in teaching.

Many of Rosenblatt's concepts can be related to the material presented by Martha King in Chapter 1. With her description of the collaborative way mothers and children build meaning in talk and her extension of the collaborative metaphor to children's acquisition of written language, King, like Rosenblatt, puts language activities—including writing, reading, and speaking—firmly in a social context. In addition, King's analysis of story structure highlights the importance of the individual's reservoir of past experience with language and the world—a view that complements Rosenblatt's concept of the importance of the individual in transactions with text.

Although King's and Rosenblatt's views are similar in many respects, King adds an important dimension to Rosenblatt's theoretical framework: the dimension of development. King's work on the development of children's ability to elaborate the functions of stories and to employ cohesive devices is one of the most thorough and interesting investigations of the growth of language competence in areas central to literacy acquisition. Her work makes it clear that in addition to product, process, and context, development should be a key variable in research on the teaching and learning of writing and reading.

Although their theoretical frameworks are complementary, Rosenblatt and King do appear to have theoretical differences in relation to the concept of "text" as defined by Halliday and Hasan. King's definition of text sounds suspiciously like an autonomous code, something that Rosenblatt debates. Halliday and Hasan define text as "a piece of language use that is internally consistent and interpretable without reference to anything outside of the context of the discourse itself. Texts are semantic units that are encoded in sentences and have meaning within themselves and in relation to the context in which they occur" (p. xxx). When we consider that definition, we have to be careful to emphasize the last phrase, "in relation to the context in which they occur." If we forget that phrase, or if we ignore the well of personal meanings the individual brings to a transaction with text, then we are in danger of falling into the trap that Rosenblatt warns us about: viewing language as a self-contained system. Definitions of text that focus too narrowly on products or outcomes fail to capture the complexities of meaning-making processes, as well as the kinds of collaborative activity that occur during instruction. We need to consider new ways of characterizing how communities of language users create meaning while employing multiple modes of language—reading, speaking, and listening, as well as writing.

The instructional studies presented in Part Two complement the themes that run through the two theoretical chapters and are valuable extensions of the reported studies in Part One. Rosenblatt concludes her chapter with the comment that "research methodologies and designs will need to be sufficiently complex, varied, and interlocking to do justice to the fact that reading and writing are at once intensely individual and intensely social activities." The instructional studies show a movement in the direction Rosenblatt suggests, toward a more complex and interlocking research design—one that accounts for the complexities of the social context and the roles of participants.

Teachers were intimately involved in many of these studies, not treated as objects of study, as is so often the case. As a result, the interaction between the researchers and the teachers enriched the information gained. When teachers are collaborative partners with researchers, both practice and research benefit. In addition to providing rich data for analysis, collaboration of this kind can help teachers become reflective and ultimately more effective.

The studies in Part Two also raise new issues. The research reported by Raphael, Englert, and Kirschner in Chapter 12, for example, shows that instruction that focuses on the characteristics of text structure and that emphasizes audience and purpose can improve students' ability to write expository text. In future studies, we need to consider the implications of instructional practices that provide structure for the child. By providing the structure, we may simplify the demands of the task and speed acquisition of a particular structure, but we may also be fostering formulaic writing. By focusing on form, we may be creating situations in which form drives meaning, instead of the reverse.

As researchers and educators, we need to ask whether we should be providing the structure or helping the child find the structure by ensuring that he or she works out particular problems that arise in particular communicative situations. We also need to consider the long-term effects of these two approaches. Would, for instance, the long-term effects of explicit instruction in text structure produce the same kinds of results as problem-solving writing tasks? And, finally, we also need to consider the issue of development. We need to ask whether different approaches are better for different ages. Would, for instance, instruction in a particular type of text structure be more helpful for students during the middle-school years than during elementary school?

All the chapters in Part Two suggest a need for coherently drawing together information from different theoretical perspectives and research paradigms, for interweaving process, product, development, and context in order to obtain new insights about the teaching and learning of language. As we proceed to develop this new approach, we must consider its implications. For researchers, does this mean that different methodologies should be developed? Is the "old dualistic experimental research design" insufficient, as Rosenblatt suggests? Should new methods for analyzing data be devised? For practitioners, even more difficult questions arise. For example, what implications does a theoretical framework that incorporates social context have for the evaluation of writing? If we advocate collaborative activities in instruction, can we justify models of evaluation that focus only on products? Will our old methods of evaluating writing suffice? And if we value aesthetic experience, how do we go about assessing our progress in fostering its development? The problem of evaluation may well be the most difficult problem we will have to solve.

R E F E R E N C E S

Duffy, G. G. (1982). Fighting off the alligators: What research in real classrooms has to say about reading instruction. *Journal of Reading Behavior, 14,* 357–373.

Freedman, S. W., Dyson, A. H., Flower, L., & Cnafe, W. (1987). *Research in writing: Past, present and future* (CSW Report No. 1). Berkeley: University of California, Graduate School of Education, Center for the Study of Writing.

Halliday, M., & Hasan, R. (1976). *Cohesion in English.* London: Longman.

7

WRITING AND READING
The Transactional Theory

Louise M. Rosenblatt

In the light of the post-Einsteinian scientific paradigm and Peircean semiotics, reading and writing are seen as always involving individuals, with their particular linguistic and experiential resources, in particular transactions with particular environments or contexts. Analyses of the reading and writing processes reveal parallels in patterns of symbolization and construction of meaning. This chapter gives special attention to a dimension usually ignored: the processes associated with "literary" and "nonliterary" reading and writing. Differences, however, defeat the notion of an automatic cross-fertilization of reading and writing activities. Conditions are set forth for creating a teaching environment favorable to such cross-fertilization.

The purpose of this chapter is to present a coherent theoretical approach to the interrelationship between the reading and writing processes.[1] Recent decades have seen much publication concerning these two kinds of linguistic activity, and their connections have not been entirely neglected. Why, then, a chapter devoted to theory? The answer is that any research project, any teaching method, rests on some kind of epistemological assumptions and, in this field, on some models of the reading and writing processes. The effort will be to present a basis for scrutinizing current practices and for judging how they relate to long-term educational goals.

In recapitulating my transactional theory, I am aware that in the past decade an atmosphere favorable to this point of view has developed. To refer to the various theorists and researchers on reading and writing who have drawn on this approach or to differentiate it from other theories would, however, require extended discussion of points of agreement and disagreement beyond the scope of this chapter.

The relationship between reading and writing encompasses a network of similarities and differences. Sharing a necessary involvement with texts, both reading and writing lack the nonverbal aids to communication afforded the speaker and listener. Yet writing and reading obviously differ in that the writer starts with a blank page and must produce a text, while the reader starts with the already written or printed text and must produce meaning. A similarity, however, is currently being stressed: the writer "composes" a presumably meaningful text; the reader "composes," hence "writes," an interpreted meaning. This metaphor, though useful for similarities, glosses over certain differences in the two ways of composing. Another parallel is being increasingly recognized: reading is an integral part of the writing process. But the writer's reading both resembles and differs from the reader's. This chapter identifies at least two kinds of reading special to the writer. It also presents a distinctive view of the writing and reading processes implied by such generally accepted contrasts as "expository/poetic" or "literary/nonliterary."

THE TRANSACTIONAL PARADIGM

The terms *transaction* and *transactional* as used in this chapter are consonant with the contemporary twentieth-century shift in thinking about the relationship of human beings to the natural world. In *Knowing and the Known*, John Dewey and Arthur F. Bentley pointed out that the term *interaction* had become too closely tied to Cartesian or Newtonian philosophical dualism, the paradigm that treats human beings and nature as separate entities. The newer paradigm, reflecting especially Einsteinian and subatomic developments in physics, emphasizes their reciprocal relationship. The scientist—or "observer," to use Niels Bohr's phrasing (1959, p. 210)—is seen as "part of his observation." Instead of separate, already defined entities acting on one another (an interaction), Dewey and Bentley (1949, p. 69) suggested that the term *transaction* be used to designate relationships in which each element conditions and is conditioned by the other in a mutually constituted situation. This view requires a break with entrenched habits of thinking. The old stimulus-response, subject-object, individual-social dualisms give way to recognition that such relationships take place in a context that also enters into the event. Human activities and relationships are seen as transactions in which the individual and the social, cultural, and natural elements interfuse. The transactional mode of thinking has perhaps been most clearly assimilated in ecology. Current writers on philosophy and semiology (e.g., Bruner, 1986; Rorty, 1982; Toulmin, 1982), though they may differ on metaphysical implications, find it necessary to come to terms with the new paradigm.

Language

The transactional concept has profound implications for understanding language activities in general and reading and writing in particular. Language traditionally has been viewed as primarily a self-contained system or code, a set of arbitrary rules and conventions, manipulated as a tool by speakers and writers or imprinting itself on the minds of listeners and readers. This way of thinking is so deeply engrained that it continues to function, tacitly or explicitly, in much supposedly innovative literary theory and rhetoric. The influence of the great French semiotician Ferdinand de Saussure plays a part in this. Despite his recognition of the difference between actual language and the abstractions of linguists and lexicographers, his formulation of a dyadic, or two-element, relationship between "signifier and signified," between word and object, has lent itself to the conception of language as an autonomous system.

In contrast, Charles Sanders Peirce, the American founder of semiotics, offered a triadic formulation congenial to a transactional sense of human beings in their environment. "A sign," Peirce wrote, "is in conjoint relation to the thing denoted and to the mind. . . . The sign is related to its object only in consequence of a mental association, and depends on habit" (3.360). Since Peirce evidently did not want to reinforce the notion that "mind" was an entity, he typically phrased the "conjoint" linkage as among sign, object, and "interpretant" (6.347). This triadic model grounds language and the processes involved in speaking, listening, writing, and reading firmly in the individual's transactions with the world.[2]

Psychologists' studies of children's acquisition of language support the Peircean triad. For example, Werner and Kaplan, in their work on *Symbol Formation,* concluded that a vocalization or sign becomes a word, a verbal symbol, when the sign and its object or referent are linked with the same "organismic state" (1962, p. 18). William James noted such a linkage when he said that not only the words referring to objects but also the words naming the relationships among them carry "an inward coloring of their own" in the stream of consciousness (1890, p. 245). This rich experiential aura of language is different for each of us. As L. S. Vygotsky pointed out, "the sense" of a word is "the sum of all the psychological events aroused in our consciousness by the word" (1962, p. 146).

Language, we know, is a socially generated public system of communication—the very bloodstream of any society. But it is often forgotten that language is always internalized by an individual human being in transaction with a particular environment. "Lexical concepts must be shared by speakers of a common language, . . . yet there is room for considerable individual difference in the details of any concept" (Miller & Johnson-Laird, 1976, p. 700). And traces of cumulatively funded personal experiences remain. Bates (1979, p. 66) uses the image of an iceberg for the total sense of a word; the tip of the iceberg represents the public aspect of meaning, while the submerged base represents private meaning. The dictionary lists the public, lexical meanings of a word. No language act, however, can be thought of as totally public or totally private. Always anchored in individuals, it necessarily involves both public and private elements, the base as well as the tip of the "iceberg." And although we speak of individual signs or words, we know that words do not function in isolation, but always in particular verbal, personal, and social contexts.

The individual's share in the language, then, is that part, or set of features, of the public system that has been internalized in the individual's experiences with words in life situations. The residue of such transactions in particular natural and social contexts constitutes a kind of linguistic-experiential reservoir. Embodying our funded assumptions, attitudes, and expectations about the world—and about language—this inner capital is all that each of us has to start from in speaking, listening, writing, and reading. We make sense of a new situation or transaction by applying, reorganizing, revising, or extending elements selected from our personal linguistic-experiential reservoir.

Selective Attention

William James tells us that we are constantly engaged in a "choosing activity," which he termed "selective attention" (1890, 1:284). We constantly select from the stream, or field, of consciousness "by the reinforcing and inhibiting agency of attention" (1:288). This activity is sometimes called "the cocktail-party phenomenon." In a crowded room, where various conversations are in progress, we focus our attention on only one of them at a time, and the others become a background hum. Similarly, we can turn our attention toward a broader or narrower area of the field.[3] The transactional concept will prevent our falling into the error of envisaging selective attention as a mechanical choosing from among an array of fixed entities; rather, we will see it as a dynamic centering on areas or aspects of the contents of consciousness.

Thus, while language activity implies an intermingled kinesthetic, cognitive, affective, associational matrix, what is brought into awareness, what is pushed into the background, or what is suppressed depends on where the attention is focused. The linguistic reservoir should not be seen as encompassing verbal signs statically linked to meanings, like typewriter keys to fixed letters, but as a fluid pool of potential triadic symbolizations. Such residual linkages of sign, object, and organic state, it will be seen, become actual symbolization as selective attention functions under the shaping influence of particular times and circumstances. In the linguistic event, any process will be affected also by the physical and emotional state of the individual (e.g., by fatigue or stress). Attention may be controlled or wandering, intense or superficial. In the discussion that follows, it will be assumed that such factors enter into the transaction and affect the quality of the process under consideration.

THE READING PROCESS

The Reading Transaction

The transactional nature of language and the concepts of transaction and selective attention illuminate what happens in reading. Every reading act is an event, a transaction involving a particular reader and a particular configuration of marks on a page, and occurring at a particular time in a particular context. Certain organismic states, certain ranges of feeling, certain verbal or symbolic linkages, are stirred up in the linguistic reservoir. From these activated areas, selective attention—conditioned by multiple personal and social factors that enter into the situation—picks out elements that synthesize or blend into what constitutes "meaning." Meaning does not reside ready-made in the text or in the reader; it happens during the transaction between reader and text.

When we see a set of marks on a page that we believe can be made into verbal signs (i.e., can be seen as a text), we assume they should give rise to some more or less coherent meaning. We bring our accumulated experience to bear. Multiple inner alternatives resonate to the words as they fall into phrases and sentences. From the very beginning, some expectation, some tentative feeling or principle or purpose, no matter how vague at first, guides selection and synthesis. As the eyes encounter the unfolding text, one seeks cues on which, in the light of past syntactic and semantic experience, to base expectations about what is forthcoming. The text as a linguistic pattern is part of what is being constructed. Possibilities open up concerning diction, syntax, linguistic and literary conventions, ideas, themes, and the general kind of meaning that may be developed. Each additional sentence will signal certain options and exclude others, so that even as "the meaning" develops, the selecting, synthesizing impulse is itself constantly shaped and tested. If the marks on the page evoke elements that cannot be assimilated into the emerging synthesis, the guiding principle or framework is revised. If necessary, it is discarded, and a complete rereading occurs. New tentative guidelines, new bases for a hypothetical structure, present themselves. A complex, nonlinear, self-correcting transaction between reader and text continues—the arousal and fulfillment (or frustration) of expectations and the construction of a growing, often revised, "meaning." Finally, a synthesis or organization, more or less coherent and complete, emerges, the result of a to-and-fro interplay between reader and text.

The Reader's Stance

The reading process that produces the meaning, say, of a scientific report differs from the reading process that evokes a literary work of art. Neither contemporary reading theory nor literary theory has done justice to this important distinction. The tendency in the past generally has been to assume that such a distinction depends entirely on the texts involved. The character of the "work" has been held to inhere entirely in the text. Such classifications of texts as literary or nonliteray ignore the contribution of the reader. We cannot look at the text and predict the nature of the resulting work in any particular reading. Before we can assume, for instance, that a poem or novel, rather than a statement of facts, will be evoked from the texts, say, of Frost's *Mending Wall* or Dickens's *Great Expectations*, we must postulate a particular kind of relationship between the reader and the text.

Essential to any reading is the reader's adoption, conscious or unconscious, of a stance. As the transaction with the printed text stirs up elements of the linguistic-experiential reservoir, the reader adopts a selective attitude, bringing certain aspects to the center of attention and pushing others to the fringes. A stance reflects the reader's purpose. The reading event must fall somewhere in a continuum, determined by whether the reader adopts a "predominantly aesthetic" stance or a "predominantly efferent" stance. The difference in stance determines the proportion or mix of public and private elements of sense that fall within the scope of attention.

The term *efferent* (after the Latin *efferre,* to carry away) describes the kind of reading in which attention is centered predominantly on what is to be carried away or retained *after* the reading event. An extreme example is the man who has accidentally swallowed a poisonous liquid and who is rapidly reading the label on the bottle to learn the antidote. Here, surely, we see an illustration of James's point about selective attention and our capacity to push into the periphery of awareness those elements that do not serve our present interests. The man's attention is focused on learning what is to be done as soon as the reading ends. He concentrates on what the words point to, their barest public referents, and on constructing the directions for future action. Reading a newspaper, a textbook, or a legal brief would usually provide a similar, though less extreme, instance of the predominantly efferent stance. In efferent reading, then, we focus attention mainly on the public "tip of the iceberg" of sense: the meaning results from abstracting and analytically structuring the ideas, information, directions, or conclusions to be retained, used, or acted upon after the reading event.

The predominantly *aesthetic* stance covers the other half of the continuum. In this kind of reading, the reader adopts an attitude of readiness to focus attention on what is being lived through *during* the reading event. Welcomed into awareness are not only the public referents of the verbal signs but also the rest of the "iceberg" of sense: the sensations, images, feelings, and ideas that are the residue of past psychological events involving those words and their referents. Attention may even include the sounds and rhythms of the words themselves, heard in "the inner ear." The aesthetic reader experiences and savors the qualities of the structured ideas, situations, scenes, personalities, and emotions that are called forth and participates in the tensions, conflicts, and resolutions as they unfold. This "lived-through" meaning is felt to correspond to the text; this meaning shaped during the aesthetic transaction constitutes "the literary work," the poem, story, or play. This evocation, and not the text, is the object of the reader's "response" and "interpretation" both during and after the reading event.

To recognize the essentiality of stance does not minimize the importance of the text in the transaction. Various verbal elements— for example, divergence from linguistic or semantic norms, metaphor, or formal or stylistic conventions—have even been said to constitute the "poeticity" or "literariness" of a text. None of these arrangements of words could make their "literary" (i.e., aesthetic) contribution, however, without the reader's prior shift of attention toward the qualitative or experiential contents of consciousness. Such verbal elements actually often serve as cues to the reader to adopt an aesthetic stance.

The Efferent-Aesthetic Continuum

Thus one of the earliest and most important steps in any reading event is the selection of either an efferent or an aesthetic stance toward the transaction with the text. Although many readings may fall near the extremes, many others—perhaps most—may fall nearer the center of the continuum, where both parts of the "iceberg" of meaning are more evenly involved. Also, within a particular aesthetic reading, attention may turn from the experiential synthesis to efferent analysis, as the reader recognizes some technical strategy or passes a literary judgment. Similarly, in an efferent reading, a general idea may be illustrated or reinforced by an aesthetically lived-through illustration or example. Despite the mix of private and public aspects of meaning in each stance, the two dominant stances are clearly distinguishable: someone else can read a text efferently for us and acceptably paraphrase it, but no one else can read aesthetically—that is, experience the evocation of a literary work of art for us.

Since each reading is an event in particular circumstances, the same text may be read either efferently or aesthetically. The experienced reader usually approaches a text alert to cues offered by the text and, unless another purpose intervenes, automatically adopts the appropriate predominant stance. Sometimes the title suffices as a cue. Probably one of the most obvious cues is the arrangement of broad margins and uneven lines that signals the reader to adopt the aesthetic stance and undertake to make a poem. The opening lines of any text are especially important from this point of view because of their signaling of tone, attitude, and conventional indicators of stance to be adopted. Of course, the reader may overlook or misconstrue the cues, or they may be confusing. And the reader's own purpose or schooling that indoctrinates the same undifferentiated approach to all texts may dictate a different stance from the one the writer intended. For example, a student reading *A Tale of Two Cities* who knows there will be a test on facts about characters and plot may be led to adopt a predominantly efferent stance, screening out all but the relevant data. Similarly, readings of an article on zoology could range from analytic abstracting of factual content to an aesthetic savoring of the ordered structure of ideas, rhythm of sentences, and images of animal life brought into consciousness. Figure 7.1 indicates how different readings of the same text may fall at different points of the efferent-aesthetic continuum.

The Problem of Validity of Interpretation

The polysemous character of texts—that there is no one absolutely "correct" meaning—creates the problem of the relation between the

READING OR WRITING EVENTS

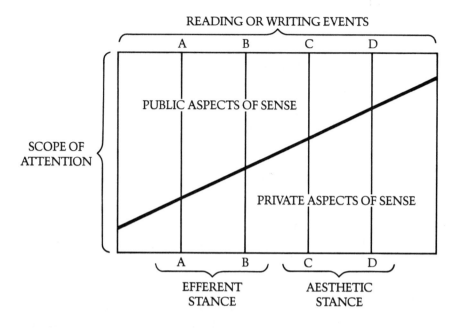

FIGURE 7.1. The Efferent-Aesthetic Continuum. Any linguistic activity has both public (lexical, analytic, abstracting) and private (experiential, affective, associational) components. Stance is determined by the proportion of each component admitted into the scope of selective attention. The efferent stance draws mainly on the public aspect of sense; the aesthetic stance includes proportionally more of the experiential, private aspect. Reading or writing events *A* and *B* fall into the efferent part of the continuum, with *B* admitting more private elements. Reading or writing events *C* and *D* both represent the aesthetic stance, with *C* according a higher proportion of attention to the public aspects of sense.

reader's interpretation and the author's probable intention. Here we find ourselves moving from the reader-text relationship to the author-text relationship and to the interdependence of the two transactions. The reader, we recall, transacts with the text, not directly with the author. And readers may bring to the text past linguistic and life experiences and purposes very different from those of the author. Of course, we are often very much interested in inferring the author's intention from textual or extratextual evidence. But agreement on the intention cannot determine our interpretation. We must again transact with the text to decide whether our interpretation fulfills that intention. Of course, questions also arise concerning how what we bring to the text relates to the author's horizons. Moreover, since texts are also an important means of communication or communion among readers, the problem of interpretation is broader than the author-text relationship.

The deconstructionists, following certain Nietzschean French writers and treating language as an autonomous system, have concluded from the indeterminancy of meaning that the reader can "write" whatever meaning can be made from any point of view.[4] Such complete relativism is not a necessary conclusion from the premises, however. John Dewey (1938, p. 11), accepting the new epistemological paradigm but foregoing the quest for absolutes, set conditions for "warranted assertibility" in scientific investigation. Such a position makes possible agreement concerning the most defensible interpretation according to shared criteria of evidence, but leaves open the possibility that alternative explanations for the same facts may be found or that different criteria or paradigms may be developed.

Similarly, as argued elsewhere (Rosenblatt, 1978, Chap. 7; 1983, p. 151ff.), given a shared cultural milieu and shared criteria of validity of interpretation, we can, without claiming to have the single "correct" meaning of a text, agree on an interpretation. Or we may find that alternative interpretations meet our minimum criteria. In contrast to the notion of readers locked into a narrow "interpretive community" (Fish, 1980), the emphasis on making our underlying assumptions explicit provides the basis not only for agreement but also for understanding the tacit sources of disagreement—hence the possibility of change and of revision of the criteria. Such self-awareness on the part of readers can also foster communication across social, cultural, and historical differences between author and reader, as well as among readers.

In short, the concept of shared criteria of validity of interpretation in a particular social context recognizes that different interpretations of the same physical text may be acceptable and that some readings may satisfy the criteria more fully than others. Thus we can be open to alternative readings of the text of *Hamlet*, but we also can consider some readings superior to others according to certain criteria (e.g., as activating and organizing more of the verbal elements). Whether any of the interpretations reflect the author's intention is a separate question to be judged according to accepted criteria of scholarly investigation.

In both efferent and aesthetic reading, then, the reader may seek as much as possible to "read with the eyes of the author." The sophisticated reader at least understands the problems involved in inferring the author's intention at any point in the aesthetic-efferent continuum. Just as past experiences, prior knowledge, social and psychological assumptions, and assumptions about language and literature enter into the reader's making of meaning, so do such factors become important in recovering the author's intention.

The need for grasping the author's purpose and for a consensus among readers is usually more stringent in efferent reading—hence the importance of differentiating the criteria of validity for efferent and for aesthetic reading. In efferent reading, the student has to learn to focus attention mainly on the public, referential aspects of consciousness and to ignore private aspects that might distort or bias the desired publicly verifiable or justifiable interpretation. We have seen that selectivity is equally essential in aesthetic reading but that it involves a different scope of attention.

The transaction between author and reader through the medium of the physical text has been considered in terms of the reading process. Recognizing the symbiotic situation, we can proceed to consider in what ways the basic transactional concepts sketched for reading apply also to writing.

THE WRITING PROCESS

The Writing Transaction

Like readers approaching a text, writers facing a blank page have only their individual linguistic captial to draw on. For the writer, too, the residue of past experiences of language, spoken and written, provides the material from which the text will be constructed; any new "meanings" are restructurings or extensions of the stock of experiences the writer brings to the task.

An important difference between readers and writers should not be minimized, however. In the triadic sign-object-interpretant relationship, the reader has the physical pattern of signs to which to relate the symbolizations. The writer facing a blank page may start with only an organismic state, vague feelings and ideas, which require further triadic definition before a symbolic configuration—a physical text— can take shape.

But writing, which is often spoken of as a solitary activity, is not a matter simply of dipping into a memory pool. Writing, we know, is always an event in time, occurring at a particular moment in the writer's biography, in particular circumstances, and under particular external and internal pressures. In short, the writer is always transacting with a personal, social, and cultural environment. (We shall see that the writer transacts also with the very text being produced.) Thus the writing process must be seen as always embodying both personal and social environmental factors.

Given the Peircean, triadic view of the verbal symbol, the more accessible the fund of organismically linked words and referents, the more fluent the writing. This helps us place in perspective an activity such as "free writing." Instead of treating it as a prescriptive "stage" of the writing process, as some seem to do, it should be seen as a technique for tapping the linguistic reservoir without being hampered by anxieties about acceptability of subject, sequence, or mechanics. Especially for those inhibited by unfortunate past writing experiences, this can be liberating, a warm-up exercise for starting the juices flowing, so to speak, and permitting elements of the experiential stream, verbal components of memory, and present concerns to rise to consciousness. Such free writing may bring onto the page something the writer will find worthy of further development.

Some established poets and novelists testify to a persistent sense of simply recording their texts, of merely opening the floodgates to, as Plato's Socrates suggested, inspiration from the gods. At the other extreme are authors who think out and revise whole poems and books, carrying them in their memories before committing the completed work to paper. Most writers fall between these extremes; each needs to develop a personal approach. The essential point is that the individual linguistic reservoir must be activated.

No matter how free and uninhibited the writing may be, the stream of images, ideas, memories, and words is not entirely random; William James (1890) reminds us that selective attention operates to some degree. Without minimizing the liberating or remedial effect of free writing, we should note the value of bringing the selective process more and more actively into play. Like the reader, the writer needs to move toward a sense of some tentative focus for choice and synthesis. This will be fostered by the writer's awareness of the transactional situation: the context that initiates the need to write and the potential reader or readers to whom the text will presumably be addressed. Often in trial-and-error fashion, and through various freely flowing drafts, the writer's sensitivity to such factors translates itself into an increasingly clear impulse that guides selective attention and integration. For the experienced writer, the habit of such awareness, manifested in the multifold decisions or choices that make up the writing event, is more important than any explicit preliminary statement of goals or purpose.

The concept of stance, developed earlier in relation to reading, is clearly also important for writing. A major aspect of the delimitation of purpose in writing is the adoption of a stance that falls at some point in the efferent-aesthetic continuum. The dominant stance will be determined by how much of public and private aspects of sense in the linguistic-experiential reservoir will be included in the scope of the writer's attention. The attitude toward the subject will manifest itself in the range and character of the verbal symbols that will "come to mind" and from which the writer will select.

Thus, when we speak of a sense of purpose guiding the selective process, we assume, on the one hand, the writer's perception of what is to be communicated and, on the other, a feeling for the factors that will shape its reception. Whether these two components will produce an intense and alert selective operation depends on a consideration too often neglected in the past and only now becoming more generally recognized by educators: the relation of all this to the writer's own self and world.

In reading, the continuing sequence of words on the page may prod the reluctant or confused reader to move ahead. But if the signs on the page have only tenuous linkages with the experiential reservoir, the reader will often give up the frustrating attempt to make new meanings. For the writer faced with a blank page, the need for "live" ideas—that is, ideas having a strongly energizing linkage with the experiential base—is even greater. We have all seen a student laboriously dragging words out of a stagnant memory, without anything there to move the process along. This happens often when ideas with no links to the reader are lifted out of someone else's text and paraphrased or when a topic or format is arbitrarily assigned.

Purpose should emerge from or be capable of constructively engaging the writer's actual experiential and linguistic resources. Past experience need not be the limit of the writer's scope. But purposes or ideas that lack the capacity to connect with the writer's funded experience and present concerns cannot activate the linguistic reservoir. A need to test ideas or to apply them to specific situations or an urge to communicate ideas to specific readers can provide such an impetus to thinking or writing.

The matter of degree of intensity of attention adds another dimension to the description of the reading or writing process. Live ideas growing out of situations, activities, discussions, or problems provide the basis for an actively selective and synthesizing process of making meaning. Live ideas have roots drawing sustenance from writers' needs, interests, questions, and values; live ideas have tendrils reaching out toward external areas of thought. A personally grounded purpose develops and impels movement forward. The quickened fund of images, ideas, emotions, attitudes, and tendencies offers the means for making new connections, for discovering new facets of the world of objects and events—in short, for thinking and writing creatively.

In writing (as in reading), an unexpected juxtaposition of words, the challenge of a new context, or an unsettling question may open up new lines of thought and feeling. Each sentence tends to eliminate certain possibilities regarding the meaning to be built up. At the same time, the newly formed sentence may reveal implicit areas not thought of before. New ideas, drawn from new combinations of words and phrases, present themselves. The writer may even choose to start all over again with a firmer guiding principle of selection, a clearer purpose. Such transactions with the text explain why, as Emig (1983) has demonstrated, writing can become a learning process, a process of discovery. This may also explain why some theorists are under the illusion that language "writes" the text.

Once inhibitions due to lack of confidence and worry about correctness are removed and words flow more readily onto the page, the aspiring writer can be helped to develop a purpose concerning a personally rooted subject, initially at least in terms of a predominant stance or process of selective attention. The writer may then discover an overall purpose, a general idea or effect, and a sense of relations among subordinate elements. We need to recognize that the essential requirement is not that the subject of the writing be always overtly "personal," but rather that there be some links, sometimes subterranean, between the subject and the interests, needs, prior knowledge, or curiosities of the writer.

Thus far we have been developing parallels between the ways readers and writers select and synthesize elements from the personal linguistic reservoir and adopt stances that guide selective attention and serve a developing purpose. Emphasis has fallen mainly on similarities in composing structures of meaning related to texts. If all readers are in that sense also writers, it is equally—and perhaps more obviously—true that all writers must also be readers. At this point, however, some differences within the parallelisms begin to appear.

Authorial Reading I

As a reader's eyes move along a printed text, the newly evoked symbolizations are tested for whether they fit the tentative meanings constructed for the preceding portion of the text. The writer, the first reader of the text, similarly peruses the succession of verbal signs being inscribed on the page. But this is a different kind of reading—a writer's, or authorial, reading—which should be seen as an integral part of the composing process. As the new words appear on the page, they must be tested not just for how they make sense with the preceding text but also against something more demanding: whether the emerging meaning serves or hinders the purpose, however nebulous and inarticulate, that is the motive power in the writing. This inner-oriented type of authorial reading leads to revision even during the earliest phases of the writing process.

Most writers have times when a word comes to mind or flows from the pen and, even if it makes sense, is not right. One word after another may be brought into consciousness and still not satisfy. Sometimes the writer understands what is wrong, perhaps the word is ambiguous or does not suit the tone. But often the writer cannot articulate the reason for dissatisfaction. The tension simply disappears when the "right" word presents itself. When it does, a match between inner state and verbal sign has happened. Such a "writer's block" can be seen as an interruption of an underlying process in which the words flowing onto the page are being matched against an inner touchstone. This gauge may be an organic state, a mood, an idea, or perhaps even a consciously constructed set of guidelines. Such reverberation or transaction between emerging text and inner state is too much taken for granted or ignored.

For the experienced writer, this kind of completely inner-oriented reading integral to the composing process depends on—and nourishes— a growing but often tacit sense of purpose, whether efferent or aesthetic. In other words, the writer is carrying on a two-way, circular, transactional relationship with the very text being written. In such inner-oriented authorial reading, the writer tries to satisfy and refine a personal conception. This kind of reading and revision can go on throughout the writing event. There are indeed times when it is the only reading component—that is, when one writes for oneself alone, perhaps to express, to give shape to, or to record an experience, as in diaries and journals, or perhaps to analyze a situation or the pros and cons of a decision.

Authorial Reading II

Although at times one may write for oneself alone, writing is usually felt to be part of a potential transaction with other readers. There comes a point in the writing process at which the writer needs to engage in a second type of authorial reading, a point that probably comes earlier the more expert the writer. In this kind of reading, the writer dissociates from the text and reads it through the eyes of potential readers (i.e., tries to judge the meaning *they* would make). This is the kind of writer's reading usually recognized. However, the writer does not simply adopt the "eyes" of the potential reader. A twofold operation is involved. The emerging text must be read in the light not only of what others might make of the text but also of how that fits the writer's own inner sense of purpose. Rereading the text at intervals, the writer may alternate attention to the two kinds of inner criteria or, if sufficiently expert, may merge them.

We must already have some hold on the stance- and purpose-oriented inner awareness if we are to benefit from reading through the eyes of others. The first becomes a criterion for the second. If communication is the aim, revision should be based on such double criteria in the rereading of the text. Thus writing can be both personally purposive and reader-oriented, reflecting the context of the total transaction. The experienced writer will probably engage in a synthesis or rapid alternation of the two kinds of reading.

Writers have spoken of sensing or addressing an ideal reader; this parallels readers' sensing a "voice" or persona often identified with the author. Another parallel suggests itself: a parallel between the authorial reading through the eyes of a potential reader and a reader's effort to sense an author's intention.

The Writer's Stance

Basic to clarification of purpose in writing is the selection of a predominant stance. In actual life situations, this choice is not arbitrary; rather, it is a function of the circumstances, the subject, the writer's motives, and the relation between writer and prospective reader. For example, someone who had been involved in an automobile collision would need to adopt very different stances in writing an account of the event for an insurance company and in describing it in a letter to a friend. The first would activate an efferent selective process, bringing into the center of consciousness and onto the page the public aspects, such as statements that could be verified by witnesses or by investigation of the terrain. Banished to the periphery of attention would be everything but the facts and their impersonal significance. In the letter to a friend, the purpose would be to share an experience. An aesthetic stance would bring within the scope of the writer's attention the same basic facts, together with feelings, sensations, tensions, sights, and sounds lived through during this brush with death. The selective process would favor words that not only would match the writer's inner sense of the felt event but also would set in motion in the prospective reader symbolic linkages evoking a similar experience. Given different purposes, other accounts might fall at other points of the efferent-aesthetic continuum. For the benefit of potential readers, it is important to choose and to provide clear cues to either a predominantly efferent or a predominantly aesthetic stance (see Figure 7.1). Sensitivity to purpose and context would bring into play both kinds of authorial reading.

Communication undoubtedly is easiest when both writer and reader share not only the same native language system but also similar cultural, social, and educational contexts. But even in these circumstances, individual differences persist (as we see among even members of the same family). Moreover, in our complex society, we all are members of a network of varied subgroups and even subcultures. As the materials for communicating a new meaning, the writer must draw on what can presumably be shared with the reader. Whether communication is achieved depends largely on the writer's taking into account the resemblances and the differences between what the potential reader will bring to the text and the linguistic and life experience from which the writing springs.

Here, again, we must underline the difference between ordinary reading of another's text and the second kind of authorial reading of one's own text in the light of others' needs. Children, we know, must be helped to realize that what was "in their heads" will not necessarily be conveyed to others by what is on the page. Inexperienced writers of college age and beyond have been found to be similarly handicapped. Actually, to dissociate from one's text in order to read it with another's eyes is a highly sophisticated activity. The writer's problem is to offer verbal cues that will set in motion the linkages in the potential reader's inner repertory that will lead to the intended meaning. To accomplish such "translation," the writer must have both self-understanding and understanding of others—awarenesses that may be intuitive but that can also be explicitly fostered.

The second type of authorial reading demands, then, a sense of what is taken for granted in the text: the knowledge that the potential reader is expected to bring, the conventional expectations based on prior reading and linguistic experience, the assumptions about social situations or the environment, the implicit moral, social, or scientific criteria. Some literary theorists make much of the gaps in an author's text that the reader will be called on to fill. From the writer's point of view, however, it is important to stress instead the gaps that must be avoided, the assumptions that should be made explicit, and the experiences that have to be spelled out before the text is sent out to make its way in the world.

Writing about Reading

It is now increasingly recognized that when a reader describes, responds to, or interprets a work—that is, speaks or writes about a transaction with a text—a new text is being produced. The implications of this fact in terms of process should be more fully understood. When the reader becomes a writer about a work, the starting point is no longer the physical text—the marks on the page—but the meaning or the state of mind felt to correspond to that text. The reader-turned-writer may return to the original text to recapture how it entered into the transaction but must "find words for" explaining the evocation and the interpretation.

The reader-turned-writer must once again face the problem of choice of stance. In general, the choice seems to be the efferent stance. The purpose is mainly to explain, analyze, summarize, and categorize. This is usually true even when the reading has been predominantly aesthetic and a literary work of art is being discussed. However, the aesthetic stance might be adopted to communicate an experience expressing the response or the interpretation. An efferent reading of the Declaration of Independence, for example, might lead to a poem or a story. An aesthetic reading of a text might also lead, not to an efferently written critical essay, but to another poem. The translator of a poem is a prime example of this process, first being a reader who evokes an experience through a transaction in one language and then becoming a writer who seeks to express that experience through a writing transaction in another language. The two modes of authorial reading become especially important in translation, since the experiential qualities generated in a transaction with one language must now be communicated to readers who have a different linguistic reservoir.

CONDITIONS FOR CONSTRUCTIVE CROSS-FERTILIZATION

Parallels and Differences

As we have seen, the reading and writing processes both overlap and differ. Both reader and writer engage in constituting symbolic structures of meaning in a to-and-fro, circular transaction with the text. They follow similar patterns of thinking and call on similar linguistic habits. Both processes depend on the individual's past experiences with language in particular situations. Both reader and writer therefore are drawing on past linkages of signs, objects, and organic states in order to create new symbolizations, new linkages, and new organic states. Both reader and writer develop a framework, principle, or purpose, however nebulous or explicit, that guides the selective attention and the synthesizing, organizing activities that constitute meaning. Moreover, every reading and writing act can be understood as falling somewhere on the efferent-aesthetic continuum, as being *predominantly* efferent or aesthetic.

Yet the parallels should not mask the basic difference: the transaction that starts with a text produced by someone else is not the same as a transaction that starts with the individual facing a blank page. To an observer, two people perusing a typed page may seem to be doing the same thing (i.e., "reading"). But if one of them is in the process of writing that text, different activities will be going on. The writer will be engaged in some form of authorial reading. Moreover, since both reading and writing are rooted in mutually conditioning transactions between individuals and their particular environments, a person may have very different experiences with the two activities, may differ in attitudes toward them, and may be more proficient in one than in the other. Writing and reading are sufficiently different to defeat the assumption that they are mirror images; the reader does not simply reenact the author's process, nor will the teaching of one automatically improve the student's competence in the other.

Still, the nature of the transaction between author and reader through the text and the parallels in the reading and writing processes described in this chapter make it reasonable to expect that the teaching of one can affect the student's operations in the other. But how fruitful that will be depends on the nature of the teaching and the educational context. *Constructive cross-fertilization will happen at the level of reinforcement of linguistic habits and thinking patterns resulting from sensitivity to the basic transactional processes shared by reading and writing.*

The Total Context

Here we return to our basic concept, that human activity is always in transaction, in a reciprocal relationship, with an environment, a context, a total situation. Teachers and pupils in the classroom are transacting with one another and with the school setting; their context broadens to include the whole institutional, social, and cultural environment. None of these aspects of the transaction should ultimately be ignored in thinking about education and especially about the "literacy problem." The contextual and personal elements that enter into the transaction can inhibit or foster the reading and writing processes. Such elements may, for example, affect the individual's attitude toward the self, toward the reading or writing activity, and toward the purpose for which it is being carried on.

Viewing the text always in relation either to author or reader in specific situations makes it difficult to treat the text as an isolated entity or to overemphasize either the author or the reader. Recognizing that language is not a self-contained system or static code avoids, on the one hand, the traditional obsession with the product—with skills, techniques, and conventions, essential though they are—and, on the other, a pendulum swing to overemphasis on the personal aspect or on process. Nor can the transactional view of the reading and writing processes be turned into a set of stages to be rigidly followed. Such extremes are avoided by treating the writer's drafts and final texts—or the reader's tentative interpretations, final evocation, and reflections—as the stopping points in a journey, as the outward and visible signs of a continuing process in the passage from one point to the other. A "good" product, whether a "well-written" paper or a sound textual interpretation, should not be an end in itself, a terminus, but should be the result of a process that builds the strengths for further journeys—or, to change the metaphor, for further growth. "Product" and "process" become interlocking concerns.

Such teaching will permit constructive cross-fertilization of the reading and writing processes. Effective communication must be rooted in, must grow out of, the ability of individual writers and readers to generate meaning. The teaching of reading and writing at any level should have as its first concern the creation of environments and activities in which students are motivated and encouraged to draw on their own resources to make "live" meanings. With this as the fundamental criterion, emphasis falls on strengthening the basic processes shared by reading and writing. The teaching of one can then reinforce linguistic habits and semantic approaches useful in the other.

Enriching the individual's linguistic-experiential reservoir and enabling the student to freely draw on it become underlying aims broader than the particular concern with either reading or writing. Many current teaching practices—the kinds of questions asked, the way assignments are phrased, the types of tests given, the atmosphere created in the classroom—counteract the very processes presumably being taught and foster manipulation of empty verbal abstractions. Treatment of either reading or writing as a dissociated set of skills (though both require skills) or as primarily the acquisition of codes and conventions (though both involve them) inhibits sensitivity to the organic linkages of verbal signs and their objects. Purposive writing and reading will enable the student to build on past experience of life and language and to practice the kinds of selective attention and synthesis that produce new structures of live meaning.

Collaborative Interchange

In a favorable educational environment, speech is a vital ingredient. Its importance in the individual's acquisition of a linguistic-experiential capital is clear. Moreover, it can be an extremely important medium in the classroom. Interchange and dialogue between teacher and students and among students can foster growth and cross-fertilization in both the reading and writing processes. Such transactions can help students develop metalinguistic insights in a highly personal and hence instructive way. The aim should be not simply improved performance but also metalinguistic understanding of skills and conventions in meaningful contexts.

Students' achievement of insight into their own reading and writing processes should be seen as the long-term justification for various curricular and teaching strategies. Peer reading and discussion of texts, for example, have been found effective in helping writers at all levels understand their transactional relationship to their readers. The questions, varied interpretations, and misunderstandings of fellow students dramatize the necessity of the writer's providing verbal signs that will enable readers to draw on their own resources to make the intended meaning. The writer can become aware of the responsibility for providing verbal means that will help readers gain required facts, share relevant sensations or attitudes, or make logical transitions. Such insights make possible the second, reader-oriented kind of authorial reading.

Group interchange about the texts of established authors can also be a powerful means of stimulating growth in reading ability and critical acumen. When students share their responses and learn how their evocations from transactions with the same text differ, they can return to the text to discover their own habits of selection and synthesis and can become more critical of their own processes as readers. Interchange about the problems of interpretation and a collaborative movement toward self-critical interpretation of the text can lead to the development of critical concepts and criteria of validity of interpretation. Such metalinguistic awareness is valuable to students as both readers and writers. The teacher, no longer a dispenser of ready-made ideas and formulas, becomes the facilitator of such interchange among students.

The dynamic discovery of metalinguistic insights contrasts with the static and formalistic analysis of "model" or canonical texts, typical of traditional composition and literature courses alike.[5] Neophyte writers and readers should be encouraged to engage, first of all, in personally meaningful transactions with the texts of established authors. In this dynamic way, texts can serve as sources from which to assimilate a sense of the potentialities of the English sentence and an awareness of strategies for organizing meaning and expressing feeling. Formal analysis can then serve a valuable function, explaining to a reader how the verbal signs enter into the transaction or answering a writer's own problems in expression.

A rounded, humanistic education necessarily encompasses the efferent-aesthetic continuum, the two basic ways of looking at the world. Students need to learn to differentiate the circumstances that call for one or the other stance. But recall that both stances involve cognitive and affective, public and private elements. Despite the over-emphasis on the efferent in our schools, failure to understand this complexity has prevented successful teaching even of efferent reading and writing. Teaching practices and curricula should from the very beginning include both efferent and aesthetic linguistic activity, should foster the habits of selective attention and synthesis that draw on relevant elements of the semantic reservoir, and should nourish the ability to handle the mix of private and public aspects appropriate to any particular transaction. Especially in the early years, these things should be done in a largely indirect way—for example, through choice of texts, phrasing of assignments in writing and reading, and implications concerning stance in the questions asked. Unfortunately, much current practice is counterproductive, either failing to encourage a definite stance or implicitly requiring an inappropriate one. A favorite illustration is the third-grade workbook that prefaced its first poem with the question, "What facts does this poem teach you?" Small wonder that graduates of our schools (and even colleges) often read poems and novels efferently, and political statements and advertisements with an aesthetic stance.

Research

The old dualistic experimental research design, with its treatment of student and text as separate, static entities acting on one another in a presumably neutral context, cannot suffice for the questions and hypotheses that the transactional paradigm presents.[6] Although the experimental model may still have its uses, extrapolation of results to practical situations should be very cautious. Moreover, no matter how much we may generalize quantitatively about groups, reading and writing are always carried on by individuals. If research is to serve education, the linguistic transaction should be studied above all as a dynamic phenomenon in a particular context, as part of the ongoing life of the individual in a particular educational, social, and cultural environment. We need to learn how the student's attitudes and self-understanding are formed and enter into the reading and writing events. Increasing interest in this area is evident in the use of case-study and ethnographic methods. Research methodologies and designs will need to be sufficiently complex, varied, and interlocking to do justice to the fact that reading and writing transactions are at once intensely individual and intensely social activities.

N O T E S

[1] For a fuller presentation of transactional theory, dealing with such questions as openness and constraints of the text and relationship of evocation, interpretation, and criticism, see Rosenblatt, 1978, 1983.

[2] The spoken sign, the vocalization, usually comes first, of course, and its connection with the written sign is a complex question being explored by linguists, psychologists, and philosophers. By grounding language in the individual's transactions with the environment, the triadic model can serve the written, as well as the spoken, sign.

[3] According to Myers (1986, p. 181), during the first half of the twentieth century, "a combination of behaviorism and positivism [led to neglect of] the concept of attention. . . . By the 1970s, however, the concept was resurrected, and today's psychologists have reasserted its importance for professional psychology." (See also Blumenthal, 1977, Chap. 2.)

[4] Since this chapter is concerned primarily with the processes essential to the making of meaning in reading and writing, it is not possible to discuss the currently controversial question of the critical framework that students should be helped to apply to their evocations (see Chap. 7 of Rosenblatt, 1978, and Pt. II and Pt. III of Rosenblatt, 1983). Deconstructionists (e.g., Jacques Derrida and his American disciple, J. Hillis Miller) are mentioned here only to clarify the transactional position on the matter of validity of interpretation (see Culler, 1982).

[5] A course combining the traditional teaching of "composition" and "introduction to literature," for example, compounds the obstacles in both fields. Approaching the text with a set of literary categories and topics for the conventional critical essay, the student is hindered from savoring the aesthetic transaction that could provide the springboard for "live" writing. In many classes, the teacher, even when permitting personal comments, reverts to the traditional fixation on the text and expounds the "correct" or "sound" interpretation of the story or essay. The result is that students soon lose interest or confidence in their own interpretive activities and fail to develop the actively selective attention necessary for effective reading, both efferent and aesthetic.

[6] For fuller discussion of the implications of the transactional theory for research, see Rosenblatt, 1985a (pp. 40–51), 1985b.

R E F E R E N C E S

Bates, E. (1979). *The emergence of symbols.* New York: Academic Press.

Blumenthal, A. L. (1977). *The process of cognition.* Englewood Cliffs, NJ: Prentice-Hall.

Bohr, N. (1959). Discussion with Einstein. In P. A. Schilpp (Ed.), *Albert Einstein, philosopher-scientist.* (pp. 201–241). New York: Harper.

Bruner, J. (1986). *Actual minds, possible worlds.* Cambridge, MA: Harvard University Press.

Culler, J. (1982). *On deconstruction.* Ithaca, NY: Cornell University Press.

Dewey, J. (1938). *Logic: The theory of inquiry.* New York: Holt.

Dewey, J., & Bentley, A. F. (1949). *Knowing and the known.* Boston: Beacon Press.

Emig, J. (1983). *The web of meaning.* Upper Montclair, NJ: Boynton/Cook.

Fish, S. (1980). *Is there a text in this class?* Cambridge, MA: Harvard University Press.

James, W. (1890). *The principles of psychology* (2 vols.). New York: Holt.

Miller, G. A., & Johnson-Laird, P. N. (1976). *Language and perception.* Cambridge, MA: Harvard University Press.

Myers, G. (1986). *William James: His life and thought.* New Haven, CT: Yale University Press.

Peirce, C. S. (1931–1935). *Collected papers* (Vols. 1–6) (P. Weiss & C. Hartshorne, Eds.). Cambridge, MA: Harvard University Press.

Rorty, R. (1982). *Consequences of pragmatism.* Minneapolis: University of Minnesota Press.

Rosenblatt, L. M. (1978). *The reader, the text, the poem: The transactional theory of the literary work.* Carbondale: Southern Illinois University Press.

Rosenblatt, L. M. (1983). *Literature as exploration* (4th ed). New York: Modern Language Association. (Originally published 1938)

Rosenblatt, L. M. (1985a). The transactional theory of the literary work: Implications for research. In C. Cooper (Ed.), *Researching response to literature and the teaching of literature* (pp. 33–53). Norwood, NJ: Ablex.

Rosenblatt, L. M. (1985b). Viewpoints: Transaction versus interaction—A terminological rescue operation. *Research in the Teaching of English, 19,* 96–107.

Toulmin, S. (1982). *The return to cosmology.* Berkeley: University of California Press.

Vygotsky, L. S. (1962). *Thought and language* (F. Hanfmann & G. Vakar, Eds. and Trans.). Cambridge, MA: MIT Press.

Werner, H., & Kaplan, B. (1962). *Symbol formation.* New York: Wiley.

8

CONNECTING WRITING

Fostering Emergent Literacy in Kindergarten Children

William H. Teale and Miriam G. Martinez

This chapter describes how writing has been integrated into an emergent literacy program in kindergartens around San Antonio, Texas. The idea of "connecting writing" with other activities in the children's lives and with other subject areas in the curriculum proved especially important in fostering the kindergartners' literacy development. Three such connections are described: (1) connecting writing to functional purposes, (2) connecting writing with children's reading of their own writing and with children's literature, and (3) connecting kindergarten writers with each other.

No doubt five-year-old Sommer was smitten the first time she saw Tommy's picture on the pen pals' chart in the kindergarten classroom. Tommy, from the afternoon class, had been chosen as pen pal to Sommer, who attended the morning session. The pen pal activity began in February, when the teacher explained to the children that they would write to each other for the remainder of the school year and

The Kindergarten Emergent Literacy Program described in this chapter is a cooperative project of the University of Texas at San Antonio and schools in several independent school districts in the greater San Antonio area. William H. Teale and Miriam G. Martinez direct the project. We especially want to thank kindergarten teachers Cynthia Cates, Judith Bercher, Frances Hernandez, Nancy Pfrang, and Connie McBroom; vice-principal (and former kindergarten teacher) Kay Montgomery; kindergarten coordinator Mary Armstrong; and Wanda Glass. All have been intimately involved in the implementation and research that has occurred, and without their help and insights this chapter could not have been written.

would get to meet their pen pals on the kindergarten trip to the zoo in May. A rather typical correspondence commenced between Tommy and Sommer, focusing on such vital statistics as age, hair color, and favorite toys. In March Sommer brought the teacher a letter she had written to Tommy. After reading the letter aloud, Sommer finally got up the gumption to mention that she thought Tommy was very cute. The teacher suggested that Sommer might like to add something to that effect to her letter.

The final text of Sommer's letter to Tommy was as follows:

UROTUMENS [You wrote to me nice.]
I LOEV YOU
TOMM SOMMER [To Tommy from Sommer]
URC BKZURITRIN [You are cute because you write real nice.]

Not moved by this addendum in the direction Sommer had hoped, Tommy unflinchingly replied, as shown in Figure 8.1, "I don't love you."

When the teacher finished helping Sommer read this missive, Sommer, crushed, promptly burst into tears. After much consolation and attempted mending of the broken heart, the teacher suggested that the best thing Sommer could do was to write back, expressing

FIGURE 8.1 Tommy's Letter to Sommer

3-19-86
NoIDTLU UTMFeLZ
UBWRMTH
IHU
IHU

Tommy Sommer

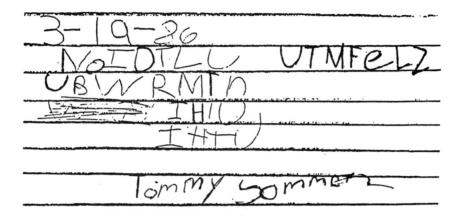

FIGURE 8.2 Sommer's Letter to Tommy

her feelings. Though not so terse as Tommy's message, Sommer's message was, as shown in Figure 8.2, just as much to the point. She had written, "No, I don't love you. You hurt my feelings. You better watch your mouth. I hate you. I hate you." The teacher, also disturbed by Tommy's reply, turned over Sommer's letter and added her own message, shown in Figure 8.3. After the teacher read aloud to Sommer what she had written, Sommer promptly took the message and added some finishing touches of her own—in red.

FIGURE 8.3 Teacher's Letter to Tommy

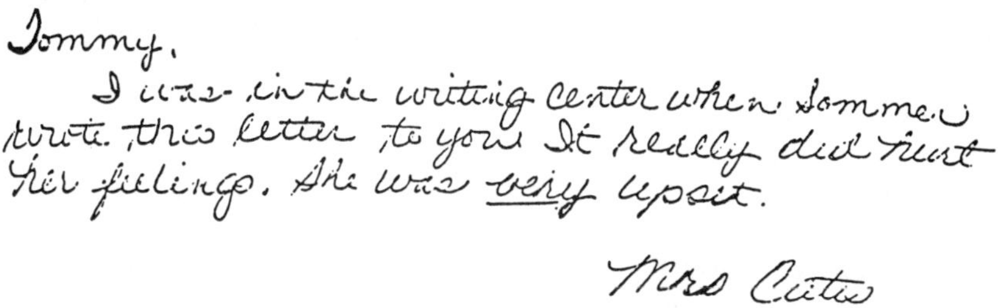

Tommy,
I was in the writing center when Sommer wrote this letter to you It really did hurt her feelings. She was very upset.

Mrs Cates

FIGURE 8.4   Sommer's Additions to Teacher's Letter

As can be seen in Figure 8.4, Sommer had emphatically added exclamation points throughout the teacher's text and a final three-line message of her own. Sommer read it to the teacher: "I hate you forever! I will never love you again! Unless you say sorry." (Sommer read the final phrase even though she had written no equivalent.)

Having had Sommer's printed wrath read to him, Tommy, appropriately contrite, wrote the following reply:

SREFIHETUFANE [Sorry if I hurt your feelings.]
BY TOMMY

When Tommy took his letter to the teacher to read what he had written, it was obvious that he himself was upset. The teacher discussed the matter with him, trying to get him to express why he was so displeased with Sommer's previous letter. After some conversation, Tommy summed up, saying, "Well, I just don't like it when she says she loves me," to which the teacher replied, "Then you need to write her and tell her that. But tell her in a nice way." He added this to his message.

ESTEVLEVILCU TOMMY [Instead of love, I like you. Tommy]

Apparently, this letter resolved the conflict by setting the appropriate interactional conditions: liking was all right, loving was not.

Correspondence between the two was nothing but pleasant thereafter. May came, and Tommy and Sommer finally got to meet each other on the class trip. For the entire day two absolutely inseparable companions, hand in hand, visited every corner of the zoo.

WRITING IN AN EMERGENT LITERACY PROGRAM FOR KINDERGARTNERS

Sommer and Tommy's correspondence comes from a kindergarten classroom in San Antonio, Texas, one of the several in which we have been attempting over the last few years to implement a reading and writing program. It serves to illustrate the central role writing can play in the lives of kindergarten children. The curriculum development and research being conducted in the classrooms are based on an emergent literacy perspective. Such a perspective assumes that listening, speaking, reading, and writing abilities develop concurrently and interrelatedly in early childhood, rather than in a sequential fashion; that the functions and uses of reading and writing are as much a part of literacy learning as are the formal skills; that children's early behaviors are a legitimate phase of, rather than a precursor to, literacy development; and that these behaviors and conceptualizations develop in predictable ways in a progression toward conventional literacy. In essence, our program has sought to foster reading and writing abilities in ways that are developmentally appropriate for young children.

Though to our minds too extreme in the conclusions drawn, the line of reasoning that prompted Chomsky (1971) to propose a philosophy of "write first, read later" for early literacy instruction has certainly affected our curriculum. Writing is a central activity for the kindergartners from the first day of school for a variety of reasons. It helps children develop their concept of words (Henderson, 1985; Morris, 1981); it promotes their ability to segment words phonemically, as well as their knowledge of letter-sound mapping, spelling, and decoding (Dyson, 1984, 1985; Ehri & Wilce, 1987; Temple, Nathan, & Burris, 1982), and it facilitates their more general abilities in composing and comprehending (Dyson, 1983, 1984; Graves, 1983; Sulzby, 1985, 1986; Tierney & Pearson, 1985). In short, writing is a means of teaching the character of written language. Each day the children in our program visit the writing center, where they write, "pretend-write" or "write the way five-year-olds do" on teacher-assigned topics or topics of their own choosing.

In attempting to integrate writing into the kindergarten curriculum, we have been struck by how important it is to "connect" writing to other aspects of the curriculum if it is to have maximum impact on fostering children's emergent literacy. Other authors' descriptions of the development of young children's writing in the classroom accord with such a conclusion (Dyson, 1982, 1983, 1986; Schickedanz, 1986). We have found three types of connections particularly powerful: connecting writing with functional purposes, connecting writing with reading, and connecting child writers with each other.

WRITING FOR A PURPOSE

"It is not too simple to say that children begin to write because they want to" (Gundlach, 1982, p. 136). But why would children want to write? One suggestion comes from the work of Gibson and Yonas (1968). Operating on the assumption that if children are given appropriate graphic instruments and surfaces they will begin producing graphics spontaneously, Gibson and Yonas studied the scribbling of children ranging in age from fifteen months to thirty-eight months. The study took place in the children's homes in a free-play situation. By providing the children with two writing instruments, one that left a mark and one that did not, Gibson and Yonas found that the children wrote not simply to exercise their hands and arms but because they could actually see and manipulate their productions. Thus there seems to be something inherently pleasing to the young child about the process of creating marks with a writing instrument. However, the satisfaction that results from making marks on a page soon dissipates without the presence of an additional factor: a reason for writing. Writing, like literacy in general, is a social process. It functions not as an isolated event but as a component of social activity. In other words, writing cannot be reduced to a process of representing sounds through symbols; it is an activity typically performed to achieve some goal beyond the act of writing itself. As several recent ethnographic studies have indicated, writing and reading are essentially functional, purposeful activities (Heath, 1983; Reder & Green, 1983; Taylor, 1983; Teale, 1986).

Such a foundation is important to keep in mind when planning literacy instruction for beginning writers and readers. As Taylor (1982) has stated, without an emphasis on making literacy socially significant in the lives of children, we may unwittingly be undercutting the teaching of the skills of writing and reading. Part of "solving the written language puzzle" (Dyson, 1982) is the child's sorting out of the complex relations between what is spoken and what is put on the page. But even before writing becomes a puzzle in this sense, young children face the mystery of understanding just what it is their parents or older siblings are doing when they make marks on paper. An awareness of writing as a goal-directed, functional activity is basic to developing as a writer. Children continue *wanting* to write long after the initial fascination with making marks on the page has worn off; the reason for this continuing motivation is that they see writing as a new way of achieving objectives they had previously accomplished in other ways. Furthermore, writing can serve as a vehicle leading to new social goals.

For all these reasons, we have attempted to emphasize the functions of writing as the basis for the writing aspect of the curriculum in the kindergarten classroom. Writing begins and ends with the functions involved. Such a perspective means that audience and purpose become especially important. Many of the children's assigned writings are directed to a particular audience for a particular purpose. The pen pal activity is one example. Each child writes to his or her pen pal—another kindergartner—communicating, informing, entertaining, and even arguing and resolving arguments. The purpose of writing to one's pen pal is immediately apparent, and the audience is familiar (though initially unknown in some ways). Teachers have also corresponded with the children. In one school, the kindergartners know that if they deposit a message to the teacher in the classroom mailbox, they will receive a personal reply.

The children's writing is connected with as wide a range of activities as possible. They make menus, construct shopping lists, and write invitations for the annual Thanksgiving feast and Mother's Day tea. They are encouraged to incorporate writing in their activities in the dramatic play center, much in the fashion used at the Boston University Laboratory Preschool (Schickedanz, 1986). Encouragement comes from the way the teacher sets up the dramatic play center. For example, the emphasis at one point in the year may be on a doctor's office. The teacher provides appropriate clothing and props, such as toy medical instruments. Also included in the props are items like appointment books and prescription forms, which encourage the children to make writing an integral part of their play.

In addition to performing functional writing tasks assigned or directly encouraged by the teacher, children engage in self-sponsored functional writing. After the first few weeks of school in one teacher's class, the children on their own initiative lined up each morning after entering the room to read to the teacher personal letters they had written at home the night before. A number of parents also reported that their children wrote many notes to them at home. Schickedanz (1986) has described another interesting form of self-sponsored functional writing among young children in the classroom: signs on block structures or art projects telling other children "Do Not Touch" and signs reading "Save This to Show My Mom."

In short, children want to write because they come to see writing as a way of getting things done. Often, and perhaps most obvious, are things that connect with the daily routines of the classroom or day-to-day activities, including communicating with each other. The motivation to engage in such writing is high, precisely because it is so functional and meaningful. That is not to say, of course, that other, less "pragmatic" types of writing, like creating or re-creating stories, are not highly motivating for and prevalent among young children. However, we have found writing for functional purposes to be an important bridge into the forms and processes of writing for many five- and six-year-olds.

CONNECTING WRITING WITH READING

If the 1970s were the years of schema theory in reading research, then the 1980s may be remembered as the time when research on the reading-writing connection began. Goodman and Goodman (1983), Smith (1982, 1983), and Tierney and Pearson (1985), among others, have discussed from a theoretical standpoint the significance of the reading-writing connection. In addition, Dyson (1982, 1984, 1985), Ferreiro (1984, 1985, 1986), Ferreiro and Gomez Palacio (1982), Ferreiro and Teberosky (1982), and Sulzby (1981, 1985, 1986) have provided empirical or case-study information on the relations between reading and writing for young children. This work has shown that reading and writing, although not mirror images of each other, mutually reinforce each other in the process of literacy development.

Our observations have revealed two aspects of the connection between writing and reading that are especially important for young children. One is the children's reading of their own writing. The other is connecting literature for children with the children's writing.

Children's Reading of Their Own Writing

As many authors have pointed out, writing involves reading one's own writing. We have attempted to reinforce the children's perceptions of themselves as writers by saying to them each time they complete a piece of writing, "Read me what you wrote." In addition to encouraging children to view themselves as writers, this process provides the teacher with significant insights into the child's developing concepts and strategies for writing. It also serves important instructional purposes for young children.

The diagnostic significance of having children read what they have written is perhaps best illustrated by the extensive research conducted by Sulzby (1981, 1985, 1986). Sulzby's 1985 study of children's rereading of their own story compositions (both handwritten and dictated) led to the development of a 7-point scale to assess different levels of sophistication in rereading attempts. The scale includes behaviors like the following: "Child may produce random-looking marks but will refuse to re-read them" [score of 2]. . . . Child attempts to re-read story but does not keep eyes on print. The story recited is similar to original production but is not stable with it [score of 4]. . . . Child's eyes are tracking print and child is matching voice to print [score of 7]." Thus, with careful observation of the child's rereading behaviors, the teacher can learn a great deal about a child's emerging literacy concepts and skills.

Children's reading of their own writing can also promote development by increasing their sensitivity to the distinctions between oral and written language. The requirement that they read their writing places children in the position of having to produce a variety of language when they speak. Even though many five-year-olds' productions may initially resemble oral language, listening to other children's readings and to storybook readings helps them develop the idea that productions that resemble written language are appropriate when one reads.

The process of reading one's own writing has been described as "becoming the reader over one's own shoulder." We have attempted to influence this aspect of children's emerging sense of authorship with a regularly scheduled activity called "author of the week," which is patterned after the notion of "author's chair" (Graves & Hansen, 1983). Individual children read their writing to the other members of the writing group, and a discussion about the piece ensues. Initially the children have little, if anything, to say about their peers' writing, and at this stage modeling by the teacher is critical. The teacher demonstrates the kinds of questions one can ask and the comments one can make about the writing of others and ultimately about one's own writing. This feedback can focus on the writing process itself and/or on the content of the piece (e.g., "What made you decide to write about your trip?" or "You told us your cat's name. What can you tell us about the things she liked to do?"). It is hard to find direct evidence that teacher modeling affects the way children "read over their own shoulders" during composing. Yet as the year progresses, the children appear to internalize the teacher's approach, as evidenced by the feedback they begin to give their peers during this activity.

Children's Literature and Children's Writing

A host of studies has indicated the numerous positive effects of storybook reading on young children's literacy development. These effects range from increased comprehension to improvement in decoding. (See Teale, 1987, for a review of important recent studies, such as those of Feitelson, Kita, & Goldstein, 1986, and Wells, 1982, 1985.) Storybook readings are therefore a central component of our emergent literacy program. To extend the positive effects, various response activities are planned in conjunction with many of the books read in the classroom. Children may produce art work—for example, by making thumbprint caterpillars after reading *The Very Hungry Caterpillar* (Carle, 1979)—or they may reenact a story with feltboard characters or dramatize it after or during the reading. Writing is also frequently used as a means of responding to stories or in conjunction with the other forms of response just mentioned.

A particular type of book widely used in the classrooms is the "predictable book" (Bridge, 1986; Rhodes, 1981). Predictable books are meaningful texts that use repetitive (and thus predictable) language patterns and/or are structured according to set patterns. Children can use the language patterns of the text read to them to produce new stories, poems, or songs. For example, the teacher in one room read the book *Sing a Song* (Melser, 1980), whose pattern is as follows:

Sing, sing, sing, a song,
Sing a song together;
Sing, sing, sing, a song,
Sing a song together.

The story utilizes this pattern to describe a range of activities engaged in by the tiger family at home. For the response activity, the teacher asked the children to write about their activities in school, using a similar language pattern. Scott wrote the ten-page production shown in Figure 8.5. Such writing tasks have proven extremely popular with the children and have resulted in well-formed and interesting pieces, possibly because the model gives them a support framework without restricting them to too great a degree.

Writing has also been used in conjunction with other responses to literature. Creative dramatics and writing are an especially intriguing combination, whose effects we are only beginning to investigate. A preservice teacher who had worked extensively in the classroom implemented the first planned use of such activities. She began by leading the students through an exercise in which they demonstrated and discussed certain personality characteristics and acted out various emo-

AS A SONG
BY SCOTT F.

SING SING
SING A SONG
TOGETHER

DO DO DOTH
CALENDER
DO THE
CALENDER
TOGET T EA

DO DO DOTH
WETHER HOUND
TOGEYTER

PICK PICK
RICK A HESAR
HESAR HELPER PICK
A HELP...
TO...

DO DO DO
THE CHALK
BOARD
DO THE CHAL
BOARD TO GETH

FIGURE 8.5   Scott's "Sing-a-Song" Book

BRAKE BRAKE
BRAKE INTC
THREE
GROUPS
BRAKE INTO
THREE
GROUPS TOGETHE

GO GO GOTO
MISS MONTGOMERY
TABBLE TOGETHE
GO GO GOTO
THE ARTTABL
TOGETHER

GO GO ... UT HE
CENTER
GOTOTHE CENTER TOGETHE
FIRST TOGE
CLEN CLEN
CLENUP UP
CLE NUP TOGETHE

DO DO DOTHE
WETHER HOUND
TOGETHER
PICK PICK
RICK A
HELPER DICK
A HELPER
TOGETHER

FIGURE 8.5 (continued)

188

Uo!

MATH OO

MATH tOGETHER

GO GO Go ouH side
TOGEt H-ER

COME & COME
COME
iNsLDE ICOME
i NsDE tog
TOGEt 4FR
GEt Gt
OUR
GE OU R stUUF
GE OUR STUUF
TOGETHER

RIDE RIDE
RIDE tHE
BuS RIDtHEBu:
tOGEtHER
9-16-ch

FIGURE 8.5 (concluded)

tions: happiness, sadness, anger, mischievousness, and so on. After that, she read *Caps for Sale* (Slobodkina, 1940) straight through to the children. She then read it again but stopped at various points so that the children could act out scenes, stressing especially the personal attributes or emotions of the characters. Afterward she asked the children to write about how they would have felt if they had been either the peddler or the monkeys.

As the teacher reviewed the children's writing, she was struck by one aspect in particular: the writing systems, or spelling strategies, the children used. Table 8.1 summarizes the strategies the children used in two pieces they wrote immediately before the story reading and creative dramatics and those they used immediately afterward. (The labels for the spelling strategies are taken from Henderson & Beers, 1981, and from Sulzby, Chap. 2, this volume.) The striking feature of the change is that after listening to *Caps for Sale* and acting it out, fifteen of the sixteen children (the exception being the child in group 6) used strategies that involved taking into account letter-sound relationships, whereas previously only four children (groups 3, 4, and 5) had used such systems.

Descriptions of developmental patterns in children's writing are by no means conclusive. The studies of Dyson (1985) and Sulzby (1985, 1986) have produced ample evidence of a range of individual differences in children's writing and of children having a repertoire of writing systems that they may use at particular points in their growth as writers. Nonetheless, children show a general tendency to use increas-

TABLE 8.1 Writing Systems before and after Reading of *Caps for Sale* and Creative Dramatics

	Previous Strategies (11/8/85; 11/11/85)	*Subsequent Strategies* (11/12/85)
Group 1 (*N* = 8)	Scribble, random-appearing letters, or combination of the two	Letter name or letter name with random-appearing letters
Group 2 (*N* = 3)	Scribble, random-appearing letters, or combination of the two	Early phonemic or early phonemic with random-appearing letters
Group 3 (*N* = 2)	Letter name and random-appearing letters	Letter name
Group 4 (*N* = 1)	Early phonemic and random-appearing letters	Letter name
Group 5 (*N* = 1)	Letter name	Letter name
Group 6 (*N* = 1)	Random-appearing letters	Random-appearing letters

ingly sophisticated strategies, usually progressing from nonphonemic systems (e.g., scribble, random-appearing letters) to a phonemic strategy (e.g., early phonemic, letter name). In this respect, the results shown in Table 8.1 are particularly interesting, showing as they do that children used more sophisticated systems after the storybook reading and creative dramatics. Observations of children in other creative dramatics performed in conjunction with storybook readings and examination of their subsequent writings suggest that there is something very engaging about such activities and that consequently they have important effects on children's writing.

Perhaps these effects can best be understood in the light of studies by Galda (1982) and Pellegrini and Galda (1982). These researchers found that enacting stories through play improved story comprehension. Furthermore, the children who had "played" the stories were more likely when retelling them to use a dramatic tone, to include details, and to re-create conversations between characters. In effect, the children who acted out stories appeared to have experienced them more fully. This may be the key to understanding the changes we have observed in children's writing. Acting out the story meant *experiencing* the story in the fullest sense of the word, and experience underlies successful writing. The children had something to say, and they made every attempt to say it. Much research remains to be done in this area, but the connections appear to be very promising ones for promoting young children's writing growth.

CONNECTING WRITERS WITH EACH OTHER

The final writing connection of significance that we have observed among emergent writers involves connecting the children with each other. Of course, since writing is fundamentally a social process, it naturally brings individuals into contact with each other. Nonetheless, we believe teachers should make every effort, both formally and informally, to facilitate and maximize interactions among children about their writing.

The benefits of permitting, indeed encouraging, interactions among writers are numerous. For one thing, such interactions promote the development of a community of writers; writing becomes part of the fabric of the classroom. A community atmosphere like this gives support to each child's efforts to become a better writer.

Also, children when interacting frequently teach each other about writing—a point well illustrated by the interactions of Scott, Ben, and Jason. Scott was in one writing group; Ben and Jason, in another.

On his first day at the writing center in September, Scott wrote with invented spelling. His stories were easily read by the adults in the room; Figure 8.6 shows a story he wrote on September 17. In contrast, Ben, Scott's best friend, began the year using a scribbling strategy to write. On November 12 Ben was still writing with scribble (see Figure 8.7). On November 13 he accompanied his teacher to the bulletin board to help her place several of his pieces of writing on display because he was to be "author of the week" in his writing group. Scott, who had been chosen for the same role in his writing group, already had a number of pieces on the bulletin board. The teacher observed

FIGURE 8.6   Scott's Story on September 17: "One day my cat and me went walking by the woods. We saw a bear."

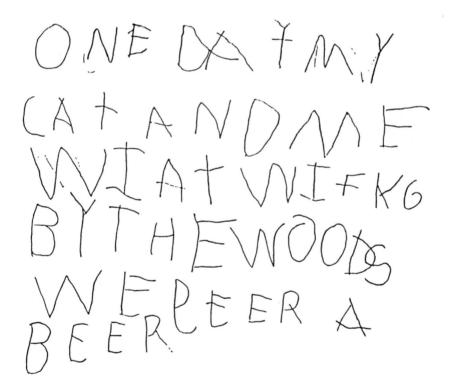

FIGURE 8.7 Ben's Story on November 12: "One day coconut and his friends were playing until a dry starfish fell into the water. The birds dropped the starfish in."

that Ben intently studied Scott's writing for a long time. Then he went to the writing center where he wrote the piece shown in Figure 8.8. Notice that Ben used letters and that he wrote with invented spelling, a strategy he consistently employed for the remainder of the year. Moreover, Ben's writing had the same effect on Jason. When Jason saw how Ben was writing, Jason also began to use invented

IM. tqc ho
the hol day. Bcs I HAvuvuLTui
FUN

Bi Ben

FIGURE 8.8   Ben's Story on November 13: "I am thankful for the holidays because I have a lot of fun."

spellings instead of the scribble strategy he had been utilizing for seven weeks.

The changes in Ben's and Jason's writing demonstrate why the writing center is an area where chatting and sharing are encouraged. Children discuss and read each other's writing. They often hear the oral language that accompanies a companion's composing efforts. They also watch and listen as a child reads his or her piece to the teacher. Teachers attempt in these informal ways to promote interaction and to capitalize on peer influence.

In addition, they use some formal means of encouraging interaction. Children are occasionally asked to read pieces during sharing time. Teachers display the children's work throughout the room and encourage children to read what their classmates are writing. Children's own books become part of the classroom library. Activities like "author of the week," the kindergarten postal system, and the pen pal program are other means of putting children in touch with each other.

The importance of connecting writers with each other cannot be overemphasized. Such a practice aids in creating functional contexts for writing, and it also fosters positive attitudes toward writing, encouraging children to view writing not as a solemn ritual but as another facet of social interaction. Hickman (1979) proposed the notion of a "community of readers" to describe how children, in conjunction with classmates and the teacher, work together to help each other learn to read. It might be said that our goal has been to create a community of writers as well.

CONCLUSION

During the past decade, writing has been identified, or perhaps re-identified, as a skill of critical importance. It also has finally been widely recognized as a very powerful learning tool and as a fundamentally social process. Simultaneously, early literacy development has been "discovered," and the perspective known as emergent literacy has begun to take hold. Like many other researchers and teachers, we have attempted to use the new and exciting knowledge about these areas to devise better educational opportunities for young children.

We described in this chapter three types of connections that, in our attempts to implement a developmentally appropriate kindergarten literacy program, we found to have a powerful effect on young children's writing development. In so doing, we mentioned several types of activities that have been used to help children make those connections. It is important to stress that it is not the activities themselves that make an emergent literacy program work. The fundamental connection is between children and writing. We must create in the classroom an atmosphere that promotes writing, that makes it desirable to be a writer, and that lets the child know that by writing he or she becomes a member of a community. To quote Gundlach (1982, p. 136) again, "It is not too simple to say that children begin to write because they want to." It is also not too simple to say that children continue to write and that they become writers because they want to. The key to making that happen lies in the teacher's interactions with the children.

R E F E R E N C E S

Bridge, C. (1986). Predictable books for beginning readers and writers. In M. R. Sampson (Ed.), *The pursuit of literacy: Early reading and writing* (pp. 81–96). Dubuque, IA: Kendall/Hunt.

Carle, E. (1979). *The very hungry caterpillar.* New York: Philomel Books.

Chomsky, C. (1971). Write now, read later. *Childhood Education, 47,* 296–299.

Dyson, A. H. (1982). Reading, writing, and language: Young children solving the written language puzzle. *Language Arts, 59,* 829–839.

Dyson, A. H. (1983). The role of oral language in early writing. *Research in the Teaching of English, 17,* 1–30.

Dyson, A. H. (1984). Emerging alphabetic literacy in school contexts. *Written Communication, 1,* 5–55.

Dyson, A. H. (1985). Individual differences in emerging writing. In M. Farr (Ed.), *Advances in writing research: Vol. 1: Children's early writing development* (pp. 59–125). Norwood, NJ: Ablex.

Dyson, A. H. (1986). Children's early interpretations of writing: Expanding research perspectives. In D. B. Yaden & S. Templeton (Eds.), *Metalinguistic awareness and beginning literacy* (pp. 201–218). Portsmouth, NH: Heinemann Educational Books.

Ehri, L. C., & Wilce, L. S. (1987). Does learning to spell help beginners to read words? *Reading Research Quarterly, 22,* 47–65.

Feitelson, D., Kita, B., & Goldstein, Z. (1986). Effects of listening to stories on first graders' comprehension and use of language. *Research in the Teaching of English, 20,* 339–356.

Ferreiro, E. (1984). The underlying logic of literacy development. In H. Goelman, A. Oberg, & F. Smith (Eds.), *Awakening to literacy* (pp. 154–173). Exeter, NH: Heinemann Educational Books.

Ferreiro, E. (1985). Literacy development: A psychogenetic perspective. In D. R. Olson, N. Torrance, & A. Hildyard (Eds.), *Literacy, language, and learning: The nature and consequences of reading and writing* (pp. 217–228). Cambridge: Cambridge University Press.

Ferreiro, E. (1986). The interplay between information and assimilation in beginning literacy. In W. H. Teale & E. Sulzby (Eds.), *Emergent literacy: Writing and reading* (pp. 15–49). Norwood, NJ: Ablex.

Ferreiro, E., & Gomez Palacio, M. (1982). *Analisis de las perturbaciornes en el proceso aprendizaje de la lecto-escritura* [Analysis of perturbations in the process of literacy development] (5 vols.). Mexico City: Office of the Director General of Special Education.

Ferreiro, E., & Teberosky, A. (1982). *Literacy before schooling.* Exeter, NH: Heinemann Educational Books.

Galda, L. (1982). Playing about a story: Its impact on comprehension. *The Reading Teacher, 36,* 52–55.

Gibson, J. J., & Yonas, P. A. (1968). A new theory of scribbling and drawing in children. In *The analysis of reading skill* (Final report, Project No. 5-1213, U.S. Office of Education). Ithaca, NY: Cornell University.

Goodman, K. S., & Goodman Y. M. (1983). Reading and writing relationships: Pragmatic functions. *Language Arts, 60,* 590–599.

Graves, D. H. (1983). *Writing: Teachers and children at work.* Exeter, NH: Heinemann Educational Books.

Graves, D. H., & Hansen, J. (1983). The author's chair. *Language Arts, 60,* 176–183.

Gundlach, R. (1982). Children as writers: The beginnings of learning to write. In M. Nystrand (Ed.), *What writers know: The language, process, and structure of written discourse* (pp. 129–147). New York: Academic Press.

Heath, S. B., (1983). *Ways with words: Language, life and work in communities and classrooms.* Cambridge: Cambridge University Press.

Henderson, E. H. (1985). *Teaching spelling.* Boston: Houghton Mifflin.

Henderson, E. H., & Beers, J. (Eds.). (1981). *Developmental and cognitive aspects of learning to spell.* Newark, DE: International Reading Association.

Hickman, J. G. (1979). *Response to literature in a school environment, grades K-5.* Unpublished doctoral dissertation, Ohio State University, Columbus.

Melser, F. (1980). *Sing a song.* San Diego, CA: Wright Group.

Morris, D. (1981). Concept of word: A developmental phenomenon in the beginning reading and writing processes. *Language Arts, 58,* 659–668.

Pellegrini, A., & Galda, L. (1982). The effect of thematic-fantasy play training on the development of children's story comprehension. *American Educational Research Journal, 19,* 443–452.

Reder, S., & Green, K. R. (1983). Contrasting patterns of literacy in an Alaska fishing village. *International Journal of the Sociology of Language, 42,* 9–39.

Rhodes, L. K. (1981). I can read! Predictable books as resources for reading and writing instruction. *The Reading Teacher, 34,* 511–518.

Schickedanz, J. A. (1986). *More than the ABCs: The early stages of reading and writing.* Washington, DC: National Association for the Education of Young Children.

Slobodkina, E. (1940). *Caps for sale.* New York: Scholastic.

Smith, F. (1982). *Writing and the writer.* New York: Holt, Rinehart, and Winston.

Smith, F. (1983). Reading like a writer. *Language Arts, 60,* 558–567.

Sulzby, E. (1981). *Kindergarteners begin to read their own compositions: Beginning readers' developing knowledges about written language* (Final report to the Research Foundation of the National Council of Teachers of English). Evanston, IL: Northwestern University.

Sulzby, E. (1985). Kindergarteners as writers and readers. In M. Farr (Ed.), *Advances in writing research: Vol. 1. Children's early writing development* (pp. 127–199). Norwood, NJ: Ablex.

Sulzby, E. (1986). Writing and reading: Signs of oral and written language organization in the young child. In W. H. Teale & E. Sulzby (Eds.), *Emergent literacy: Writing and reading* (pp. 50–89). Norwood, NJ: Ablex.

Taylor, D. (1982). Children's social use of print. *The Reading Teacher, 36,* 144–149.

Taylor, D. (1983). *Family literacy: Young children learning to read and write.* Exeter, NH: Heinemann Educational Books.

Teale, W. H. (1986). Home background and young children's literacy development. In W. H. Teale & E. Sulzby (Eds.), *Emergent literacy: Writing and reading* (pp. 173–206). Norwood, NJ: Ablex.

Teale, W. H. (1987). Emergent literacy: Reading and writing development in early childhood. In J. Readance & R. S. Baldwin (Eds.), *Research in literacy: Merging perspectives: Thirty-sixth yearbook of the National Reading Conference* (pp. 45–74). Rochester, NY: National Reading Conference.

Temple, C. A., Nathan, R. G., & Burris, N. A. (1982). *The beginnings of writing.* Boston: Allyn & Bacon.

Tierney, R., & Pearson, P. D. (1985). Toward a composing model of reading: Writing, reading and learning. In C. Hedley & A. Baratta (Eds.), *Contexts of reading* (pp. 63–78). Norwood, NJ: Ablex.

Wells, G. (1982). Story reading and the development of symbolic skills. *Australian Journal of Reading, 5,* 142–152.

Wells, G. (1985). Preschool literacy-related activities and success in school. In D. R. Olson, N. Torrance, & A. Hildyard (Eds.), *Literacy, language and learning: The nature and consequences of reading and writing* (pp. 229–255). Cambridge: Cambridge University Press.

9

RESEARCH TO PRACTICE

Integrating Reading and Writing in a Kindergarten Curriculum

Alice J. Kawakami-Arakaki, Madelline E. Oshiro, and Dale C. Farran

This chapter describes the development of two classroom activities—a "morning message" and a writing-process approach—in a laboratory school setting and the subsequent dissemination of these activities in other classrooms in private and public schools. Based on studies of emergent literacy, both activities integrate reading and writing at the kindergarten level. The chapter also describes the teacher-researcher collaboration that went into developing the activities, which were ultimately implemented in seventeen classrooms. A study of the dissemination phase showed different patterns of implementation and indicated that activities are modified to fit the constraints of different classroom settings. Differences in implementation also appeared to be related to the characteristics of the activity itself, suggesting that task demands, as well as classroom constraints, must be considered when research-based activities are installed in real-world classrooms.

The work described in this chapter was conducted in the Kamehameha Schools, a major private school in Honolulu, Hawaii, at the Center for the Development of Early Education (CDEE), and in public schools that were implementing the Kamehameha Elementary Education Program (KEEP). KEEP is a language arts program specifically designed to increase the reading achievement of educationally at-risk Hawaiian and part-Hawaiian students. The program, which focuses primarily on reading comprehension, was first developed in the laboratory school at CDEE for use with first through third grades. After a five-year period, during which achievement results were consistently near national norms (Tharp, 1982), KEEP was disseminated to public schools that enroll a high proportion of Hawaiian and part-Hawaiian children who are educationally at risk. It is currently being used in over seventy classes in public elementary schools across the state of Hawaii.

In 1981 a teacher in the laboratory school and two curriculum developers began to work on a kindergarten curriculum that would allow teachers to integrate both reading and writing with current research on early literacy (Crowell, Kawakami, & Wong, 1986). The curriculum included parts of the standard KEEP program, but it added writing-process activities (Graves, 1983), large-group story-reading sessions (Kawakami, 1984), and the "morning message" (Kawakami & Wong, 1986), a unique activity developed to integrate the teaching of reading and writing. Although other teachers and CDEE staff were kept informed of progress during the two-year developmental effort, the curriculum was developed in a single kindergarten classroom. It was subsequently disseminated among other kindergartens in the laboratory school and in public schools, and in 1984 a research team was formed to examine various aspects of it (Farran, 1985). This study provided the opportunity to examine the dissemination of the "morning message" and the writing process.

THE DEVELOPMENTAL PHASE

The Morning Message in the Laboratory School

Research by Taylor (1983), Heath (1983), Anderson, Teale, and Estrada (1980), Teale (1982), and Snow (1983) has suggested that experiences in which children engage in meaningful communication are critical in developing a child's awareness of the usefulness of literacy and a desire to become literate. This research includes many detailed accounts of observations of children being introduced to reading and writing in their own homes by such devices as notes left on the refrigerator or invitations to birthday parties. Bedtime story reading, note and letter writing, and sign making also help children become aware of the value of reading and writing as a natural and necessary form of communication. The morning message was developed as a school activity that would demonstrate the processes of reading and writing as part of the classroom communication system.

Using research information, classroom observation, suggestions, and negotiations, the teacher and researchers developed the morning message in the kindergarten of the laboratory school, planning to modify the activity as it evolved through observation and discussion. Even in the best collaborations, a classroom is always the domain of the teacher; the researchers strove to become informed and influential participant observers. They met with the teacher once a week to discuss both what they had observed in the kindergarten classroom and the teacher's concerns. Each meeting began with proposed agenda items and a review of the previous week's notes. Discussions were often based on the morning message itself and on the teacher's goals for it. The discussion frequently brought to mind a research article or paper that would be circulated and read before the next group meeting. At times, researchers' feedback on the students' reactions to the morning messages was especially helpful in evaluating modifications to the routine.

The morning message, the first activity of the day, was deliberately structured to demonstrate the importance of reading and writing in the classroom. The whole class was seated on the floor while the teacher took attendance and conducted a short blackboard lesson. This unremarkable activity, which accomplished the business routines of roll call, morning circle, and calendar discussion, was modified to maximize opportunities for the children to participate in integrated reading and writing classroom communication.

After the teacher took attendance and added another date to the calendar, she wrote the date on the board. Children were encouraged to read along or to chime in as she simultaneously spelled out and wrote the letters and numbers. Early in the school year, when many of the children could read only a few words, she also wrote a simple sentence about something of interest to the class that day. In September she wrote:

Today is Thursday, September 17, 1984.
We will go to art class today.

The teacher encouraged the children to read along with her, identifying letters and words. She led the class in reading and discussed the message of the written text. When problems in decoding occurred, the teacher and children worked together to use context and phonic cues to identify words and to develop meaning. The children were actively involved in the process of written communication.

As the year progressed, to maintain an appropriate instructional level, the messages became more complex. In December of the first year of development, after the message had been written and read, one of the children raised his hand and announced to the class, "If you take the *e-r-s* away from *Founder's* you have the word *found."* This revelation came about because of a message concerning the school's Founder's Day program. The student's observation was to become the topic of the teacher and researchers' group discussions for a few weeks. The discussions included notions regarding the zone of proximal development (Vygotsky, 1978), the writing-process approach (Graves, 1983), and emergent literacy (Clay, 1977; Holdaway, 1979; Mason, 1981). These discussions and the insights of the teacher resulted in the second phase of the morning message, which involved a focus on conventions of writing.

As the second phase got underway, the teacher began focusing on developing the children's awareness of the writing process. In January she wrote the following message:

January 9, 1985
Today is Wednesday. Don't forget your art aprons before recess. We also have music at 2:00. Did you have a nice time with Miss Murakami?

As she wrote the message, the children chimed in and read the words. When she had completed the message, she and the children read it together. She then asked the class if they noticed any interesting things about the written message. Children went to the board and pointed out upper- and lower-case letters, plural forms, contractions, question marks, and periods at the ends of sentences. Each example was underlined and discussed. This second phase of the morning message gave the teacher and the students opportunities to discuss the kinds of things to which a writer needs to attend in constructing a written message.

In April the teacher wrote the following message:

April 17, 1985
Good Morning. It's Wednesday, an art day. There's no music at 1:30 today because we are invited to a Spring Fling. Older boys and girls will be dancing and jumping rope. Please be on your best behavior.

The children watched and read along. The teacher guided the reading, introducing comprehension strategies as needed to understand the message. Children then proceeded to call attention to the following conventions of writing:

1. The contraction *it's* means *it is.*
2. The letter *s* in *boys* and *girls* makes these words plural.

3. The root word *day* is in *Wednesday* and *today.*
4. The word *be* is found twice in the message.
5. *Spring* and *Fling* rhyme.
6. The word endings -*ed,* -*ing,* and -*er* are used in *invited, dancing, jumping,* and *older.*

The morning message had thus become an activity that presented reading and writing as an integrated process. The simple business routines of the morning were now an instructional event, based on principles of emergent literacy research. The teacher found herself planning morning messages that would make students aware of writing conventions. Children's written pieces suggested the need to present specific techniques. Instructional goals were also taken from the scope and sequence chart of the KEEP reading program. The message then became a means of teaching literacy skills by bringing components from a formal reading program into a meaningful context for direct instruction.

The morning message remained an appropriate instructional activity throughout the kindergarten year because it was adjusted to levels of the children's development, thus adhering to Vygotskian principles. It taught from a text that was a natural part of the communication system in the classroom, while integrating written with spoken language.

The Writing Process Approach in the Laboratory School

By the time we began to teach writing in kindergarten, Graves and Hansen (1983) had studied the writing-process approach with first graders, and Clay (1982), Taylor (1983), and Dyson (1984) had observed writing and drawing by young children in home-based studies. Jane Hansen visited the lab school and demonstrated prewriting discussion and conferring with small groups of children and adults. Although the writing-process approach had no guidelines for teaching beginning writing to kindergarten children, we decided to use it because it could be adjusted to the levels and needs of our children. Our classes occasionally included children who had no idea of the difference between a letter and a jagged line, as well as others who lacked the fine motor coordination required to make a pencil or crayon follow the route they intended. With these kinds of kindergartners in mind, we began to try to understand the principles of the writing-process approach and to modify them to fit these children.

Constructing appropriate procedures for the writing-process approach in kindergarten was a more difficult task than it was for the morning message. By allowing the children to compose their own written message, the teacher and researchers were put in the position of having to guide development at the child's pace. The writer, not the teacher, determined the text for instruction. The major problem was to provide instruction for each child's message, be it scribbles, pictures, or pages of sentences written in invented spelling. The teacher and researchers addressed many unexpected issues as they modified the writing-process approach for kindergarten.

As the team met and discussed the morning message, they simultaneously discussed ideas about the writing process. Issues included topic choice, conferring, dictation, invented spelling, publication, and "author's chair." Each issue was resolved by tinkering with existing procedures under close observation, discussing the goals and outcomes for each strategy, and, after a number of these cycles, deciding on a procedure that seemed to best meet the goals of the classroom and to be consistent with the research on literacy.

Early in the first year of development, the children were assigned topics for writing. However, they sometimes did not have the information to write about these teacher-selected topics, and in other instances they wanted to write about personally relevant experiences. Thus, after a few months, the procedure was amended, and children were encouraged to talk and write about topics of their choice. Child-generated writing topics prevailed during the prewriting discussion period, and topics chosen by the children replaced those assigned by the teacher.

Strategies for conferring with children during the writing period needed to follow a consistent strategy that supported the development of writing. Without guidelines, the three adults in the room had been giving the children inconsistent and confusing feedback. Common conferring procedures were developed for use with children whose writing spanned a wide range of competence. The following four steps were sufficient:

1. Focus on the message or the meaning of the piece.
2. Make a statement about the child's knowledge of the writing process.
3. Elicit additional information from the child about the topic.
4. Close each conference with an encouraging comment.

Guidelines were also established for coaching children with their writing. We found the following four guidelines to be most effective:

1. Invented spelling and the use of environmental print should be encouraged. Initial and/or final consonant sounds used in conjunction with a blank line seemed to be the easiest way

for children to begin labeling pictures and constructing words. As they became more familiar with sound-symbol relationships, they began filling in more letters and eventually could manage to write a few words in conventional spelling. Written labels, charts, and books also became a resource for correctly spelled words.

2. Verbatim dictation should be banned. The issue of adults' writing the children's message on paper arose very soon after development of the curriculum began. Dictation often resulted in lengthy text that made no sense at all to the children later. We decided that if the child had started writing some words and was aware of a sound-symbol relationship, adults could write the standard spelling beneath the child's written text. Our rationale was that such a model of standard spelling would enhance writing development.

3. Standards for book publication should vary according to individual abilities. When a child had written a piece that contained enough information to be turned into a book, classroom publication occurred. Many of the kindergarten children were not able to construct three sentences in one piece to meet the criterion for publication that many first-grade classes use. We set an initial kindergarten criterion of allowing publication of picture books if three objects were labeled. For more advanced children, three sentences related to a main idea were required for publication. As the year progressed, the criterion for publication increased in complexity; only a few children continued to label pictures throughout the year. The range of written pieces is evident in Figures 9.1–9.3, showing books published in April.

4. Sharing of children's writing should feature the most and the least advanced pieces of writing in the class. Adults in the classroom had often been overly impressed by the complex writing of a few star students and had focused "author's chair" on their sentences and elaborate illustrations. It was important to remember that children progress at different rates and that each child needs encouragement. A wide range of writing pieces was included during sharing time. Barely recognizable pictures that had taken twenty minutes of effort received just as much attention as published books of five pages. The content of the teacher's praise went back to the basic conferring strategy of focusing on the meaning of the message and the effort that was put into the communication.

The Writing Sessions. Writing time followed the morning message and was initiated with a request for children to write the teacher

FIGURE 9.1 "Things I Like," by Chris

a message on paper. Writing time was divided into three phases: prewriting discussion, writing and conferring, and sharing. The entire writing period lasted about thirty-five minutes.

The prewriting period usually began with a discussion of topics the children wanted to write about. The class sat together on the carpet, facing the chalkboard. The teacher, stressing the communicative nature of writing, asked for ideas the children wanted to include in a message to her. She generated enthusiasm for unique ideas and asked children for suggestions on how they could convey their ideas in writing, encouraging them, for example, to use the chalkboard to demonstrate invented spelling or to look for print in the classroom to aid conventional spelling. Because some children were not yet able to write letters and words, the teacher was always careful to talk about illustration as an acceptable way of communicating ideas.

After about a five-minute discussion, the teacher handed out writing booklets to the children, and they went to their seats. Some drew pictures and wrote letters and names next to the pictures. Others had barely enough control of a crayon to render a recognizable picture. The teacher circulated around the classroom; each piece received admiration and sincere interest. She always focused first on the message of the piece and the communication of ideas. A secondary focus was

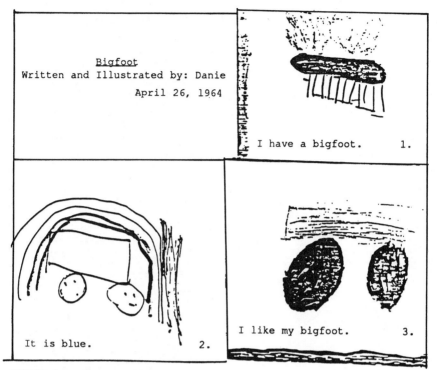

FIGURE 9.2 "Bigfoot," by Danie

on the mechanics of writing, and a final comment usually encouraged the children to keep working until the end of the period. Each day they spent about twenty minutes engaged in actual writing.

At the end of the writing time, the class gathered on the carpet for the sharing time, which usually lasted about ten minutes. Basic procedures for the "author's chair" (Graves & Hansen, 1983) were followed. The teacher was careful to select pieces that displayed a range of writing levels. Early in the school year, pieces included scribbled pictures and letterlike forms, as well as recognizable, labeled pictures. Later in the year, pieces included not only labeled pictures but also sentences with illustrations that often were "published" as books. Throughout the year, the writings displayed many levels of sophistication.

The Writing Process and Two Children. A comparison of two children illustrates how the writing process was incorporated into the classroom in ways appropriate to the variability in children's writing development. In September Jay produced a picture resembling a house (see Figure 9.4). When the teacher asked him about his message, he said that it was his house. The teacher responded by telling him

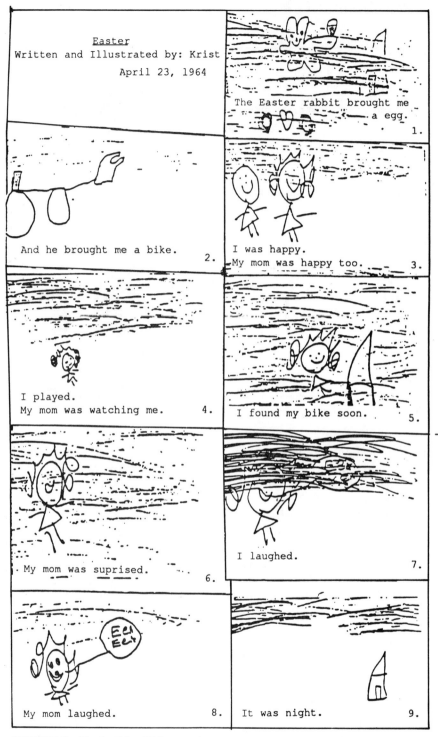

FIGURE 9.3 "Easter," by Krist

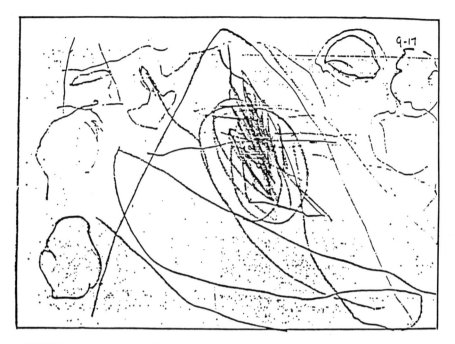

FIGURE 9.4 Jay's House, Drawn in September

that his piece showed he knew that pictures and lines can give people a message on paper. She then praised the effort he had made and encouraged him to continue. In September the teacher also conferred with Misty, who said that her piece was about a birthday party at Noel's house (see Figure 9.5). The teacher acknowledged Misty's skill in labeling the sounds in the words *balloon* and *table.* She also encouraged Misty to add more to the piece.

Throughout the year, the children acquired an increasing number of writing skills. In February Jay wrote his first piece with complete sentences (see Figure 9.6). He was determined to write three sentences so that he could "publish" a book. He copied the first sentence from the morning message. After pondering the word *fish,* he suddenly stood up and dashed to the library corner. There he added a figure of a fish and then wrote *"fish"* into his sentence, which read, "I like to fish." He completed his piece with, "After I went to Pizza Hut." His piece showed that he knew sentences were comprised of words and also that he could use invented spelling and environmental print. On the same day Misty wrote, "Our school has new fishes from science, because Miss Viser bought the fishes at the store" (see Figure 9.7). This variability in the sophistication of written products continued throughout the year.

FIGURE 9.5 Misty's Rendition of a Birthday Party at Noel's House, Drawn in September

THE DISSEMINATION PHASE

In preparation for implementation in other classes, videotapes of the morning message were made in September, January, and April of the final year of work in the laboratory school classroom. These segments were used in a training tape for teachers who were interested in learning about the morning message (Kawakami & Wong, 1985). The teacher and one of the researchers began leading discussions about the morning message and sharing ideas with other kindergarten teachers and researchers. The developmental team also held seminars and workshops on the concepts underlying the writing-process approach, distributed lists of necessary writing materials and supplies, and compiled videotapes showing the phases of the writing period (Kawakami & Wong, 1986).

Logs of classroom observations and notes from meetings had been the sources of information during the developmental phase. To carry out their assignment of monitoring the implementation of recently developed kindergarten activities in classrooms during the dissemination phase, the research team devised a "Teacher Checklist of Kindergarten Classroom Activities" (Kawakami & Oshiro, 1985). Data from the checklist described the sequence and format in which activities were implemented. Teachers were first asked to review and to contribute to a list of common kindergarten activities. This list formed the categories for observation. Teachers were also asked to indicate common organizational schemes that comprise the contexts of classroom

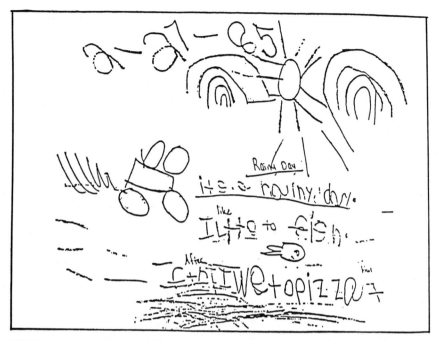

FIGURE 9.6 Jay's First Piece with Complete Sentences, Produced in February

instruction. Teachers' input was thus instrumental in developing the checklist for reporting the classroom activities during a one-week period each month of the school year. During the first data-collection period, researchers were present in the classrooms to answer questions about procedures for completing the checklist. At that time, a few more activities were added to the list, and revised definitions of classroom context were adopted.

The Morning Message in the Real World

The "Teacher Checklist of Kindergarten Classroom Activities" provided information on the number of teachers who were using the morning message during the school year. Seventeen participating kindergarten teachers, four from the laboratory school and thirteen from public schools, were implementing the standard program and other optional activities. Sixteen teachers reported using the morning message as an activity for the whole class throughout the year. One teacher implemented the morning message as a large-group activity in all but one reporting period, when it was used for small-group instruction. This activity seemed to have transferred quite easily to many different classrooms.

FIGURE 9.7   A Sample of Misty's Writing, Produced in February

Classroom observations and demonstrations provided other opportunities to note modifications that took place in the schools. A curriculum specialist presented the morning message in workshops for all the teachers at the beginning of the year, in demonstrations in each of the classrooms as the year progressed, and through videotapes (Kawakami & Wong, 1985; Kawakami & Iwahashi, 1985). The teachers at different sites continued to change the procedure to suit their needs. One teacher added the use of colored chalk to highlight and teach letter formation and discrimination early in the year. This idea was shared and was eventually widely used to color-code different types of letters, word forms, and grammatical structures. Another innovation included writing the message on a chart so that teachers could refer to messages written earlier in the week. Children also took parts of the messages home to read to their families. The morning message had thus become an activity that reached from school to home.

The Writing Process in the Real World

The "Teacher Checklist of Kindergarten Classroom Activities" included the three phases of the writing sessions: prewriting discussion, writing, and sharing, based on "author's chair." Teachers were asked to indicate on the checklist whether the instruction took place in large groups, small groups, or independent centers. The results are presented in Table 9.1.

During every reporting period, at least eleven of the seventeen classes were implementing all three components of the writing sessions. There was a gradual increase in implementation, from an average of thirteen classes in September to fifteen in March. Another change involved the way the writing process was implemented: in the beginning of the year, most of the teachers conducted writing as a whole-class activity; later in the year, some teachers had the writing phase take place at independent centers and in small groups.

The process approach to kindergarten writing that was developed in the laboratory school did not transfer intact to the "real world" of the public schools. Public school teachers reported that it was an exciting idea but difficult to maintain. Progress in writing with the process approach was hard to observe. Teachers had problems in circulating and talking with all the students during a single writing period. They would occasionally become impatient and discouraged over some of the slower students' apparent lack of progress. As they conferred with students, they often found it difficult to say something meaningful and encouraging about squiggles and other forms of beginning writing.

Many of the problems reported seemed to occur among teachers who lacked specific goals and strategies for use with children who were at different stages of writing development. Many teachers requested information on appropriate responses to specific pieces of writing. In retrospect, these requests, although they appeared to center on the form of students' written texts, were actually indications that teachers needed information on the principles of instruction and on the key features of children's written texts. One solution was to shift the writing periods into small groups. Teachers who shifted writing into the context of direct instruction maintained this pattern and occasionally scheduled writing time as independent-center work. Although in a few classes the actual writing took place in small groups, in most of the classes the prewriting discussion and the sharing continued as large-group activities.

TABLE 9.1 Number of Classrooms Using Writing Activities in Large Groups, Small Groups, and Independent Centers

	September			October			November			January			February			March			April		
	L	S	I	L	S	I	L	S	I	L	S	I	L	S	I	L	S	I	L	S	I
Prewriting discussion	14	0	0	13	0	0	13	2	0	13	1	0	16	0	0	15	0	0	13	2	0
Writing	14	0	0	14	0	1	15	3	0	13	2	1	13	2	1	14	1	3	11	3	2
Sharing/ author's chair	11	0	0	13	0	0	15	0	0	13	0	0	14	0	0	16	0	0	11	1	0

Note: L = large group; S = small group; I = independent center.

Summary of Dissemination Results

The results for both the morning message and the writing process suggest that activities developed in a laboratory school do not transfer intact to other schools. Both activities had to be modified to fit teaching styles and routines.

The morning message was easily installed in many classrooms. Teachers had to make only minor modifications to fit this activity into their classroom routines. Its easy assimilation was due to a number of factors. First, the morning message provided a fresh approach to a familiar routine. Second, teaching objectives and goals for the morning message were drawn from the structured language arts program and from research on emergent literacy; teachers could teach familiar skills through a meaningful communicative activity. A final reason for the ease of implementation was that the morning message consisted of the familiar routine of student responses to text provided by the teacher. The task demands for teaching the morning message were not very different from those of many other classroom routines.

Process writing in kindergarten was a new activity, and it was more difficult to implement than the morning message. Most kindergarten classes had not included written composition as part of the curriculum, and the goals of the writing-process activity had not been clearly spelled out. As the writing-process approach for kindergarten was developed in the laboratory classroom, the teacher and researchers had to struggle with many of the issues that became problematic topics for discussion in the public school classes. Unfortunately, an efficient method of working through those issues on a class-by-class basis had not yet been developed by the time dissemination had begun. Successful writing periods depended on the teacher's understanding of the long-term course of writing development and of the principles of instruction.

Unfortunately, this raises the perennial problem of introducing child-centered literacy activities in schools that view progress in terms of scope and sequence charts and standardized tests. The literature on writing development suggests that there are many different paths and sequences for acquiring competence in writing (Dyson, 1984). We were therefore reluctant to lay out anything that could be misconstrued as a scope and sequence chart for writing development. Our reluctance was based on the very real possibility that teachers would teach these objectives to every child in a fixed sequence. Our more flexible method of teaching the writing process was almost revolutionary. Within each writing period, teachers had to base writing instruction on many different and unfamiliar child-generated texts.

IMPLICATIONS FOR CURRICULUM RESEARCH AND POLICY

This chapter has described how a team in a laboratory school, using emergent literacy research, developed two kindergarten activities that integrate reading and writing. The data on implementing these activities in other classrooms suggest that they may require different types of in-service training. Whereas the morning message was easily and quickly accepted and adapted by virtually all the teachers, problems arose in implementing the writing process. Although both activities were disseminated with similar consultative support, teachers may have required a different kind of support in writing process, one centered on principles of instruction rather than on demonstrations of techniques.

The morning message seems to be easily adapted to the routine of many classrooms as an extension of morning business time. As in most instructional situations, the text is a message controlled by the teacher. It is often constructed with various objectives in mind in order to provide opportunities for instruction within a meaningful context. Teachers can use the morning message by combining the goals of a structured reading program with insights from recent research on literacy development. It provides a fresh approach to the familiar routine of student responses, to text provided by the teacher.

The writing-process activities, however, seem to require further examination. In kindergarten classes, writing to communicate is rather uncommon. During the actual writing period, the teacher must recognize the strengths of each child's piece and lead the child onward by gentle questioning and encouragement. This requires teachers to react and respond to each child in a manner that cannot be preplanned. Teachers need to understand the principles of instruction and to recognize the manifestations of writing development. Because of the various stages of writing development present in any one class, teachers must contend with instructional materials (each child's writing) on many different topics and at many different levels of expertise. Finally, writing instruction, unlike most instructional sequences, is based on a model of teaching that starts from the drawing or the written text constructed by each child.

During the development of the morning message and the writing-process approach in the laboratory school, three adults observed and worked with children's writing. They developed a set of goals and benchmarks of writing progress for kindergartners and were able to identify some basic strategies for instruction. Beyond the experimental setting, however, during dissemination, teachers who were able to implement this writing activity encountered some difficulty using the information and strategies that had been developed. Implementation might have been easier had there been a more comprehensive and systematic program of in-service training in principles of instruction for developing writing skills and in general strategies for conferring and for selecting pieces for sharing.

Some public school teachers who participated in the project managed to use or to adapt the approaches developed in the laboratory school. They helped us realize that further work is needed on both the content of activities and the process of developing training and support to match the task demands of the activities. Curriculum development must also include a closer look at task demands. If research is to find a place in real-world classrooms, researchers must expect and facilitate development of practices that ease the transfer of activities from experimental settings to public school classrooms. Training and support services must be provided to address many of the concerns that arise because of the need to adapt a curriculum to different classrooms. Continued collaboration on these issues should help make the transition from research to practice a smoother one. Collaborative curriculum development cannot end at the laboratory school. Task demands of the activities must be considered in terms of both the teacher's role and the children's performance.

R E F E R E N C E S

Anderson, A., Teale, W., & Estrada, E. (1980). Low-income children's preschool literacy experiences: Some naturalistic observations. *The Quarterly Newsletter of the Laboratory of Comparative Human Cognition, 3,* 59–65.

Clay, M. M. (1977). *Reading: The patterning of complex behaviors.* London: Heinemann Educational Books.

Clay, M. M. (1982). *Observing young readers.* Exeter, NH: Heinemann Educational Books.

Crowell, D. C., Kawakami, A. J., & Wong, J. L. (1986). Emerging literacy: Experiences in a kindergarten classroom. *The Reading Teacher, 40,* 144–149.

Dyson, A. H. (1984). Emerging alphabetic literacy in school contexts: Toward defining the gap between school curriculum and child mind. *Written Communication, 1,* 5–55.

Farran, D. C. (1985). *The kindergarten project team study.* Paper presented at the meeting of the kindergarten project team, the Kamehameha Schools, Center for the Development of Early Education, Honolulu.

Graves, D. H. (1983). *Writing: Teachers and children at work.* Exeter, NH: Heinemann Educational Books.

Graves, D. H., & Hansen, J. (1983). The author's chair. *Language Arts, 60,* 176–183.

Heath, S. B. (1983). *Ways with words*. New York: Cambridge University Press.

Holdaway, D. (1979). *The foundation of literacy*. Auckland, NZ: Heinemann Educational Books.

Kawakami, A. J. (1984). *Promoting active involvement with text through story reading*. Paper presented at the annual meeting of the National Reading Conference, St. Petersburg, FL.

Kawakami, A. J., & Iwahashi, A. (1985). *Morning message potpourri* (Videotape). Honolulu: Kamehameha Schools, Center for the Development of Early Education.

Kawakami, A. J., & Oshiro, M. E. (1985). *The teacher checklist of kindergarten classroom activities*. Honolulu: Kamehameha Schools, Center for the Development of Early Education.

Kawakami, A. J., & Wong, J. L. (1985). *The morning message training tape* (Videotape). Honolulu: Kamehameha Schools, Center for the Development of Early Education.

Kawakami, A. J., & Wong, J. L. (1986). *Kindergarten writing program* (Videotape). Honolulu: Kamehameha Schools, Center for the Development of Early Education.

Mason, J. (1981). *Acquisition of knowledge about reading: The preschool period*. Paper presented at the annual meeting of the American Educational Research Association, Los Angeles.

Snow, C. E. (1983). Literacy and language: Relationships during the preschool years. *Harvard Educational Review, 53*, 165–189.

Taylor, D. (1983). *Family literacy*. Exeter, NH: Heinemann Educational Books.

Teale, W. (1982). Toward a theory of how children learn to read and write naturally. *Language Arts, 59*, 555–570.

Tharp, R. G. (1982). The effective instruction of comprehension: Results and description of the Kamehameha Early Education Program. *Reading Research Quarterly, 17*, 503–527.

Vygotsky, L. S. (1978). *Mind in society: The development of higher psychological processes*. Cambridge, MA: Harvard University Press.

10

PRESCHOOL CHILDREN'S READING AND WRITING AWARENESS

Janice Stewart and Jana M. Mason

We explored prekindergarten children's awareness about literacy— their ability to express varying facets of learning to read and write— by asking them to describe how they were learning, to read a picture-phrase book, and to write something. We found that most of the children were aware of how they were learning and, though not able to read, they pretended to read by labeling pictures in the book. For the writing task, they usually drew pictures or wrote single letters and then produced meaningful descriptions of their writings or drawings. Variations in their literacy awareness were related to the instruction provided in school and the quality of home support for literacy.

When preschool children are asked to tell how they are learning to read and write, some will say nothing, while others will talk about how a parent is helping them or about what they do to learn. When asked to read words, some will ignore the letters, listing instead their favorite words; others will whisper the word slowly, analyzing the words into letter sounds. When asked to read a book, some will name the pictures or make up a story; others will use the print and picture information to read a few of the words. When asked to write something, preschool children will again react in very different ways; some will scribble or draw a picture, and others will make letters or try to construct words.

   In responding to these reading and writing tasks, young children demonstrate an *awareness* of reading and writing, both in their ability to talk about how they are learning and in demonstrating what they know and can do. Such responses ought to provide insights into how we can best help children learn to read and write. When these responses are coupled with information about how parents help their children learn about reading and writing at home, practitioners should be able to plan appropriate activities in school and to recommend other activities for home use. This chapter focuses both on the effects of the home environment and on three sorts of awareness that young children have about literacy—namely, knowing what and how they are learning, knowing how the sounds of letters are mapped onto words, and knowing how to derive meaning from printed texts.

TYPES OF LITERACY AWARENESS

Researchers (e.g., Johns, 1972) have measured children's awareness of their learning with such interview questions as, "What is reading?" and "How are you learning to read?" Other researchers (e.g., Liberman & Shankweiler, 1985) have tested children's awareness that spoken words can be separated into letter sounds and that these sounds can be blended to make words. Children's awareness that written language is meaningful in the sense that they realize they can in some ways map their oral language onto written language has been described by Chafe (1985) and Perena (1984), among others; this awareness can be measured by interpreting the extent of children's text comprehension.

Awareness of Learning to Read and Write

Research in the 1950s and 1960s indicated that kindergarten and first-grade children had serious difficulty talking about the purpose of written language and held only a vague understanding of how they learn to read (Denny & Weintraub, 1966; Reid, 1966; Vernon, 1957). More recent work on the subject has determined that children can demonstrate how they read and can talk about an ongoing reading activity, although they do so in a simple way (Pramling, 1983). Furthermore, the quality or maturity of their answers is related to their reading performance at the end of first grade (Stewart, 1986). Children who give a more complete explanation of how they are learning tend to be the better readers later.

Awareness of thinking and learning requires an ability to analyze and talk about one's own actions. From work by Vygotsky (1962), we know that children are able to analyze their own actions beginning at about age four. This ability is apparent from listening to their speech, which at that age is either social (i.e., talking to others) or private (i.e., talking to oneself). When children first begin to use private speech, they speak aloud, even though the speech is directed to themselves; later they turn it underground into the silent speech we all use to monitor and evaluate our thoughts and actions. Extending Vygotsky's work, Diaz (1986) found that when young children are engaged in learning tasks, they use private speech to analyze their own actions; they verbalize the steps they are carrying out and the difficulties they encounter in trying to solve various problems. Since beginning reading and writing activities often involve problem-solving, young children are likely to use private speech when they are learning to write and read. We assume that they ought then to be able to tell others what they are doing and how they are learning.

Awareness of Letter Sounds

Reading and spelling draw on knowledge about the regularity of letter sounds (phonemes). Phonological awareness enables children to represent letters and letter clusters in terms of sound patterns in words. As experienced readers, we can read words we have never seen before. Take, for example, the nonword *thut*. We can separate and recognize the *th* sound and blend it with short *u* and *t* sounds to produce the correct word sound, and we do this without being conscious of the process. We can agree about the pronunciation of *thut*, as well as about the way it is spelled, because we have an awareness, explicit or implicit, of the regularities in our language.

We believe young children become aware of letter-sound patterns and their relation to words as they learn letter names, as they recognize and print or spell words, and as they try to read and write new words (see Chapter 3). However, not all children acquire an awareness of letter-sound regularity in the primary grades. Those who do not are at a considerable disadvantage in learning to read, and research shows that many of them do not become good readers. Information about letter-sound awareness could provide a means of early identification of children who might otherwise have difficulty learning to read and write.

Awareness of Meaning in Print

It is not known how young children become aware that the words they see in printed texts are meaningful and related to their speech, but certainly children do make such connections. Soderbergh (1977) described her child's awareness of word meaning as beginning with an unwillingness to read words that did not make sense to her (e.g., the word *have*). The child also imagined at first that printed words were real entities (e.g., telling her mother she got worried when she read the word *frightened*). Snow (1983) suggested that the process of understanding ideas in print can take place as parents read to their children and talk about pictures, words, and the children's related personal experiences. Assessing children's developing understanding of print meaning would indicate whether they need more help.

HOME INFLUENCES ON EARLY READING AND WRITING AWARENESS

Most children begin to recognize meaningful written words before they are taught to read in first grade, and some also begin to hear and write letters and to spell words before then. It must therefore be true that reading and writing awareness is, or can be, initiated at home. A home environment supportive of literacy fosters the early development of useful concepts for reading and writing. In such an environment, children are provided with printed materials, are read to regularly from a very early age, are helped to read and write, and have opportunities to see that literacy can be functional (Clark, 1976; Durkin, 1966; Stewart, 1986; Teale, 1981; Wells, 1986).

There is some evidence that drawing at home facilitates later writing. Genishi, Dyson, and Hass (1984) found that writinglike drawing was a means of symbolizing significant people and objects in the child's world. Children use many variations in their writing strategies, and they move freely among writing, art, and drama to express themselves. Because they can depict their ideas more completely in art, they continue to use drawing as a writing form even after they can print (see Chapter 6). It is also the case that children use art to rehearse for writing (Graves, 1983); that is, they may first express an idea in a drawing and use the drawing as a repository for meaning while they work on the written message. This concept finds support in Vygotsky's remark that "make-believe play, drawing and writing can be viewed as different moments in an essentially unified process of written language development" (1978, p. 116).

A READING AND WRITING STUDY

The findings presented here are from a study of the reading and writing development of low-income black children in an inner-city community. We chose to study these children because a better understanding of their progress toward literacy is needed if we are to learn how to intercede for their benefit.

The study began in March of the prekindergarten year and ended in September as the children were entering kindergarten. We gave children tasks related to reading and writing awareness, and in March parents filled out a questionnaire regarding children's awareness during the prekindergarten year. For the next three months, we instituted classroom reading and writing activities. We retested the children in May and after the summer break, when they were entering kindergarten. We looked for connections between their reading and writing performances and their home support, as well as at their awareness about reading and writing.

Research Method

The study was carried out with two prekindergarten classrooms of black children who attended a church school near their inner-city homes. The teachers had college degrees and were certified teachers. The forty-five children ranged in age at the onset of the study from four years and two months to four years and ten months. The setting was unusual in that the school believed in providing formal reading instruction beginning in the prekindergarten year. The teachers taught prekindergartners to recognize letters, to copy words, and to carry out reading-readiness tasks. During the last three months of prekindergarten, we added instruction for one group to listen to and discuss stories and had another group recite and then read picture-phrase books, an approach used by McCormick and Mason (1986). Informal classroom writing experiences were added for both groups. Although possible differences between the two groups could not be considered because of high attrition for one group, responses and changes over time for the remaining eighteen children were analyzed and are reported here.

We measured children's awareness with three sources of data. Children's awareness about the process of learning to read and write was evaluated with interview questions. Letter-sound knowledge was measured with spelling and writing tasks (adapted from Mason & McCormick, 1979). The Wide Range Achievement Test (WRAT) (Jastak & Jastak, 1965) was also used to assess children's letter and word knowledge. Children's understanding of written text was based on analyses of book-reading tasks (adapted from an early literacy test by Mason and Stewart, in preparation). Analysis of writing attempts and talk was adapted from Mason, Peterman, Powell, and Kerr (see Chapter 5).

To assess children's awareness of learning to read, the interviewer asked them two things: (1) "Tell me, how are you beginning to learn to read?" (2) "Now we're going to play a game. You go over there and pick a doll or stuffed animal. Let's pretend that it can't read but wants to learn. Show me what you might do to help it learn." The children's responses were scored according to a four-level scale (Stewart, 1986). *Level 0* identifies children who can give no information and who respond with "I don't know" or "I'm not learning." At *level 1* the response describes only one actor. The child says, "I read" or "She reads." There is neither an elaboration of who helps nor is the child described as interacting with the text. At *level 2* the response describes the procedure and actions between significant others or the text but does not describe the nature of the interaction. Children at level 2 typically respond by saying, "My mother tells me" or "My teacher say to read it." Responses at *level 3* include a description of the interaction; for example, the child might say, "I listen to the teacher and then I try to read it the same way" or "My mommy reads the words and then I sound them out and read them to her." *Level 4*, which was not found among these young children, demonstrates the use of conditional knowledge, such as, "Well, you have to figure out the words. First you sound them out and say them real fast and then you read them to see if you know what it says" (examples are from Stewart, 1986).

Awareness of learning to write was assessed from responses to the question, "How did you learn to write?" The responses, scored in the same way as responses to questions about reading awareness, determine whether children perceive other people as significant helpers and what process they use for learning to write. *Level 0* indicates no response. At *level 1* children describe writing in terms of one actor, saying, for example, "I write" or "My mommy writes." Responses at *level 2* indicate that the child is aware of others' help; for example, "My teacher tells me to write the words down." At *level 3* children describe an interaction between themselves and the text or another person; a child at this level might typically answer, "My teacher writes the words on the board and then I copy them on the lines." *Level 4*, describing conditional knowledge, was not found among these prekindergartners.

Letter-sound awareness was measured with a spelling task in which children were asked to use magnetic letters to spell three- and four-letter words (e.g., *pat* and *tape*). Each correctly identified letter, placed in its approximately appropriate position, was assigned a point (see Chapter 3 for clarification of this kind of analysis). Thus *pat* spelled as *p* would receive one point, *pt* or *pa* would receive two points, and *pat* would receive three points.

Awareness of letter-sounds was also assessed by analyzing the writing children did during testing and during class time. Some writing situations were unstructured; that is, children were simply asked to "write something." Others were structured, and they wrote after hearing a short story or participating in an activity the class had done together, such as a field trip. Writing samples were scored according to the maturity of the writing form, as follows: (0) *no response,* (1) *free form* (scribble), (2) *pictures or isolated letters,* (3) *groupings of letters with space boundaries to represent words,* and (4) *real words.*

Awareness of meaning in print was evaluated with a book-reading task in which children were asked to read a picture-phrase book. The book contained a six-page story with an illustration and three to four words on each page. Since most children could not read, we scored their movement toward meaningful reading as follows: (0) *no response or don't know,* (1) *one-word labeling of picture* (e.g., "cat"), (2) *phrase or sentence labeling of pictures* (e.g., "The cat is in the street"), (3) *connection of one picture with the next* (e.g., "Now, they all stop"), and (4) *reading attempt* (e.g., "stop for the cat").

We evaluated children's awareness of meaning in their own written attempts (whether printed letters or drawings) by asking them to describe what they had written. Evaluation of responses centered on meaningfulness, disregarding form, using the following scores: (0) *not related to task, don't know, or no response,* (1) *single labeling of each picture or print* (e.g., "Here is a car" or "It's an *f*"), (2) *two or more ideas about a written product* (e.g., "A girl who wants to go home"), (3) *connection of one piece of text or drawing with another* (e.g., "This is Sesame Street and Oscar is in the garbage can. I saw him when I went to Sesame Street and here is me"), (4) *reading attempt* (e.g., "The fat cat. The cat sat on the mat. This is what we copy off the board" or "This says *house* and this says *Pat,* and that's my mom's name").

A parent questionnaire (reported by Mason & Dunning, 1986, and Stewart, 1986) was used to assess the amount and type of literacy support provided at home. Questions about the type and frequency of home reading and writing experiences were analyzed to determine whether parents' support for literacy was related to children's awareness.

Results and Discussion

The pretreatment (March) and posttreatment (May and September) measures for reading and writing are displayed in Table 10.1. There were no overall changes in children's awareness of learning to read and write, but there were improvements over time in their understanding of letter sounds, in awareness of print meaning, and in their letter and word recognition (WRAT).

TABLE 10.1 Average Levels of Pretreatment and Posttreatment Awareness

Awareness	March (Pre)	May (Post 1)	September (Post 2)
Learning about reading	1.9	1.8	1.9
Learning about writing	—	1.6	1.6
Letter sounds, reading	.4	3.2	4.4
Letter sounds, writing	—	2.3	2.6
Print meaning, reading	2.3	3.4	3.2
Print meaning, writing	—	2.4	2.4
WRAT score	22.5	23.9	24.9

Most children talked about how they were learning to read and write by describing their own actions or another person's help, and some described the nature of their interaction with others. The measures of letter-sound awareness showed that in March most of the children had no awareness of letter sounds, but by May they had begun to place a few letters correctly when trying to spell words, and they continued to improve over the summer. Progress in writing letters lagged behind progress in reading them and changed less over time. Tests of print-meaning awareness showed that children were more likely to label pictures in March, but by May they were connecting the pictures. No additional improvement occurred during the summer. Finally, the scores on letter and word recognition (WRAT) indicated that the children were able to name most of the upper-case letters in March (a score of 25 signifies recognition of all the letters on the test) and that they improved slightly over time.

Relating Reading Awareness to Writing Awareness. As children became aware of reading constructs, they also became aware of writing. Table 10.2 shows the correlation values between the reading and writing measures. Although the data represent only eighteen children (those who returned to the school in September and who were tested

TABLE 10.2 Correlations between Reading and Writing Awareness in May of Prekindergarten Year

	Reading		Writing			
	Sounds	Meaning	Learning	Sounds	Meaning	WRAT
Learning about reading	.25	.60	.42	.50	.34	.47
Letter sounds, reading	—	.45	.29	.12	.40	.23
Print meaning, reading	—	—	.25	.58	.11	.48
Learning about writing	—	—	—	.05	.33	.57
Letter sounds, writing	—	—	—	—	.67	.61
Print meaning, writing	—	—	—	—	—	.48

all three times), reading and writing are moderately well related, a result also reported by Dobson (see Chapter 4). Moreover, most of the measures are moderately related to the standardized measure, the WRAT, which suggests that letter-name knowledge and reading and writing awareness are acquired together.

One explanation for the tie between reading and writing awareness is that children who try to read also try to write, as the studies described in Chapters 2, 3, 4, and 6 demonstrate. We found that as children began to recognize a few printed words, some began to write letters and words, as well as to draw. Their descriptions of what they produced reflected an ability to elaborate in meaningful ways. For example, in May one child drew a picture and wrote his name. He described his picture by saying, "This is about a man name bad Joshua. He kicked out the glass and went to jail. I saw this story on TV." In September the child began printing words and after a long deliberation, he said, "I write about the honey." He pointed to a picture of a honeycomb in the book from which he had copied the words and said, "I write *I* but I don't know what's this name," as he pointed to the letters *TROT* that he had written. "I got this from the book. I just made up my mind on this one." He had figured out what one word was but did not attempt to read the other words he copied. This example, typical of children who are beginning to acquire letter-sound awareness, indicates that young children can use their partial knowledge about how to read for both reading and writing attempts.

Relating Literacy Awareness to Home Support. Because children's responses about how they learn described their home environments—who helped them learn, their learning activities and materials, and the nature of their interactions with family members—we used these responses, as well as the responses to the parent questionnaire, to analyze connections between the children's literacy awareness and home support. Table 10.3 lists all the different responses children made regarding learning to read and to write.

Children described a wider range of materials and activities and types of adult-child interactions when they talked about learning to read than when they talked about learning to write. The reading activities they described reflected their notion that reading could be watching, writing, drawing, and talking, as well as actual reading. Their writing activities were limited to watching, copying, and practicing writing. They described only one type of writing interaction but mentioned six different types of reading interaction.

One explanation for the paucity of learning-to-write responses may be the constricted view that these teachers and parents had regarding writing. Children practiced copying letters and words in school and took the worksheets home for further practice. Creative and free

TABLE 10.3. Children's Responses about How They Learn to Read and Write

	Helpers	Activities	Materials	Nature of Interaction
Writing	Family members, friends, teacher	Watches, copies, and writes	Alphabets, letters, names, words, numbers	Child told to copy or write
Reading	Family members, friends, teacher	Spells, writes, does homework, says words, reads, draws, talks, watches, traces, does repeated reading	Letters, notebooks, words, homework, stories, books, flash cards, numbers, scribbles	Child and parent solve reading problem, child and parent do repeated reading, parent drills, child listens and repeats words, child tries to sound out words alone, child's reading errors are corrected

writing and writing with drawing had not been encouraged until we began working with the teachers. A typical description of learning to write was, "My big sister teach me." School reading activities, by contrast, had included story reading, as well as filling in of worksheets and copying words from the board. At home, some parents had books, magazines, and other reading materials for their children to use. The children's learning-to-read responses were more elaborate than their learning-to-write responses. For example, one child said, "My mommy buys books and flash cards. And we practice them." Another child said, "My mommy reads to me and then I read the book back to her. If I have a problem with a word she tells me. I can read good."

Table 10.4 compares the responses of these children's parents to the questionnaire with the responses of a sample of one hundred mostly middle-income, black and white families from rural regions and small towns in Illinois (Mason & Dunning, 1986). Responses to nearly every item reveal less support for reading by the inner-city black parents. Rural and small-town parents began reading to their child at an earlier age, were more likely to set up a regular time for reading, read to the child more frequently, and provided more help for reading; however, they provided less help for writing. Despite these differences, most parents in both groups said their children were inter-

TABLE 10.4 Parents' Responses to Questionnaire Regarding Support of Literacy at Home

	Response	
Questionnaire Item	*Low-Income Inner-City Parents*	*Middle-Income Rural and Small-City Parents*
Frequency of reading to child (1 = never, 2 = occasionally, 3 = weekly, 4 = daily)	2.8	3.3
Child's age when reading was begun	2.1	1.6
Regular time for reading (2 = yes, 1 = occasionally, 0 = no)	0.9	1.3
Number of children's books in home	28.6	81.4
Frequency of help to child in reading (1 = never, 2 = occasionally, 3 = weekly, 4 = daily)	2.2	2.8
Frequency of help to child in writing (1 = never, 2 = occasionally, 3 = weekly, 4 = daily)	3.4	2.9
Number of literacy items child likes to look at	5.7	4.8
Number of literacy items child tries to read	5.4	5.5
Number of literacy items child tries to write	3.4	2.9

ested in reading and writing, suggesting that one source of inner-city black children's difficulty in learning to read is an insufficient amount of reading support from home, not a lack of interest. The results also suggest that schools might be able to change the level of support by distributing literacy materials to homes. Writing may have been better supported in this inner-city school because teachers assigned home writing, limited though it was. If the home assignments had covered a broader range of writing activities and had included books and other reading materials, it is conceivable that a larger proportion of inner-city parents would have provided better support for their children's reading and writing.

Vignettes of Three Children

Our results indicate that children in prekindergarten can talk about how they are learning to read and write, that they have an emerging awareness of letter sounds, and that they are aware of text meaning. They can also talk about learning to write, they can draw pictures to write, and they can present meaningful descriptions of their pictures. A more concrete sense of these children's awarenesses and how they changed can be gained by looking more closely at three particular children: Odessa, who was behind her classmates in learning to read and write; Myesha, about average with respect to classmates; and Senai, above average.

Table 10.5 summarizes the reading awareness of these children over time. It includes scores on the beginning-reading portion of the Wide Range Achievement Test (WRAT), in which the children were asked to name and match a set of letters and then to print their name and to identify some common words. A score of 25 indicates letter-naming and printing ability; a higher score indicates recognition of words as well. All three children could name letters, and Senai also knew a few words.

TABLE 10.5   Reading-Awareness Measures for Three Children

	WRAT		Letter Sounds		Text Meaning		Learning to Read	
	May	*Sept.*	*May*	*Sept.*	*May*	*Sept.*	*May*	*Sept.*
Odessa	24	23	0	1	1	1	0	2
Myesha	24	22	0	10	4	4	3	3
Senai	26	27	0	10	2	3	2	3

The letter-sound task had children try to spell three- and four-letter words. Although none of these children could do this in March or May, Odessa's score of 1 in September indicates an emerging awareness because she put down one letter correctly (spelling *pat* as *pfi*). Senai's and Myesha's September scores indicate a substantial change in awareness, with ten letters correctly placed. Myesha correctly identified one or two consonant sounds in every word. Senai spelled *pat* correctly and got several other words partly correct (e.g., spelling *sack* as *sar*).

The text-meaning task required children to read a thirteen-word picture-phrase book. It was one that had been read in school to Odessa and Myesha, but Senai had not heard it (which explains his lower scores). Odessa's scores of one in May and September indicate one-word labeling of the pictures on each page (saying, "Go" for each picture). Myesha read many of the words correctly on both occasions, getting one point, for instance, when she read the text "Go pig" as "Go out." Senai elaborated on the pictures, saying on the "Go pig" page, for example, "A pig is running," a response that secured one of his three points in September.

On the learning-to-read awareness task, Odessa's response in May was at Level 0 because she said she did not know how she was learning to read. However, in September she explained, "My mommy and daddy, we read books." Myesha's responses were more complex, one being, "My mommy teach me, my mommy read me a story and then I teach her, then I read my mommy a story and then she read me a story again." Senai was able to talk about learning to read with more focus on his interaction with his parents, particularly in September when he said, "They talk to me, they buy me some school cards. They read me a story. I do my flash cards and my mommy writes some numbers on it and some words." In May he had not mentioned his mother or father but had said, when referring to a favorite book, "I know how to read *Clifford*, I read stories."

The children's writing awareness was evident from their writing form, the meaningfulness of their descriptions of what they had written, and their descriptions of how they were learning to write. Their scores are shown in Table 10.6. Table 10.7 shows their descriptions of their responses in September to the three writing situations.

Odessa's writing, completely pictorial, contained no letters. When asked to write "something" in an unstructured situation, she usually produced only a smiling face. But when asked in a structured class situation to write about springtime, she made several pictures and gave an extended description. When asked how she was learning to write, however, she either did not respond or said, "My mommy."

TABLE 10.6   Writing-Awareness Measures for Three Children

	Form of Writing		Writing Descriptions in Class		Learning to Write	
	May	*Sept.*	*May*	*Sept.*	*May*	*Sept.*
Odessa	2	2	3	3	1	0
Myesha	3	4	3	4	2	2
Senai	2	2	3	4	2	2

TABLE 10.7   Children's Descriptions of Their Responses to Writing Situations

	Unstructured Test	*Structured Test*	*Structured Class Situation*
Odessa:	"It's a happy face."	"A girl who wants to go home."	"These are kites that are floating on the water. Two boys are flying their kites. The sun is shining. It's a nice day. I also see a large rainbow."
Myesha:	"This is the moon and this is the rainbow."	"This is rain and she got an umbrella, she put her umbrella on her but it was still raining and then she held on her umbrella and went walking."	"The girl was crying because she didn't went to Sesame Place. Then she went to Sesame Place by herself."
Senai:	"Cat and my name." "It's a tree."	"Jan wanted to to go outside so she put on her rain—no she put on her dress first, put on her dress and she wanted to put on her raincoat and she put on her boots and she said it's fun to jump in the rain."	"This is a museum. There are cats and snails. There is a lady at the museum who sells souvenirs. There are space ships all at the museum, also an elevator and an alarm system. The name of the museum is the Senai Brown Museum [this was written on the picture]."

Myesha's writing form was also pictorial but sometimes included letters. Her descriptions were more elaborate in the structured tasks than in the unstructured, as she connected her pictures into storylike forms. Regarding learning to write, she reported on both occasions, "My daddy taught me."

Most of Senai's writing samples were pictures that usually included his name. His descriptions of his art were more meaningful when he was asked to respond to a story or to an activity than when he was asked to write "something," and in these structured situations he connected his pictures into story or report forms. When asked how he was learning to write, his response was similar to Myesha's: "My mommy teaches me."

Odessa's responses to questions about learning to read and write indicate that she was aware she was not learning to read alone, but she was unable to describe what or how she was learning. We suspect that Odessa's low level of awareness was due in part to the low level of her literacy experiences at home (see Table 10.8). Her mother said that she read to Odessa only occasionally, that there was no regular time for reading, and that she never helped the child in reading, although she helped daily in writing. Children's books but no magazines were available at home. Odessa liked to look at a few literacy materials but tried to read only traffic signs, billboards, and a favorite story. She tried to print only her name and alphabet letters.

As is evident from Table 10.8, Myesha, who was able to describe how she was learning to read, received more literacy support at home than did Odessa. Myesha's mother reported that she read weekly to the child, "occasionally" had a regular time for reading, and helped daily with writing but hardly ever with reading. The child looked at

TABLE 10.8 Parents' Responses Regarding Support of Literacy at Home

Questionnaire Item	Odessa	Myesha	Senai
Frequency of reading to child (1 = never, 2 = occasionally, 3 = weekly, 4 = daily)	2	3	4
Child's age when reading was begun	1	1	1
Regular time for reading (2 = yes, 1 = occasionally, 0 = no)	0	1	2
Number of children's books in home	25	15	50
Frequency of help to child in reading (1 = never, 2 = occasionally, 3 = weekly, 4 = daily)	1	1	3
Frequency of help to child in writing (1 = never, 2 = occasionally, 3 = weekly, 4 = daily)	4	4	4
Number of literacy items child likes to look at	4	7	6
Number of literacy items child tries to read	3	7	9
Number of literacy items child tries to write	2	3	7

and tried to read many types of materials, though few children's books and no magazines were available in the home.

Senai gave an extensive description about learning to read, though a less extensive one about learning to write. His parents said that Senai was read to daily, that there was a regular time for reading, and that he was helped weekly to read and daily to write. Many children's books and magazines were available at home. He looked at and tried to read a wide variety of materials, including books, labels, and magazines. He also attempted to write a substantial number of things at home, including letters, words, telephone messages, shopping lists, reminder notes, and labels on pictures.

Parents' responses to the questionnaire could be related to the children's reading-awareness responses. Senai and Myesha were given considerable support for reading and were furthest along in awareness of how to read, of letters and sounds, and of print meaning. Odessa was behind Senai and Myesha in reading awareness and received the least amount of support. However, parents' responses did not concur with children's writing awareness. All three parents said they helped in writing every day; yet the children's writing awareness was less well developed than their reading awareness. Why was not Odessa better able to write if she was helped every day, and why were all three children less able to describe how they were learning to write than to read? We suspect that the writing practice—copying letters and words and circling, underlining, tracing, and matching them—did little to foster children's awareness of writing. Table 10.3, which shows that children gave more elaborate descriptions of learning to read than of learning to write, supports this explanation.

CONCLUSION

Even before preschool children are able to read and write, they can talk about how they are learning. Moreover, the quality of their responses indicates their emerging awareness of literacy. With help from adults at home and at school, some can assign a few letters correctly for spelling, though most cannot write words. They can talk about what they have written or drawn, and they have begun to understand that print has meaning and can be construed as a story or report. Some can even produce stories with titles and story endings.

Parents differ in their support for their children's early literacy experiences and in how they interact with their children, and those differences appear to be related to children's awareness of reading and writing. Although the children in this study had received a very limited view of reading and writing at school—a view that seems to have been affected by parents' support—the added experiences of free writing and book reading that we provided during the spring of the prekindergarten year may have encouraged parents to use a wider range of literacy activities and to help children become more aware of how to read and write.

Until additional classroom and home reading and writing samples are gathered from a larger group of children, we hesitate to recommend instructional changes. There is no doubt, however, that young children, even those who can be labeled at risk of failure to learn to read, are aware of concepts about literacy. Children's perceptions of reading and writing and knowledge about the process of learning appear to be linked to the extent and quality of the support they receive for literacy. Children given more support at home express higher levels of awareness. In addition, classroom reading and writing activities seem to make a difference, with a wider range of activities furthering literacy awareness.

Young children's responses to reading and writing tasks do communicate a developing knowledge of literacy. This means that teachers and researchers could obtain more complete pictures of children's understanding of reading and writing by employing some of the techniques described in this chapter. They could evaluate children's talk about how they are learning, their knowledge of letter sounds, and their reactions to a story. Teachers and researchers could evaluate children's writing attempts as well. They could also obtain measures of the extent of support for literacy at home with a set of questions to parents.

More complete information about children's literacy awareness ought to enable teachers to intercede more effectively on children's behalf. If teachers were given a broader viewpoint about literacy development, they could initiate programs that introduce children to a wide range of literacy activities at school and offer a variety of ideas to parents for home use.

REFERENCES

Chafe, W. (1985). Linguistic differences produced by differences between speaking and writing. In N. Torrance, D. Olson, & A. Hildyard (Eds.), *Literacy, language, and learning* (pp. 105–123). Cambridge: Cambridge University Press.

Clark, M. M. (1976). *Young fluent readers: What can they teach us?* Portsmouth, NH: Heinemann Educational Books.

Denney, T., & Weintraub, S. (1966). First graders' response to three questions about reading. *Elementary School Journal, 66,* 441–448.

Diaz, R. (1986). The union of thought and language in children's private speech. *The Quarterly Newsletter of the Laboratory of Comparative Human Cognition, 8* (3), 90–97.

Durkin, D. (1966). *Children who read early.* New York: Teachers College Press.

Genishi, C., Dyson, I., & Hass, A. (1984). *Language assessment in the early years.* Norwood, NJ: Ablex.

Graves, D. H. (1983). *Writing: Teachers and children at work.* Exeter, NH: Heinemann Educational Books.

Jastak, J., & Jastak, S. (1965). *The Wide Range Achievement Test.* Wilmington, DE: Guidance Associates.

Johns, J. (1972). Children's conception of reading and their reading achievement. *Journal of Reading Behavior, 4,* 56–67.

Liberman, I., & Shankweiler, D. (1985). Phonology and the problems of learning to read and write. *RASE, 6,* 8–17.

Mason, J., & Dunning, D. (1986). *Proposing a model to relate preschool home literacy with beginning reading achievement.* Paper presented at the annual meeting of the American Educational Research Association, San Francisco.

Mason, J., & McCormick, C. (1979). *Testing the development of reading and linguistic awareness* (Tech. Rep. No. 126). Champaign, IL: Center for the Study of Reading.

Mason, J., & Stewart, J. (in preparation). *Early reading test manual: Testing procedures and implications for instruction.* Champaign, IL: Center for the Study of Reading.

McCormick, C., & Mason, J. (1986). *Use of little books at home: A minimal intervention strategy that fosters early reading* (Tech. Rep. No. 388). Champaign, IL: Center for the Study of Reading.

Perena, K. (1984). *Children's writing and reading: Analyzing classroom language.* Oxford: Blackwell.

Pramling, E. (1983). The child's conception of learning. *Goteborg Studies in Educational Sciences, 46.* Goteborg, Sweden: University of Goteborg.

Reid, J. F. (1966). Learning to think about reading. *Educational Research, 9,* 56–62.

Snow, C. (1983). Literacy and language: Relationships during the preschool years. *Harvard Educational Review, 53,* 165–189.

Soderbergh, R. (1977). *Reading in early childhood: A linguistic study of a preschool child's gradual acquisition of reading ability.* Washington, DC: Georgetown University Press.

Stewart, J. (1986). *Kindergarten children's awareness of how they are learning to read: Home and school context.* Unpublished doctoral dissertation, University of Illinois, at Urbana-Champaign.

Teale, W. H. (1981). Parents reading to their children: What we know and need to know. *Language Arts, 58,* 902–912.

Vernon, M. D. (1957). *Backwardness in reading.* London: Cambridge University Press.

Vygotsky, L. S. (1962). *Thought and language.* Cambridge, MA: MIT Press.

Vygotsky, L. S. (1978). *Mind in society.* Cambridge, MA: Harvard University Press.

Wells, G. (1986). *The meaning makers: Children learning language and using language to learn.* Portsmouth, NH: Heinemann Educational Books.

11

SUCCESS OF AT-RISK CHILDREN IN A PROGRAM THAT COMBINES WRITING AND READING

Gay Su Pinnell

This chapter examines processes and results of a long-term intervention study involving interrelated reading and writing instruction. Descriptions of children's reading and writing behaviors were drawn from case studies of children who were participating in Reading Recovery, an early-intervention program for first-grade children at risk of failure in reading. Teachers' daily records of children's reading and writing efforts and children's writing samples showed that with opportunities to read and write daily for several weeks, children begin connecting the processes. Comparisons between children in the Reading Recovery program with a group that participated in another program indicated that those in Reading Recovery made greater gains on both reading and writing measures. The study suggests that educationally at-risk children who are tutored daily with holistic lessons that include reading stories and writing their own messages may be able to catch up with their classmates in reading before the end of first grade.

The research described in this chapter was collaboratively accomplished with colleagues from Ohio State University: Diane E. DeFord, Carol A. Lyons, and Phillip Young.

The efficacy of teaching reading and writing together as interrelated processes seems obvious enough to justify designing a curriculum to integrate the two. We know that young children begin to construct writing at the same time or shortly before they begin to read individual words (Calkins, 1980; Clay, 1975; Ferriero & Teberosky, 1982). As children reconstruct written language for themselves, they make it truly their own. As Barr (1985) has expressed it, reading and writing "are best developed through lively and sustained interaction one with the other." The reading and writing processes are different, and those differences deserve more study, but they are clearly related. Both processes deal with text, and some researchers (e.g., Tierney & Pearson, 1983) have connected the composing processes of writing with the reader's construction of the text while reading. Research on social aspects of reading (Bloome & Green, 1984; Cochran-Smith, 1985; Taylor, 1983) recognizes that both processes are embedded in the social and linguistic contexts that the child experiences first at home and then at school. These contexts influence children's access to literacy resources for use in both reading and writing.

A theoretical framework for emergent literacy describes reading and writing as cyclical and complementary processes (Clay, 1985). As children read and write, they make the connections that form their basic understandings about both. Learning in one area enhances learning in the other. There is ample evidence to suggest that the processes are inseparable and that we should examine pedagogy in the light of these interrelationships. In short, the two activities should be integrated in instructional settings. Teachers need to create supportive situations in which children have opportunities to explore the whole range of literacy learning, and they need to design instruction that helps children make connections between reading and writing.

Assuming that an important part of the process of becoming literate is the discovery and use of reading and writing connections, it becomes especially important for children who are at risk to have maximum opportunities for exploring and relating the two processes. This chapter describes the reading progress of first-grade children initially judged to be at risk of failure in reading. These children were involved in their first-grade year in a unique intervention program, Reading Recovery, which was designed to provide opportunities for exploring literacy. The research described here, undertaken as part of the Ohio Reading Recovery project, builds on the work of Clay (1972, 1985) and draws perspectives from research in early reading and writing behavior (notably Bissex, 1980; Harste, Woodward, & Burke, 1984; Read, 1971, 1986) and on studies of the social contexts of literacy activities (Bloome & Green, 1984). The first step was to derive descriptions of children's reading and writing behavior from case studies of a sample of children in the program. These studies were undertaken to generate hypotheses about the ways children approached tasks and directed their own learning during reading and writing activities. Then, to confirm the outcomes of the program, the progress of the larger group of children in Reading Recovery was quantitatively compared with the progress of children in another intervention program.

THE READING RECOVERY PROGRAM

Several features of the Reading Recovery program make it a viable setting for studying reading and writing connections in the literacy-learning process. Developed in New Zealand by Marie Clay (1985), Reading Recovery provides short-term intensive help that results in accelerated progress for at-risk children. The program does not have a set of materials or a step-by-step, prescribed curriculum. Instead, the program depends for its effectiveness on trained teachers' ability to observe a child's reading and writing behavior, to infer the child's intentions and underlying cognitive processes, and to make instructional decisions, including whether the teacher needs to adjust his or her own behavior in response to the child.

The program targets the poorest readers in the class. They are taken out of their regular classroom for individual planned lessons for thirty minutes each day. The goal of the program is to help children discover effective reading strategies that will result in an independent system for reading. These strategies are developed while the child reads and writes stories. During each lesson, a child reads several short books that have natural and predictable language, and composes and writes a story. Every day the child is introduced to a new, more difficult book, which he or she will be expected to read without help the following day. The intervention continues until the child has developed effective strategies for independent reading and can function satisfactorily in the regular classroom without extra help.

The Reading Recovery framework stipulates that children must be involved in whole-text reading and writing tasks, rather than in isolated teaching or drill on items. Furthermore, teachers' decisions must take into account the needs of individual children. Although teachers use a designated set of procedures, they select books and specific instructional goals and practices for each child. At numerous critical points during each lesson, teachers must consciously make decisions based on analyses that are integral to the program.

To implement Reading Recovery, teachers receive a full year of special training. They are trained through clinical and peer-critiquing experiences guided by a skilled leader. Extensive use is made of a one-way glass. On one side of the glass, a member of the teacher class demonstrates by teaching a lesson to a child. On the other side, the trainees observe and simultaneously discuss the lesson. Afterward, the teacher talks with peers about the demonstration. The goal of this special in-service course is to enable teachers to learn powerful ways of working with children to help them become readers.

The success of Reading Recovery is measured in terms of outcomes for children. Children are expected to make accelerated progress to a point where they can be released, or "discontinued," without need for further extra help. Clay's initial study and replications in New Zealand showed that the procedures of Reading Recovery were effective in reducing reading failure. Her follow-up study showed that children who were discontinued from the program continued to progress at average rates without special help.

The New Zealand studies had provided some evidence to support the program's effectiveness, but Ohio represented a different educational context. The research project in Ohio was undertaken for the following reasons:

1. Clay's studies did not involve children who were receiving classroom instruction in a reading program that focused on direct teaching of a sequence of skills and that placed great emphasis on phonics. New Zealand classrooms tended to feature language experience and a variety of natural-language texts and literature as instructional material. These natural-language texts were simple and close to the children's own oral language; they did not have controlled vocabularies. Classrooms in our study featured reading groups and instruction based on a commercial reading system with heavy concentration on skills and phonics. Texts were constructed with controlled vocabularies.

2. Clay's studies did not involve teachers who were specifically trained to use a skills approach to reading. New Zealand teachers who became Reading Recovery teachers had been teaching in schools where language experience was generally used. Teachers in our study were skills-oriented and had been directed to use the basal system for reading instruction.

3. Previous studies of the impact of Reading Recovery had not utilized a randomly selected comparison group.

4. The program's instructional setting provided a laboratory for the systematic study of children's behavior in reading and writing.

DESCRIPTIVE STUDY OF READING AND WRITING CONNECTIONS

The two kinds of data produced by the research project—descriptive and quantitative—provided different and equally important kinds of information about the instruction of young children who were having difficulty in reading. The descriptive information was drawn from the following sources: children's daily writing, videotapes of one teacher and two children at eight points in time, and teachers' records, including observational notes taken daily according to instructions. In analyzing these data, we asked three questions:

1. Is there evidence that children connect reading with writing processes during individual lessons that include both activities?
2. Are teachers who receive special training in observing children's reading and writing behavior able to capture in their daily notes those behaviors that indicate children are making connections between the two processes?
3. What kinds of links between reading and writing do children make?

Our observations provided insight into how children responded to the instruction. We tried to identify specific behaviors that occur when children have the opportunity to find their own links between reading and writing. The behaviors described here seemed to coincide with the accelerated progress that is the goal of the program.

Children

All children in the Reading Recovery program were first-grade students in urban schools that had high failure rates and high proportions of children on free or reduced-price lunch. The children were distributed over fourteen schools and were taught by specially trained teachers. Of the entire group of Reading Recovery children, 73 percent were successfully released by the end of the year. Because we wanted to study some children in more detail, we selected four teachers who were considered good record keepers and generally insightful observers. From the group of students taught by those four teachers, we identified the children who made accelerated progress and then randomly selected twenty-three for in-depth analysis of their records.

Materials

We examined three kinds of recorded information, each of which offered checks and confirmation of the others. The primary source of information was teachers' lesson plans for work with individual children. Except for selecting the new text to be read that day, Reading Recovery teachers do *no* preplanning for the daily lesson. Instead, teachers are expected to "follow the child's lead," to respond in accordance with their analysis of the child's behavior, and to look for the "teachable moment." The "lesson plan," then, is not a traditional plan but an open-ended observational record.

The teacher notes on the lesson-plan form significant observations that over time build a detailed record of behavior. In their weekly seminars, which continue throughout the year, teachers are trained in observational skills and the types of behaviors to attend to and to note in the plans. Evidence that the child is making connections between reading and writing is one of the areas to be noted. Teachers consciously look for this evidence as a sign of progress toward independent reading.

We also examined children's daily writing samples. Each day, as part of the lesson, the child is invited to compose and write a message in the writing book. The teacher supports the child when necessary, but the written products must be the child's own composition. The child writes and then reads at least one sentence each day. Although time does not permit the writing of lengthy stories, some children continue the same theme over several days. After the writing is completed, the teacher rewrites the sentence on a strip of paper and then cuts the words apart. The child then reassembles the sentence and checks the reconstruction for accuracy by reading or checking with the original text. The entire sentence is always reread. The teacher records the child's responses in the daily lesson plan.

The third source of data was a series of videotapes made of one teacher working with two children. The tapes were made over a period of six weeks and provided a means of checking the validity of teachers' plans.

Lessons

Reading Recovery lessons are individual half-hour sessions and include several components. First, the child reads several books that he or she has read before. This process allows the child to work on reading in a context that is easy and full of meaning. The stories are natural-language texts. Each day, the teacher keeps a running record of the child's reading of a new book that had been introduced to the child the day before. This record is a kind of shorthand reproduction of the exact reading behavior on that text. While an accuracy record is calculated, that is not the most important information from the running record; this useful tool provides a way of analyzing behavior to determine whether the child is developing effective reading strategies. As already noted, the lesson also includes writing a message. The child, helped by the teacher when necessary, constructs the words in the sentence. The teacher encourages the child to hear sounds in words and to represent them with letters. The sentence is then read many times, copied on a strip of paper, cut apart into words, and reconstructed by the child. These "cut-apart" words are not used out of context but are always read as part of the whole message. Finally, the teacher introduces a new book by first talking about it and then asking the child to read it. The child will read this new book independently the next day while the teacher takes a running record.

Procedures

We used the selected teachers' lesson plans to draw up a list of specific instances of behavior that in our judgment constituted evidence that children were making connections between reading and writing. These instances were listed and categorized for each child in the sample. We also examined these children's writing books and related them to the texts they had read on the same day or previous days. We then looked at the videotapes to see if the kinds of behaviors suggested by the written documents occurred in the actual lessons. The tapes generally confirmed the accuracy of the teachers' record keeping.

Results

Our analysis of the information seemed to confirm that children search for ways to connect what they have learned in reading and writing. The children we studied appeared to use information gained in one area to help them solve problems in the other area. These preliminary observations revealed at least four types of behavior apparently characteristic of the children in our sample, all of whom were successful in making the transition to literacy.

Behavior 1: *Children drew on previously read texts for specific words and phrases to use in writing.* For example, Debbie remembered the phrase *boo hoo* from a story, searched for it, and copied it to produce the message shown in Figure 11.1. Teachers' responses actively

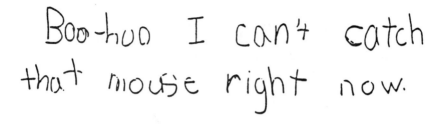

Boo-huo I can't catch that mouse right now.

FIGURE 11.1   Debbie's Message

supported this kind of searching behavior. In another instance, Eli was trying to write the word *cat*. Noticing that the boy glanced toward a simple book he had read earlier, *Cat on the Mat* (Wildsmith, 1982), his teacher said casually, "Do you notice anything that will help you?" Eli reached for the book and used it to help him write the word. When asked about this teaching technique, the teacher said she would not have told the child to look for the book and seldom encouraged copying because she liked the children to construct words from their own analyses of the sounds. However, her intervention in this instance let Eli know the importance and power of taking the initiative to solve his own problems.

Behavior 2: *Through writing, children developed an awareness of visual information, which they could then use as an aid in solving problems in reading.* This strategy was evident both in children's spontaneous actions and in teacher-guided actions. Lawndale was reading a new story that had the word *how*. After looking at the word for a moment, he reached for a scrap of paper and wrote the word *cow*, which was in his fluent vocabulary. Then he went back to his story, said the word *how*, and proceeded to read the rest of the text. On another occasion, Lawndale was reading this text: " 'Go home,' said the cows." He read, " 'Go home,' said the horse." Then he stopped, looking puzzled. Pointing to the word *cows*, the teacher said, "Could that be *horse?*" "No," said the child, looking at the word and glancing swiftly at the picture, "It's cows."

Behavior 3: *Children used reading to check their construction of their cut-up sentences, often correcting their own work independently.* Teachers encouraged them to "check" their work by reading it, and as the children did so, they usually corrected words placed in the wrong order or wrong orientation. The child's own language provided a highly supportive and meaningful context that made it easy for the child to pay close attention to print. For example, Lawndale put together a cut-up sentence containing the word *I'll*, a difficult word in the context of this task. Lawndale placed that word upside down, but when he read the sentence, he turned it right side up without prompting from the teacher. Checking and self-correcting were frequently observed by teachers, with examples occurring in the records of every child examined. It appears that this task, which elicited the use of reading as a check on writing, supported links between the two processes.

Behavior 4: *Children used previously read texts as a resource for composing their written messages.* For example, Kerry initially composed sentences that were obviously drawn from the books she was reading in the classroom. Those preprimers focused on several characters, among them Sara, Ana, and Ken. The sentence shown in Figure 11.2 is typical of those Kerry wrote for several weeks. Then, in Reading Recovery, Kerry read a story called *The Pumpkin* and another called *If You Meet a Dragon.* Drawing on these natural-language texts, she wrote the sentences shown in Figures 11.3 and 11.4. These examples show that Kerry's concept of text was strongly influenced by her experiences in classroom reading. It took many experiences with a variety of texts to expand her awareness. Finally, she was ready to risk a departure from known patterns, as evidenced by the text reproduced in Figure 11.5. One of her final stories, which she wrote just before leaving the program, began as shown in Figure 11.6.

Henry began the program with the sample of writing shown in Figure 11.7. Several weeks later, he produced a series of sentences that formed a continuing text, which he wrote over several days (see Figure 11.8). Each day, he read the previous day's writing before composing the new sentence. The resulting text reflects the repeating patterns Henry encountered in the simple stories he was reading in individual lessons. Just before writing the last entry, he read a story called *To Town,* in which each page repeats the phrase *all the way to town.*

FIGURE 11.2   Kerry's Sentence Based on a Classroom Preprimer

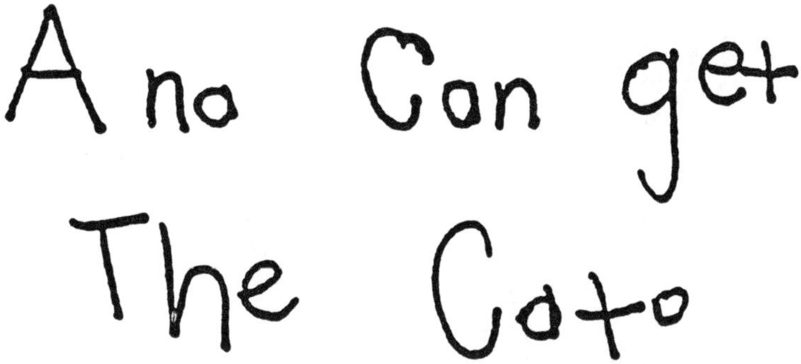

Ana can go get The pumpkin.

FIGURE 11.3   Kerry's Sentence Based on *The Pumpkin*

FIGURE 11.4   Kerry's Sentence Based on *If You Meet a Dragon*

Sara Cango get The dragon.

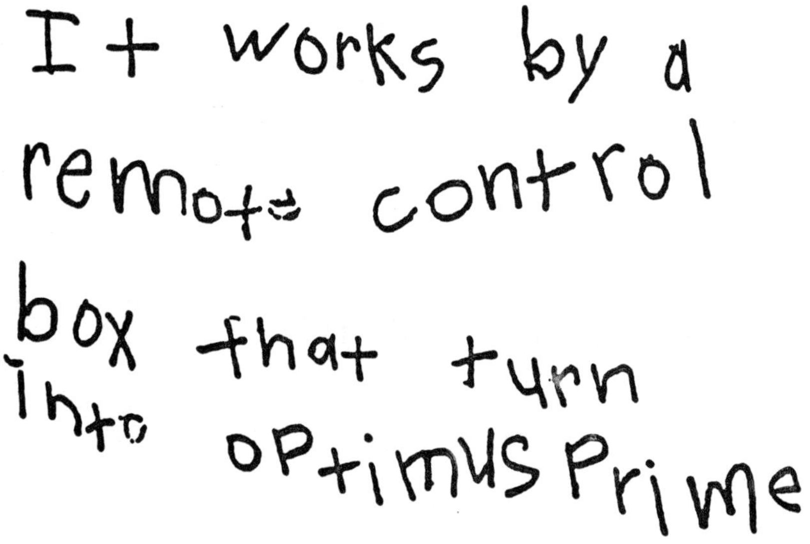

I+ works by a
remote control
box that turn
Into oPtimus Prime

FIGURE 11.5 Kerry's Departure from Known Patterns

One day there lived
a little pig

FIGURE 11.6 The Beginning of One of the Last Stories Kerry Wrote Before Leaving Reading Recovery

Henry demonstrated his use of available literacy resources as he composed his own text. The supportive context allowed him to do so.

Discussion

Our descriptive analysis provides evidence that when given opportunities to engage in related reading and writing and when supported by a sensitive and aware teacher, children do connect the two processes. Those connections vary in nature and are highly idiosyncratic, depending on the child's own experience and interests. The analysis justifies further investigation of children's behavior in situations in which they are expected to link reading and writing within "whole-task" literacy activities. Information on children's behavior must be more detailed

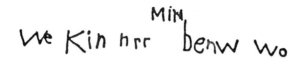

FIGURE 11.7   Henry's First Writing Attempts in Reading Recovery

than the teachers' records, made during instruction, provide. More
controlled data collection and analysis could increase our knowledge
about the ways children make connections between reading and writing. For example, detailed analysis of children's reading and writing
connections during Reading Recovery lessons would be a fruitful area
for investigation. The following investigations might be undertaken:

1. Behaviors indicating reading and writing connections could
   be measured and mapped through microanalysis of videotapes
   of a sample of children.
2. Since children's rate of progress in reading is very carefully
   monitored in Reading Recovery, children's behavior might be
   analyzed in detail during periods of acceleration. A common
   observation of teachers is that when children begin to notice
   connections between texts in reading and writing, they become
   more fluent and make faster progress. This hypothesis could
   be tested through relating children's behaviors to their rate
   of progress.
3. Before entering the program, Reading Recovery children are
   the lowest readers in their classrooms. Observations like those
   suggested here might be made of kindergarten and first-grade
   children who are high achievers making rapid progress.

I Love to play in the Snow everyday

I Love to jump in the Snow every day.

I picked up a snowball and I made a big one. It got taller. I pushed it and taller

The snow is a lot and the snow is made of water,

The snow is a lot and the snow always falls down all the way to town.

FIGURE 11.8. The Progression of Henry's Writing

STUDY OF ACHIEVEMENT

The descriptions of behaviors and teacher-child interactions presented in the preceding section are powerful because they provide evidence of reading achievement brought about by connecting reading and writing; they are not simply interesting "slices of school life." The twenty-three children examined in the descriptive study were part of a larger group who were initially judged to be poor risks and who instead made good progress. The quantitative study reported in this section documents the achievement of that larger group.

We compared two groups of children who received instruction in Reading Recovery with a third group who participated in an alternative compensatory program. In contrast to Reading Recovery's deliberate linking of reading and writing, the focus of the alternative program was on skills and isolated information. Of the two Reading Recovery groups, one was from "regular" classrooms—that is, classrooms taught by teachers not trained in Reading Recovery; the other group was from "program" classrooms—that is, classrooms taught by teachers who *were* trained in Reading Recovery. As already noted, however, all Reading Recovery instruction took place outside the classroom. The children in the comparison group, who participated in the alternative program, were from regular classrooms.

To provide a perspective for viewing the achievement of the three groups, we selected a random sample of children from regular classrooms in the same schools and calculated an "average range" for the first-grade population in project schools. This "average" assisted us in determining each group's relationship to the expected range of achievement for Reading Recovery children.

Children

A total of 184 children took part in the study. All were first graders in the fourteen urban schools described earlier. They were identified for Reading Recovery and the other compensatory program by using a combination of teachers' judgments and individual assessments. Children in all three groups were in the lowest 20 percent of their respective classrooms in terms of achievement and were therefore at risk of failure in reading. There were 96 children in the Reading Recovery group from program classrooms, and one classroom of this type in each school. The Reading Recovery group from regular classrooms totaled 37. The comparison group had 51 children in it. High-risk children from regular classrooms were randomly assigned either to Reading Recovery or to the alternative program. The alternative program, ongoing throughout the school year, involved a series of skill-oriented and drill activities, which were conducted both in small groups and individual sessions by a trained paraprofessional. This program was relatively new to the school district (implemented within the preceding four years) and, like Reading Recovery, was restricted to first-grade children and viewed positively by teachers in the system. Children in all three groups continued to participate in their classroom reading activities.

Dependent Measures

Each child was tested on the following nine measures. The first six measures, included in Clay's (1985) diagnostic survey, were administered in the fall and the spring; the last three were administered at the end of the school year.

1. *Letter identification:* Children were asked to identify fifty-four different characters, including upper- and lower-case letters and conventional print for *a* and *g*.
2. *Basal word test:* Children were asked to read a list of words compiled from the most frequent words in the preprimers of the basal reading system used by the district. Three lists were constructed; the first was used in September, the second for program entry or release during the year, and the third in May.
3. *Concepts about print:* Children were asked to perform a variety of tasks during a book reading. The tasks were designed to check on significant concepts about printed language—for example, the concepts of word and letter, the use of space, and awareness of left-to-right directionality. Two versions of the test were used.
4. *Writing vocabulary:* Children were asked to write all the words they knew how to write in ten minutes, starting with their own names and including basic vocabulary and other words.
5. *Dictation:* Children were read a sentence and asked to write the words. In scoring, children were given credit for every *sound* represented correctly. This measure thus indicated the child's ability to analyze a word for sounds. Different versions of the test were used.
6. *Text reading level:* Children were asked individually to read stories while the tester used a special technique to record reading behavior and also calculated an accuracy level. Children continued reading more difficult texts until they reached a level below 90 percent accuracy. The child's score was based on the highest level he or she read with over 90 percent accu-

racy. Text reading level was based on the difficulty of certain tasks and basal readers. The first five levels used easy books and listening tasks. For the second level, for example, the teacher read *Where's Spot!* (Hill, 1980) to the child and on one page asked the child to point to the pattern of words that had been read on several previous pages. A child unable to respond to print in this very simple way was designated as "level 1," and a child able to point to the words and read them was designated as having passed "level 2." There were twenty-six levels in all, the highest level indicating approximately a sixth-grade reading level.

7. *Writing assessment:* At the end of the year, all three groups of children were asked to write a story in response to the same prompt. They received no help on the assignment and were given twenty minutes to complete it. Stories were collected and scored by "blind" scorers at Ohio State University who had no knowledge of the children or the project. A holistic scoring procedure was used; writing samples were scored from 1 (low) to 6 (high).

8. *Reading vocabulary:* Subtest 1 of the *Comprehensive Test of Basic Skills (CTBS)* (1982), Forms U and V, was administered at the end of the school year by the school district as part of an ongoing evaluation of compensatory programs.

9. *Reading comprehension:* Subtest 2 of the *CTBS* was also administered at the end of the school year by the district's evaluation department.

Procedures

The first six measures were individually administered in the fall by Reading Recovery teachers in their own schools. For the spring testing, Reading Recovery teachers went to schools other than their own, where they were given guidelines and a list of children to test on those measures and the writing assessment. The children on each tester's list were not identified by group, whether Reading Recovery, comparison, or a random sample of first graders not in one of the three groups. Testers were asked not to discuss the children's status with other teachers in the building. For the writing assignment, children were tested in groups of ten to fifteen. On standardized measures, children were assessed along with their regular groups by representatives of the school district's evaluation department.

The Reading Recovery teacher selected the lowest-achieving children from each of the first-grade classrooms in the school. Reading

Recovery children in the regular and program classrooms were considered separately because it was thought that having a classroom teacher who was knowledgeable about Reading Recovery created a situation different from that in the rest of the classrooms in the school. Of course, Reading Recovery teaching procedures were not used in the classroom setting.

Teachers and researchers on the project evaluated the two groups of Reading Recovery children (96 from program classrooms and 37 from regular classrooms) who had received 60 daily lessons or who had been discontinued (successfully released from the program). Of that group, 97 (73 percent) were discontinued by the end of the school year, having received an average of 67.5 lessons. The entire group of Reading Recovery children received an average of 76.3 lessons, the equivalent of 15.5 weeks of instruction.

When Reading Recovery teachers "discontinued" a child, they had assessed that child and judged that he or she was achieving at an average level for the population and had the range of strategies essential for continuing to make progress without extra help. Decisions concerning whether children could be discontinued were made after Reading Recovery teachers examined a variety of data for each child: (1) level of text read at 90 percent accuracy or better, (2) scores on diagnostic survey, (3) reading behavior and analysis as shown in the running record, (4) teachers' comments on lesson plans. There was no precise text level at which a child had to read in order to be discontinued. Children who could read primer texts and book 1 at the first-grade level and above were evaluated on the basis of the other three factors. Comments from classroom teachers were also considered in the evaluation.

Results

Table 11.1 shows the data used for analysis in addressing research questions; means and standard deviations on scores earned in the spring are shown for all three groups. The figures in Table 11.1 for the Reading Recovery regular group and the comparison group are based on a random sample of the children in those groups. Table 11.2 shows means and standard deviations for the full population of comparison children in the spring. Because subjects, dependent measures, design, and analysis varied for research questions, those factors are described separately, along with results, for each question.

Question 1: *Do Reading Recovery children from regular classrooms and from program classrooms perform differently?* To address Question 1, the overall performance of Reading Recovery children

TABLE 11.1   Means and Standard Deviations on Scores Earned in the Spring

Measure	Reading Recovery Program Classes[a]			Reading Recovery Regular Classes[b]			Comparison Group[b]		
	No.	Mean	SD	No.	Mean	SD	No.	Mean	SD
Letter identification	96	51.79	3.83	37	52.27	1.41	37	51.19	3.17
Word test	96	13.59	1.85	37	13.68	1.63	37	12.51	2.87
Concepts about print	96	16.62	2.77	37	15.81	2.91	37	14.30	3.08
Writing vocabulary	96	35.38	12.56	37	32.86	13.49	37	26.05	14.32
Dictation	96	31.43	5.80	37	30.62	6.13	37	24.38	6.92
Text reading	96	9.95	2.92	37	9.97	3.69	37	7.19	2.91
Writing sample	94	2.96	1.25	37	2.89	.94	37	2.39	1.12
CTBS-NCE[c] score, reading vocabulary	96	38.16	15.31	36	36.64	11.93	35	26.11	16.86
CTBS-NCE score, reading comprehension	96	38.84	15.31	36	36.67	19.27	34	28.88	14.53

[a] Considered a population mean based the entire population scores.
[b] Random sample of children.
[c] Normal Curve Equivalent Score.

from program classrooms was compared with the overall performance of Reading Recovery children from regular classrooms. For the analysis, a Hotelling's T^2 for a single sample was used. Reading Recovery children from program classrooms served as a population, and the performances of these children on the dependent variables were used as population parameters and compared with sample estimates of performance of Reading Recovery children in regular classrooms. Results from the

TABLE 11.2   Means and Standard Deviations on Scores Earned in Spring for Full Group of Comparison Children

Measure	No.	Mean	SD
Letter identification	51	49.61	8.33
Word test	51	11.98	3.92
Concepts about print	51	13.98	3.31
Writing vocabulary	51	25.37	14.33
Dictation	51	23.80	7.99
Text reading	51	6.96	3.07
Writing sample	46	2.33	1.10
CTBS-NCE score, reading vocabulary	45	28.07	17.00
CTBS-NCE score, reading comprehension	46	27.33	13.94

analysis revealed that the performance was approximately the same for both groups of children (see Table 11.3).

This result indicates that the Reading Recovery program is not more effective for children in classrooms with a teacher trained in Reading Recovery and that the program is successful in helping children develop independent reading systems regardless of whether the classroom teacher has had special training.

Question 2: *Is the performance of Reading Recovery children in regular classrooms superior to the performance of comparison children?* Children in the academically lowest 20 percent of students in each regular first-grade classroom were assigned randomly either to the Reading Recovery program or to the alternative compensatory program. At the conclusion of the school year, all students were assessed on the dependent measures. Responses to these measures were analyzed by a Hotelling T^2. Results of this analysis suggested that substantial differences did exist between the two groups. Univariate t-tests to provide partial insight with respect to differences between the two groups on each dependent variable revealed that Reading Recovery children from regular classrooms performed better than the comparison children from regular classrooms on seven of the nine dependent measures (see Table 11.4). Reading Recovery children excelled on the basal word test, concepts about print, writing vocabulary, dictation, text reading, writing sample, and *CTBS* reading vocabulary. Both Reading Recovery children and comparison children exhibited similar performance on letter identification and *CTBS* reading comprehension scores.

Question 3: *Is the performance of Reading Recovery children in program classrooms superior to the performance of comparison children?* To address this question, Hotelling's multivariate single sample test was employed. Sample values obtained for the comparison children on the performance measures were compared to parameter values assessed for the population of Reading Recovery children attending program classrooms. Results from this analysis indicated that the performance of comparison children was inferior to the overall performance of the Reading Recovery children attending program classrooms. The single sample t-test revealed that comparison children performed at lower levels than Reading Recovery children on the word test, con-

TABLE 11.3 Scores of Reading Recovery Children in Program Classrooms Compared with Scores of Reading Recovery Children in Regular Classrooms

Hotelling's $T^2 = 19.55$

$F_{9,27} = 1.68, p = .142$[a]

[a] Not significant; differences on single variables not reported.

TABLE 11.4 Analysis of Scores of Reading Recovery Children in Regular Classrooms and of Comparison Children in Regular Classrooms

Hotelling's $T^2 = 23.63$
  $F_{9,61} = 2.32$, $p = .025$
Differences on single variables:

Measure	df[a]	t[b]
Letter identification	72	1.90
Word test	72	2.14[c]
Concepts about print	72	2.17[c]
Writing vocabulary	72	2.11[c]
Dictation	72	4.11[c]
Text reading	72	3.60[c]
Writing sample	68	2.03[c]
CTBS-NCE score, reading vocabulary	69	3.04[c]
CTBS-NCE score, reading comprehension	68	1.90

[a] Degrees of freedom.
[b] Positive value of t-statistic implies that Reading Recovery mean exceeds comparison mean.
[c] $p \leq .05$.

cepts about print, writing vocabulary, dictation, text reading, writing sample, *CTBS* reading vocabulary, and *CTBS* reading comprehension (see Table 11.5).

Discussion

Results of this research indicate that the Reading Recovery program had positive outcomes for children regardless of whether their classroom teacher had received training in Reading Recovery. After an average of 67.5 lessons, over 70 percent of the children were released from the program, having been judged no longer in need of remedial services. All Reading Recovery children—even those who remained in the program at the end of the year or who moved before they could make enough progress to be discontinued—made progress during the year. Reading Recovery children scored significantly higher than an equivalent group of children in the alternative compensatory program on concepts about print, dictation, word test, writing vocabulary, and text reading. On one measure (letter identification), there was no significant difference; however, a ceiling effect was observed, with all children scoring near perfect performance. Reading Recovery children achieved mean scores within an average band, defined as +.5 standard deviation

TABLE 11.5 Analysis of Scores of Reading Recovery Children in Program Classrooms and of Comparison Children in Regular Classrooms

Hotelling's $T^2 = 82.37$
  $F_{9,38} = 7.58, p = .0000$
Differences on single variables:

Measure	Population Mean	No.	Sample Mean	SD	df	t[a]
Letter identification	51.79	51	49.61	8.33	50	−1.87
Word test	13.59	51	11.98	3.92	50	−2.94[c]
Concepts about print	16.63	51	13.98	3.31	50	−5.70[c]
Writing vocabulary	35.38	51	25.37	14.33	50	−4.98[c]
Dictation	31.43	51	23.80	7.99	50	−6.81[c]
Text reading	9.95	51	6.96	3.07	50	−6.96[c]
Writing sample	2.96	46[b]	2.33	1.10	45	−3.90[c]
CTBS-NCE score, reading vocabulary	38.16	45[b]	28.07	17.00	44	−3.98[c]
CTBS-NCE score, reading comprehension	38.84	46[b]	27.33	13.94	45	−5.60[c]

[a] Negative t-value indicates that population mean (Reading Recovery children in program classrooms) is greater than sample mean (comparison children).

[b] Number changed because group measures were administered on a day when some children were absent.

[c] $p \le .05$.

of the mean of a random sample of first graders, on all measures. Discontinued Reading Recovery children scored average and above on all measures. Of the 133 children who had at least 60 lessons or were discontinued earlier, 73 percent were discontinued from the program.

These results indicate that the Reading Recovery program, which focuses on helping children develop strategies through related reading and writing activities, is an effective program for children at risk of failure in first-grade reading. The program, as implemented with a special teacher, can be used with success regardless of whether the classroom teacher has had special training in Reading Recovery. Whether teachers will continue to work with the same success after the training year has been completed is to be determined by data collection during the second year of work. A follow-up study of the children will determine whether the effects of the program are lasting.

CONCLUSION

These investigations quantified the results of a program that connects reading and writing. They also served to uncover some basic processes that might be involved in the program. Children who were engaged each school day in holistic lessons that included reading stories and writing and then reading messages achieved accelerated progress, as measured by a variety of tests. Although we cannot conclude from this research that making reading and writing connections was a necessary factor in that progress, our observations provided evidence that children who succeeded exhibited behaviors that indicated they were searching for those connections.

Reading Recovery children were deliberately engaged in activities that would lead to reading and writing connections. Teachers sometimes guided children to make links; often, however, children spontaneously made their own links, while teachers actively supported them. Reading Recovery involves direct intervention to help children make connections and use information. Children are placed in situations in which they are most likely to notice connections between reading and writing. Such intense intervention is unnecessary for most children because they create their own connections by utilizing all literacy resources available at school and at home. It is possible, however, that all children might benefit from increased opportunities to participate in a fuller range of literacy activities in school settings.

The descriptive study served as a beginning step in sorting out the complexities of the processes involved in children's learning to read. It appears that when given the opportunity and encouragement, even very poor readers can make their own connections between reading and writing. This study confirms the belief that children use all literacy resources available to them as they attempt to construct meaning from and through written texts.

The study implies that teachers should consciously create settings that demand the use of both reading and writing and that foster children's ability in making connections between the two processes; such settings may be of greatest importance for those children who have difficulty making connections between what they already know and the new material or processes to be learned. Helping children connect reading and writing is a promising area for research and for application. On the basis of our work with the Reading Recovery program, we recommend that teachers and researchers collaborate in creating settings for the collection of data and that such settings include the full range of complex social factors involved when children encounter text. In such settings, the goals of research and practice can be jointly served.

REFERENCES

Barr, J. E. (1985). Writing and reading: A marriage between equals. In M. M. Clark (Ed.), *New directions in the study of reading* (pp. 103–111). London: Falmer Press.

Bissex, G. L. (1980). *GNYS AT WRK: A child learns to write and read.* Cambridge, MA: Harvard University Press.

Bloome, D., & Green, J. (1984). Directions in the sociolinguistic study of reading. In P. D. Pearson (Ed.), *Handbook of reading research* (pp. 395–421). New York: Longman.

Calkins, L. (1980). Children learn the writer's craft. *Language Arts, 57,* 2.

Clay, M. M. (1972). *Reading: The patterning of complex behavior.* Auckland, NZ: Heinemann Educational Books.

Clay, M. M. (1975). *What did I write?* London: Heinemann Educational Books.

Clay, M. M. (1985). *The early detection of reading difficulties.* (3rd ed.). Auckland, NZ: Heinemann Educational Books.

Cochran-Smith, M. (1985). *The making of a reader.* Norwood, NJ: Ablex.

Comprehensive test of basic skills (CTBS). (1982). Forms U and V: Grades K-3. Monterey, CA: CTB/McGraw-Hill.

Ferreiro, E., & Teberosky, A. (1982). *Literacy before schooling.* Exeter, NH: Heinemann Educational Books.

Harste, J. C., Woodward, V. A., & Burke, C. L. (1984). *Language stories and literacy lessons.* Portsmouth, NH: Heinemann Educational Books.

Hill, E. (1980). *Where's Spot?* New York: Putnam.

Read, C. (1971). Preschool children's knowledge of English phonology. *Harvard Educational Review, 41,* 1–34.

Read, C. (1986). *Children's creative spelling.* London: Routledge & Kegan Paul.

Taylor, D. (1983). *Family literacy: Young children learning to read and write.* Exeter, NH: Heinemann Educational Books.

Tierney, R. J., & Pearson, P. D. (1983). Toward a composing model of reading. *Language Arts, 60,* 568–580.

Wildsmith, B. (1982). *Cat on the mat.* Oxford: Oxford University Press.

12

ACQUISITION OF EXPOSITORY WRITING SKILLS

Taffy E. Raphael, Carol Sue Englert, and Becky W. Kirschner

While a great deal of research and many review papers have focused on the writing process, the acquisition of written literacy, and instruction in writing, less attention has been paid to the writing of expository texts. This chapter examines the acquisition of expository writing skills in upper elementary school. First, research is related to expository writing—in particular, research on the role of text-structure instruction in expository writing, the role of the social context in which such instruction occurs, and the importance of collaborative efforts between teachers and researchers. Second, a program for teaching expository writing is discussed. Third, writing samples of students who participated in this program are presented to show the impact of the instruction on students' knowledge about writing, their ability to write and convey information, and their attitudes toward writing.

As children progress through their early years in school, they develop a wealth of knowledge about language, print, and relations among language processes. However, when children reach the upper grades of elementary school, where there is greater emphasis on learning content, their ability to progress in writing often declines (National

The work described in this chapter was initially conducted by the staff of the Expository Reading/Writing Project, funded by the International Reading Association and the Institute for Research on Teaching. Our current work continuing the line of studies is conducted by those working on the Cognitive Strategies Instruction in Writing Project, funded primarily by the Office of Special Education and Rehabilitative Services and supported by the Institute for Research on Teaching.

Assessment of Educational Progress, 1986). One reason for this decline may be that children are not being taught how to read and learn from informational or content area texts—that is, from expository writing. There are several reasons for this gap in instruction. First, expository writing has generally been the concern of rhetoricians and high school English courses; most elementary schools provide basic instruction in reading, while English courses in middle and secondary schools focus on students' acquisition of skills in expository writing. Second, what writing instruction there is in elementary schools has focused on creative writing. This was as true in the past, when such activities as story starters and daily writing on different topics were in vogue, as it is today, when more sophisticated writing-process activities are recommended to teachers. These latter programs do not ignore or dismiss expository writing, but neither do they provide specific support or instruction for it. Third, little information on how expository writing should be taught has been available. Fourth, good models of expository writing are typically not available to students in these grades. Social studies and science texts are often poorly organized and "inconsiderate" to their audience (Armbruster, 1984b), and they do not provide students with examples of effective expository writing. Elementary school teachers must therefore be unusually confident about their knowledge of expository writing to teach it to their students.

Our research team at the Institute for Research on Teaching at Michigan State University has been studying effective ways to teach upper elementary students expository writing and reading skills. We began with the recently developed idea that students should be instructed about different expository text structures (Armbruster, 1984a; Meyer, 1975). Three areas of research have influenced our approach: (1) the role of text-structure instruction in expository comprehension and composition, (2) the role of the social context in which such instruction occurs, and (3) the importance of teacher-researcher collaboration in successful intervention programs. On the basis of this research, we developed a program for teaching expository writing, linking it to reading. Students' writing samples and their responses to an interview have shown that the program affects students' knowledge about writing, their ability to present information in an organized manner, and their attitude toward writing.

RESEARCH RELATED TO IMPROVING EXPOSITORY WRITING AND READING

Our interest in improving students' ability to compose in an expository form grew out of our interest in improving their ability to comprehend such texts. In some early research on question-answer relationships

(QAR), Raphael and Pearson (1985) and Raphael and Wonnacott (1985) studied elementary and middle school students' ability to use information from their background knowledge and from the expository texts they were reading to answer different types of comprehension questions. One of the most difficult types of question was text-implicit, requiring students to "think and search." They had to integrate information from across a text, as well as read and learn from differently structured portions of the text. For example, one part of a text might compare and/or contrast the adventures of two explorers; another might define a problem explorers had and then describe their solution to the problem.

Integrating across text structures is quite difficult. Spivey (1984), who examined university students as they read more than one text and wrote summaries that required integrating information across texts, suggests that it is a problem even for mature, able readers. Less able college students had difficulty in selecting important information and integrating it.

One reason readers of all ages have difficulty in synthesizing or integrating information from expository texts may be that they lack awareness about the differences among text structures (Englert & Hiebert, 1984; McGee & Richgels, 1986; Taylor & Beach, 1984). Without this knowledge, they may not have successful "search strategies" to determine and to locate important information. It was this possibility that led us to consider text-structure instruction as one means of enhancing students' comprehension of expository text, and it eventually led us to consider student composition of expository text.

Research on Text Structures

Different text structures exist (Meyer, 1975), although no single text contains only one structure (Schallert & Tierney, 1982), and they answer different types of questions (Armbruster, 1984a). Consider, for example, a comparison/contrast text structure and a problem/solution text structure. Texts using comparison/contrast structures answer essentially four questions: (1) What is being compared? (2) On what are they being compared? (3) How are they alike? (4) How are they different? The questions are addressed regardless of text format or the order in which information is presented. Problem/solution texts consider a different set of questions: (1) What is the problem? (2) What caused the problem? (3) How was the problem solved? (4) What were the steps of the solution? Again, the actual format, order, or emphasis placed on each question may vary. Yet, problem/solution texts always address some combination of these fundamental questions.

Teaching students about text structure has been found to improve both their comprehension and composition of stories, and it seems a promising way of enhancing their expository reading and writing abilities (Fitzgerald & Spiegel, 1983; Gordon & Braun, 1985; Singer & Donlan, 1982). Most research on story structure has been based on the idea that as children's concepts of story and story structure become clearer, they use that knowledge both in reading and writing stories—in reading, to comprehend major events, and in writing, to determine what information to include in a story and how to organize or sequence it. For example, after Singer and Donlan (1982) taught high school students a set of story grammar-based questions to guide their reading, their comprehension of complex stories improved. Gordon and Braun (1985) taught fifth-grade students about elements of narration based on story grammar research by first giving them a series of questions to use to identify information in texts with varying structures. Students were then led through fifteen lessons in which they learned to generate their own questions about stories and to use similar questions in planning and composing their own narratives.

Most research on expository text structure has focused on the relationship between knowledge of text structure and comprehension (Englert & Hiebert, 1984; McGee, 1982; Meyer, Brandt, & Bluth, 1980; Taylor, 1980, 1982). It has shown that students with a better understanding of text structures have higher comprehension scores (Armbruster & Anderson, 1980; Bartlett, 1980; Berkowitz, 1986; Taylor & Beach, 1984). For example, Berkowitz (1986) taught sixth-grade students how to construct maps of important text information. Another group studied a map produced by a teacher. These students' comprehension of the text was compared with the comprehension of students who reread the text and of students who answered written text questions. Not surprisingly, students who constructed their own maps performed higher on the comprehension measures than those in other groups.

Instruction in expository text structure can affect students' writing. Taylor and Beach (1984) studied the effects of a summary procedure that focused seventh-grade students' attention on structural signals (e.g., headings and subheadings) used in content area texts. They found that when students trained in this way wrote on an assigned topic, they were better able to organize the information they wished to present. Taylor and Beach suggested that this ability improved the overall quality of the students' writing. Although these findings do not address the improvement in students' ability to produce texts when the topic is not assigned, they do provide evidence that text-structure instruction has a positive impact on students' expository writing.

Research on Process-Writing Instruction

Teaching the process of writing (see Applebee, 1981; Graves, 1983; Murray, 1982) has triggered the interest of teachers and school personnel across the country. Research on this subject describes writing as a nonlinear process. That is, it does not begin with simple tasks and work toward more complex tasks; instead it consists of a number of more holistic activities: prewriting, drafting, editing, revising, and eventual publication or sharing with an audience (Flower & Hayes, 1982). Throughout the process, writers are guided by a complex awareness of their purposes for writing, the subject about which they are writing, their intended audience, and the form that best conveys their paper's message or content (Britton, 1978; Kinneavy, 1971; Moffett, 1968). Furthermore, the social context in which students engage in writing has a powerful impact on the type of writing they produce (DeFord, 1986). Key elements of successful writing programs include writing for a real purpose and a real audience in a supportive environment that provides frequent, if not daily, opportunities for sustained writing (Calkins, 1983; Graves, 1983).

Following Vygotsky's and Bruner's theories of general language learning, teachers are to play a more supportive role in helping students learn how to write (Langer & Applebee, in press). Because writing is a socially mediated process that develops over a long time and through interactions with a more mature learner, the teacher must "scaffold" learning by simplifying the task, clarifying its structure, relating subprocesses to the larger task at hand, and providing a framework of rules or procedures. The novice gradually internalizes these rules and procedures until instruction is no longer required (Vygotsky, 1962; Wood, Bruner, & Ross, 1976).

Research on mother-child interactions has conceptualized this transfer of control from the mature learner to the novice. Wertsch (1979) identified four stages in the child's movement toward self-regulation. At the first stage, the mother and child do not share the same perception of the task, and the mother must define it in terms the child will understand. This situation parallels that in which a teacher has a specific writing activity in mind (e.g., a report on animals), and the students do not have any concept of what must be accomplished. The teacher may set up a series of writing activities to help the students complete the assignment. At the second stage, the child may understand the task (or the student may understand the writing assignment) but not be able to complete the task without explicit guidance on how to do so (e.g., a set of directions or steps from the teacher). At the third stage, the child begins to see the significance of the task (e.g., writing a report to learn about a different culture), as well as the general rules of the situation, and is able to complete the task when given vague hints and suggestions. At the fourth stage, the child shifts to self-regulation and requires no assistance.

Unfortunately, many teachers today are at a distinct disadvantage in providing this kind of support when teaching writing. Few have had any methods course in writing and thus are often uncomfortable in defining writing activities. Few consider themselves writers and so are unable or reluctant to assume the role of the "mature learner." The writing curriculum is often vague, and time allotted for writing tends to be minimal (Florio & Clark, 1982).

Research on Teacher-Researcher Collaboration

Studies of teacher-researcher collaboration aided our search for procedures that would help teachers support students in the writing process. Successful staff development involves long-term, interactive programs to which both teachers and researchers contribute (Barnes & Putnam, 1981). Just as research on instruction in writing assumes that learning to write is socially mediated, research on staff development assumes that teachers' learning is socially mediated and that control should be gradually transferred from the staff developer to the teacher. This assumption led us to design a program to help teachers implement writing through levels of transfer similar to those described by Wertsch (1979); in the final stage, teachers take over and begin to transfer control to students (Schiffert, 1978; Swanson-Owen, 1985).

THE DEVELOPMENT OF AN EXPOSITORY WRITING PROGRAM

In developing an expository writing program, we conducted a series of studies based on research on text structures, process writing, and models of successful collaboration. We taught students how texts are structured, what questions different structures are designed to answer, and how an understanding of text structure can help locate and integrate important information. Our first study, a short-term training study (Raphael & Kirschner, 1985), examined how a program of instruction in expository text structure affects students' reading comprehension and writing. Our second study, a long-term instructional study focusing primarily on composition of expository text (Raphael, Englert, & Kirschner, 1986; Raphael, Kirschner, & Englert, 1986a), measured the impact of the instruction in a process-writing classroom. Third was a case study of a process-writing teacher. The fourth study extended the instructional work to younger and low-achieving students.

We aimed to create and test a writing program that could counteract the difficulties that many teachers today encounter when teaching writing. We provided teachers with (1) a basic understanding of the components of writing, (2) methods of teaching students effective writing strategies for each component, and (3) suggestions for creating a purposeful writing environment, one that allowed teachers to define meaningful writing activities and students to feel comfortable sharing their papers with a real audience of peers and adults. A critical aspect in the success of such a change from current practice was teachers' willingness to change, as well as to extend their expertise.

The long-term goal of our research was to develop a collaborative, supportive, interactive program to change teachers' thinking—a program that would allow teachers to see instruction as appropriate and that would give them ownership of their learning and freedom to internalize instruction (Day, 1985) so they could guide students in developing their own writing. A second goal was to provide students, through their participation in the program, with a range of appropriate and useful strategies that would enable them to engage successfully in all aspects of writing.

Study 1

Raphael and Kirschner (1985) examined the effects of teaching students about comparison/contrast text structure. Students had seven hours of instruction spread over six weeks. The first lesson introduced them to the concept of comparison/contrast by presenting a hypothetical situation in which their parents had given them permission to buy a puppy and so they had gone to a pet store where they had found two puppies. They considered questions they might want to ask the pet store owner about the two animals. In this way, they were led to consider the text-structure concept—comparison/contrast—as well as the role questions play in considering information that should be included in written texts. The next two lessons focused on brief comparison/contrast passages, which students read and examined in terms of (1) the things being compared, (2) on what they were being compared, (3) similarities, and (4) differences. In later lessons, students reviewed the concept of a text structure, learned how to summarize information, and were introduced to key words and phrases used to signal text structures. Students then practiced writing summaries of increasingly longer passages that used a comparison/contrast structure.

Results indicated that such instruction did improve sixth-grade students' text recall. In addition, their summaries of text were better organized and had more relevant information, and they used key words and phrases more appropriately. Unfortunately, although these students' compositions were longer and better organized, they lacked "voice," were uninteresting, and were *not* the type of papers we wanted to encourage children to produce. This result was not surprising since the students had not participated in activities designed to create a sense of authorship. They had written (1) for the researchers, not for themselves or peers; (2) for evaluation, not for learning or publication; (3) not as part of a writing process but to produce first drafts only; and (4) with no sense of ownership. We concluded that to improve students' compositions, as well as their comprehension, our instruction in text structures should stress the writing process, particularly *purpose* and *audience*.

Study 2

To test the conclusion from the first study, we extended Raphael and Kirschner's (1985) research on text structure to process-writing class-rooms. The study involved a long-term collaborative effort in which instruction occurred as part of the ongoing curriculum and in which teachers and researchers together determined the specifics of imple-mentation. Eight teachers and their fifth- and sixth-grade students participated in the study, forming four different groups. Each teacher had a minimum of twelve years of teaching experience and at least twenty hours of graduate coursework and was considered by researchers and administrators to have good classroom skills. One experimental group, the "social-context" group, was introduced to the writing process with emphasis on audience and purpose. These students participated in peer-editing sessions, author's chair (Graves & Hansen, 1983), and publication of class books. A second group, the "text-structure" group, was introduced to the writing process with emphasis on the role that knowledge of text structure plays in planning, drafting, and revising. These two groups continued the activity for six months. A third group of students, the "social-context–text-structure" group, learned about the writing process and the role of purpose and audience for three months, and for the next three months they studied text structure and the role it plays in planning, drafting, and revising. The fourth group of students served as controls by participating in a traditional writing program driven by the curriculum in their language arts text-book.

A central feature of the instruction for all groups except the control group was a series of think-sheets modified from ones used successfully with adult beginning writers as part of an undergraduate composition course (Kirschner & Yates, 1983). Each think-sheet consisted of a set of prompts that encouraged students to use strategies appropriate to the aspect of the writing process in which they were engaged. The think-sheets served as guides for the subprocesses used during composition, making "visible" the types of questions that guide authors as they write. One think-sheet was developed to guide thinking during each phase of writing: planning, drafting, reflecting on the first draft and preparing to edit it, editing, revising, and second or final drafts. The content of the think-sheets varied according to the experimental group. Figure 12.1 shows the content of the think-sheets used by the social-context group.

Teachers of all three experimental groups used the think-sheets to introduce students to the different aspects of the writing process (planning, drafting, editing, revising), and students used them as re-

FIGURE 12.1 Think-Sheets Used by Social-Context Group to Guide the Writing Process

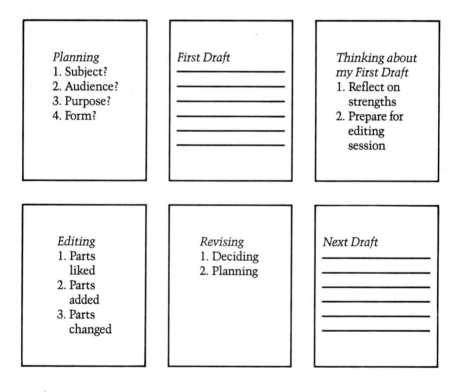

minders or prompts during their participation. Teachers initially followed procedures established and modeled by the researchers. As they internalized the knowledge, tasks, and procedures of teaching writing, they assumed more responsibility for implementing the program in their own classrooms.

Teachers established different tasks for students based on the instructional condition they were assigned. Those in the social-context group used think-sheets that did not refer to text structure, the questions the text should answer, or organizational features. Each student wrote a nonfiction narrative, an explanation, and two comparison/contrast and problem/solution papers during the fall quarter; specific topics were based on students' personal experiences and background knowledge. In the winter and spring, they wrote papers using the same structures but focusing on topics related to social studies. They never received explicit instruction in the questions or key words and phrases but did learn about and participate in planning, drafting, peer-editing and group-sharing sessions, revising, and publishing.

Teachers of the text-structure group had students practice writing a nonfiction narrative, an explanation, and two comparison/contrast and problem/solution papers, based on personal experiences, over the fall quarter. In winter, the teachers displayed good examples of each structure and had students (1) identify the type of text represented, (2) explain how they were able to recognize the type, (3) identify key words and phrases that signaled the text type, and (4) list questions answered by the paper. Students were then given the papers they had written in the fall and were asked to evaluate them in terms of text type, questions answered, and key words and phrases used. Next, students selected one paper to revise; taking into account the questions their text should answer and the key words or phrases needed to signal the type of paper, they added information, rewrote, or deleted. The think-sheets used by this group focused on text structure in planning, drafting, and revising, with no emphasis on audience or purpose through peer editing or publication. For the remainder of the year, students wrote one nonfiction narrative, one explanation, one comparison/contrast paper, and one problem/solution paper based on topics related to social studies.

Teachers of the social-context–text-structure group emphasized audience and purpose for writing throughout the year. In the fall, they had students write six papers and participate in peer editing, sharing, and publishing. In the winter quarter, however, students participated in the text-structure lessons introduced to those in the text-structure group and worked on publishing their own social studies class book.

Results indicated that students in the three experimental programs made significant gains in their free writing, surpassing students who were in the traditional program based on the language arts text (see Raphael, Englert, & Kirschner, 1986). Furthermore, students receiving instruction in text structure made specific gains in their ability to write comparison/contrast texts, a type of text that has been shown to be particularly difficult for students (Englert & Hiebert, 1984), especially in generating similarities and differences on parallel traits.

On measures of near and far transfer to reading (a summarizing activity and a measure of free recall), the results were less clear. Students in the two "pure" groups—the text-structure and the social-context groups—performed better than the students in the combined social-context–text-structure group. One possible reason for this disparity is that teachers and students in the latter group actually had two programs to implement in a single year. For students just beginning to master expository writing, the dual focus may have been somewhat confusing. Interviews with teachers of this group showed that they had just become comfortable with a new, rather complex instructional approach and had started questioning the research team in ways that showed a great deal of insight into issues surrounding the teaching of writing. With the addition of the text-structure program, their questions suggested concern for "lower-level" issues, such as timelines or management (see Kirschner, Raphael, & Englert, 1985, for a thorough treatment of the data). This hypothesis received still further support from a follow-up case study of one of the teachers in the combined experimental group.

Study 3

A key question for instructional researchers should be, What remains of a program once the formal research has ended? A case study of a fifth-grade teacher of the social-context–text-structure group provided us with some relevant data. Carol had taught in the public schools for seventeen years and was approaching retirement. She had initially voiced more concerns about implementation of the program than any of the other teachers. She had asked more questions and had seemed to rely more on the researchers and the materials provided and to take longer to internalize the concepts and procedures. However, by the end of the program, she expressed support of it, indicating that she had seen growth in her students' writing and reading. One of the most interesting comments she made was a casual remark that it was too bad she could not do the study over again now that she really understood what we were doing; in other words, she had internalized the knowledge, tasks, and procedures of teaching writing.

The researcher who conducted the case study documented Carol's participation during the formal part of the program through weekly observations, meetings, and informal discussions. Over the summer and next academic year, the researcher used notes, interviews, and student writing samples to document the program Carol implemented after her formal involvement in the study had ended. During the summer, Carol focused on adapting and modifying the program for the third grade to which she was moving. The researcher interviewed her at that time and found that she believed (1) that the gains her fifth-grade students had made in both reading and writing were attributable to the writing program, (2) that peer editing and publishing had given her fifth-grade students a purpose for writing and had helped them develop a sense of audience, and (3) that the writing program had helped demystify text as students began to view reading from a writer's perspective.

Elements of the program that Carol retained in the next academic year included a focus on peer editing and on writing for publication. In fact, instead of having students publish two class books as she had in the previous year, she had her third-grade class publish a book weekly for the ten weeks that she had a student teacher and then biweekly for the remainder of the year. Furthermore, she expanded the students' audience by involving parents, other classrooms, and other teachers. She also modified text-structure instruction substantially by introducing the four text structures—narrative, explanation, comparison/contrast, problem/solution—as she introduced students to the writing process. Other modifications included gradually allotting more time to writing than in previous years. Finally, she abandoned the use of the think-sheets, saying she was comfortable modeling each strategy and phase of writing for the students by using writing samples and thinking aloud as she wrote (on an overhead projector) or responded to students' papers. This shift indicated that she had internalized the strategies involved in teaching writing.

Study 4

The purpose of Study 4 was to extend the research to children with special needs. This study involved an extensive descriptive examination of the writing curriculum currently used in special education classrooms and with special education students in regular classrooms, and it is actually the first in a three-year line of studies. We are now examining the effects on students' expository composition and comprehension of an approach that emphasizes both text structure and audience. However, the interesting issue is not whether teachers can duplicate a program we design and can examine its impact on average students. Rather, we are interested in *how* teachers implement the program and modify it to suit the particular needs of their classroom and their students. We are also focusing on adaptations for younger (fourth grade), low-achieving, and mildly handicapped (LD) students in regular classrooms and in special education settings.

Data include narrative observations of each of sixteen teachers, eight from regular classrooms and eight from special education classrooms. They were observed during a morning and an afternoon, during two writing lessons, and during a writing activity involving a content area. Each teacher was also interviewed about her knowledge and beliefs about writing, current writing curriculum, and personal writing habits. Student data include their "think-alouds" as they wrote a paper on an animal of their choice and interview data from a subset of 40 regular and 40 special education students, as well as writing, summary, and recall measures for all 240 students. Informal analyses have suggested that special education students and low-achieving students experience difficulty writing more than a few lines and also that they have difficulty assuming the informant status needed for expository writing. The interviews with teachers indicated a wide range of writing activities, from those based on traditional language arts texts to the editing and publishing associated with the writing process. However, all teachers perceived weaknesses in their expository writing program (e.g., infrequent opportunities to engage in expository writing) and a lack of guidelines for implementing such instruction in a way consistent with the process-writing focus.

Based on our first two studies and the data available for initial analysis from our current research, we modified the program used in Study 2 by combining text-structure instruction with social context and stressing both simultaneously. A major component added to the program was a focus on dialogue, both interpersonal and intrapersonal. This program was then implemented by the sixteen teachers in Study 4. Similar measures (e.g., interviews, writing samples) are being used to assess change in both teachers and students. The next study in this sequence will focus on what remains of the program in the year after formal involvement of the researchers ends. The teachers and a subset of their students will be observed and interviewed, and student writing samples will be gathered.

The following section provides an overview of the instructional program that we are currently testing. This program again relies on the use of think-sheets as teacher and student tools, but it does not separate instruction in writing from instruction in the questions different text structures consider. Instead, the two are combined in a single approach.

THE REVISED EXPOSITORY WRITING
PROGRAM

Based on findings from the four studies reported here, we are continuing to modify materials and to adjust instructional strategies. The program presented in this section is not an "ideal" version; rather, it is a "next step" in developing an effective instructional intervention for improving expository composition and comprehension. An important component of this revised version is dialogue: teacher-student, student-student, student-self. The program uses seven think-sheets to introduce the writing process. The think-sheets are designed to prompt teachers to model and think aloud as they teach writing, to encourage teacher-student dialogue about strategies appropriate to each phase, to prompt appropriate student-student dialogue during peer editing, and to encourage useful student-self dialogue as students write independently. Sample think-sheets are presented in the following sections.

The Think Sheets

Planning: Think-Sheet 1. The planning think-sheet focuses on four elements authors consider when planning a paper: subject, audience, purpose, and form. When writers begin a paper, they initially consider the subject about which they plan to write. They focus on information their readers need to know, on what they themselves already know about the topic, on what must be gathered from external sources, and on what is particularly interesting about the topic to their readers. As they consider their topic, writers also must consider their audience—the amount of background knowledge the audience may be expected to bring to the reading and the audience's characteristics (e.g., age and interests). Writers also must consider their purpose in writing the paper. For example, if the topic is explorers of the New World, they may ask themselves whether they are writing to explain what voyages were like, to tell an adventure story that took place during that era, or to draw a parallel between preparing for such a voyage and getting ready for a field trip. Once writers have determined their topic, audience, and purpose, they select an optimal form or structure for presenting the information. The think-sheet in Figure 12.2 consists of a set of prompts to guide the reader through a consideration of these factors before beginning the first draft.

Organizing: Think-Sheet 2. The second think-sheet is actually a set of four different pattern guides designed to help the young writer organize the information generated during planning, or the young reader

Author's name _____   Date _____

TOPIC: _____

WHO: Who am I writing for?

WHY: Why am I writing this?

WHAT: What do I already know about my topic? (Brainstorm)

1. _____

2. _____

3. _____

4. _____

HOW: How do I group my ideas?

FIGURE 12.2   Think-Sheet for Planning

organize the information gathered during reading, into a format for the first draft. These pattern guides reflect the different questions each type of text is designed to answer; they display both the questions and a visual representation of the paper's organization. They thus facilitate recall of information, whether from background knowledge or from texts that have been read, by guiding the student to select important and relevant information. Figure 12.3 contains the pattern guide for the comparison/contrast text structure. Other guides are available for problem/solution, explanation, and narrative text structures. Once students have considered the most appropriate text structure in which to present their information, they then select the appropriate pattern guide to help them organize what information they have and to generate additional information.

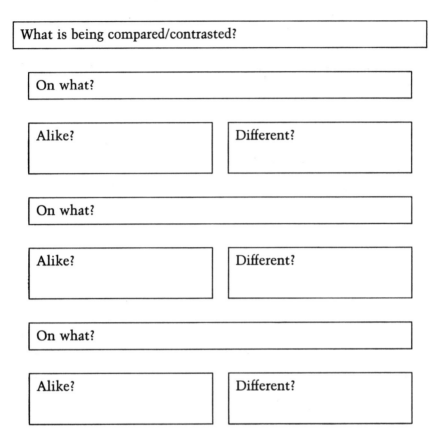

FIGURE 12.3 Think-Sheet for Organizing: Comparison Contrast

First Draft: Think-Sheet 3. Students use the third think-sheet to compose a first draft of their paper. It consists of a blank sheet of lined colored paper. Colored paper, rather than white, is used to remind students that their first writing attempt is not the final work. Writers are not usually thought to produce final copy on colored paper; thus the color serves to underscore that the paper is work in progress.

Thinking about the First Draft: Think-Sheet 4. The purpose of the fourth think-sheet is to prompt students to reflect on their first draft's strengths and weaknesses and to prepare for the editing session (see Figure 12.4). This think-sheet simulates the thoughts a writer has when he or she has completed a draft (or several drafts) and is considering asking for external response to the draft. Authors may request a general response, but they often are more specific, asking for feedback on particular sections of their paper. This think-sheet therefore asks authors to identify their favorite parts, the parts they would like to work on if they have more time, and the questions

Author's Name _____

Read to check information.

What is my paper mainly about?

What do I like best? Put a * next to the best part and explain why.

What parts are not clear? Put a ? next to the unclear parts, and tell why they are not clear.

Is the paper interesting? Tell why or why not here:

Question yourself to check organization.

Did I:

Tell what two things are compared and contrasted?	Yes	Sort of	No
Tell things they are being compared and contrasted on?	Yes	Sort of	No
Tell how they are alike?	Yes	Sort of	No
Tell how they are different?	Yes	Sort of	No
Use keywords clearly?	Yes	Sort of	No

Plan for editing conference.

What parts do I want to change? (For anything marked "Sort of" or "No," add to, take out, reorder?)

1. _____

2. _____

What questions do I want to ask my editor?

_____

_____

FIGURE 12.4 Think-Sheet for Thinking about the First Draft: Comparison/Contrast

they want to ask their editors about their papers. The goal of this activity is to have students take ownership of their paper and to provide a focus for editing.

Editing: *Think-Sheet 5.* There are five versions of the editing think-sheet, one for each of the four text structures taught and a generic version, which is used when students begin to combine the different structures as they write more complex papers. In all versions, this think-sheet focuses on five specific types of responses. First, students are reminded to listen as the author reads his or her paper aloud, and, second, they are asked what the paper was mainly about. Third, students are asked to indicate their favorite part of the paper, and, fourth, to think about ways the paper could be made clearer or more interesting. The text-structure versions contain additional prompts asking if the author presented answers to the questions appropriate to the structure; for example, the comparison/contrast version, shown in Figure 12.5, has students name what is being compared or contrasted, list the attributes for comparison, and describe their similarities and differences. The fifth prompt directs author and editor to discuss the editor's reactions. Prompts in these five areas give students concrete guidance in appropriate ways to respond to written work. As a result, the author comes into the editing session with certain questions and so is ready for feedback. The reader/editor is pushed to consider specific responses and to avoid more typical general responses, such as "I like it," "It seems fine to me," or "Work on the middle."

Revision: Think-Sheet 6. When authors receive feedback from readers, they may accept it in some form and respond, or they may ignore it. The revision think-sheet, shown in Figure 12.6, is designed to promote authors' consideration of their editor's comments but still give them control of their own papers. To ensure that they at least acknowledge the editor's suggestions, students are asked first to list all these suggestions and then to check the ones they plan to address. Next, they are directed to plan revisions that would make their paper more interesting or easier to follow.

Final Draft: Think-Sheet 7. After students have revised their first draft, they move to a final-copy (or a next-draft) think-sheet. The format of the think-sheet for the final draft is the same as for the first draft, except that it is on white paper. Students may move from revision to final draft, or they may choose to write a second draft on colored paper before moving toward final copy.

Teachers' Role in Teaching the Process

The role of the teacher in writing instruction in this program is based on the Vygotskian notion that learning is socially mediated (Gavelek, 1986; Rogoff, 1986). The acquisition of a cognitive process like expository writing is socially mediated because it first occurs on an interpersonal plane—that is, between the teacher and students. The teacher, through modeling and thinking aloud, conveys to the students meaningful activities for the different aspects of writing (e.g., Raphael, Kirschner, & Englert, 1986b). The think-sheets guide the teacher in modeling and thinking aloud about specific, appropriate strategies (e.g., during the planning phase, thinking aloud about the topic, audience, purpose, and form). They also encourage the development of a shared vocabulary

Author's Name _____   Editor's Name _____

Read to check information. (Authors: Read your paper aloud to your editor.)

What is the paper mainly about?

What do you like best? Put a * next to the part you liked best and tell why you like it here:

What parts are not clear? Put a ? next to the unclear parts, and tell what made the part unclear to you:

Is the paper interesting? Tell why or why not here:

Question yourself to check organization.

Did the author:

Tell what two things are compared and contrasted?	Yes	Sort of	No
Tell things they are being compared and contrasted on?	Yes	Sort of	No
Tell how they are alike?	Yes	Sort of	No
Tell how they are different?	Yes	Sort of	No
Use keywords clearly?	Yes	Sort of	No

Plan revision.

What two parts do you think should be changed or revised? (For anything marked "Sort of" or "No," should the author add to, take out, reorder?)

1. _____

   _____

2. _____

   _____

What could help make the paper more interesting?

Talk.

Talk to the author of the paper. Talk about your comments on this editing think-sheet. Share ideas for revising the paper.

FIGURE 12.5 Think-Sheet for Editing: Comparison/Contrast

Author's Name _____

List suggestions from your Editor.

List all the suggestions your editor has given you:

a. _____

b. _____

c. _____

d. _____

e. _____

Decide on the suggestions to use.

Put a * next to all the suggestions that you will use in revising your paper.

Think about making your paper more interesting.

List ideas for making your paper more interesting to your reader.

_____

_____

_____

Return to your first draft.

On your first draft, make all changes that you think will improve your paper. Use ideas from the lists you have made on this think-sheet.

FIGURE 12.6   Think-Sheet for Revision

between teacher and students so that students have the language with which to discuss writing and analyze their writing problems.

The teachers may initially conduct monologues, rather than dialogues with their students, as they model these strategies and the language to describe them. In effect, this level is comparable to Wertsch's (1979) description of the first stage of mother-child interactions as the child moves toward self-regulation. At this point, the students and teacher may not share the same perception of the task of writing, and the teacher's role is to define and clarify the task for the students. The think-sheets provide a structure or guide to strategies to model and language to use when explaining different aspects of writing. At this level, the think-sheets help clarify the task of writing for both teacher and students.

As a shared understanding of the task of writing is established and a shared vocabulary with which to discuss writing is created, students and teacher enter a period of dialogue and joint responsibility, with the teachers monitoring the children's understanding of the writing process and of appropriate activities and strategies. This point is comparable to Wertsch's (1979) second stage: students can complete the tasks, but they require support or explicit guidance to do so. The teacher's role at this level is to help students consider the think-sheets in terms of the writing process and as external reminders of appropriate strategies or activities.

As the students move toward the third stage in developing self-regulation, the teacher can begin to transfer responsibility for much of the process to the students, maintaining the role of an assistant who provides general hints and reminders. A part of this shared responsibility and gradual transfer of control occurs during the peer-editing sessions. Such sessions are designed to give teachers an opportunity to monitor students' relatively independent writing. As students gradually internalize the questions on the think-sheets and take ownership of the writing process themselves, they begin to work independently of the teacher. When they reach the level of self-regulation, they will no longer need external support, either from the think-sheets or from the teacher. Instead, with the process and the questions and prompts appropriate to different phases internalized, they will plan, draft, ask for feedback, and revise to achieve their own writing goals.

IMPACT OF PROGRAM PARTICIPATION

The goal of our program has been to extend students' awareness of different types of writing, as well as their ability to produce and to comprehend different expository texts. One question we had to consider was whether a program this intense could have a negative effect on students' sense of writing as communication or on their willingness to produce meaningful papers. Selected data from our research show the potential impact of such a program on students' knowledge about writing, their ability to present information in an organized manner, and their attitude toward writing.

Students' Knowledge about Writing

We interviewed a set of students randomly selected from each instructional group in Study 2. One of the questions we asked was, "What do you do when you write a paper?" The students' responses illustrated differences in their knowledge about the writing process and in how such knowledge was influenced by the program.

Keith was a student in the text-structure group, which emphasized a set of writing strategies. He responded to our question with the following comment:

> If you want to do a compare/contrast, you got to tell what you are comparing it with, and contrasting about. See what would go first, second, put them in a certain order. See if there is any misspelled words or something and try to fix it up, if there is something you have to add or take away, then you put that on a different piece of paper and then you'd go into [the] final draft. [If a friend were writing a story] I would tell him where does this take place, what is this about, and who is it about, and what came first, second, and third. Gather information if he has to, then he would write it down for his first draft, then check for misspelled words and take stuff out and add stuff, then go onto final draft.

Note that Keith recognizes the complexity of the writing process and specifically mentions the questions authors consider as they write their papers. He suggests specific, though very basic, strategies for revision, including adding or deleting certain kinds of information and gathering information if not all questions are answered. He shows a concern for copy editing in his remark about misspelled words. However, he shows no awareness of audience.

Jenny was a student who received instruction in the social-context group, which emphasized audience and purpose. Her response reflects an awareness of the many activities involved in writing a single paper, as well as a focus on the role of audience in terms of editors, but she does not seem to have any specific strategies:

> First you write down what kinds of things you're going to be doing, and you just get all your ideas out on the page. And then you try to make the first draft and you get as much stuff in as you can. Then, what we are doing in our class is, we check them over with editors. They read your paper and they say, well this doesn't sound right and maybe you should try to change this to so and so. Before that I start thinking about my first draft, and then . . . do [the] editorial. Then you just do a revision form where you decide what things you want to change, and then you put it all together in a final copy.

Note that Jenny sees an important role for her editor before completing the paper, though she maintains ownership of her paper by stating that during revision the author decides what should be changed.

Dawn participated in the combined program, and, not surprisingly, she displayed knowledge both of the complexity of the writing process and of the central role of the type of paper being written. Note that she qualifies her answer according to the structure of the type of text she is writing:

> [To write a compare/contrast], I would look at two people, find their alike and different points. Like if I was comparing my friend Stacy and my friend Tracy, I would say that Tracy is shorter than Stacy or Tracy has real dark hair and Stacy has a little light hair. [If I didn't know them], I'd have to go to the library and do some research on them. I sit down and write the first draft. Before that I do brainstorming, . . . like if I was doing George Washington and Abraham Lincoln I'd have to write [about] both Presidents . . . no full sentences, only words. Before our first draft we do prewriting and preplanning. [Interviewer asks, "What is that?"] Prewriting is like in compare and contrast, who or what is being compared on? What are they being compared on? How are they alike and how are they different? [Interviewer asks, "Then the first draft?"] Yeah, then we get these sheets with a friend, and we write, what do you think your editor said about your paper? What will you do to change the things with your editor suggestions? Your editor reads your story, and on the pink sheet they tell you what you should do to get it in better shape for your final draft or what you should take out. And what you should put in. [Interviewer asks, "And then?"] If it was published, my family would be reading it and my friends.

Dawn's comments on the need to consider similarities and differences on parallel traits in comparison/contrast texts displays a sophisticated knowledge of different strategies for different types of writing. In addition, she identifies a situation in which personal knowledge will suffice and a situation in which external knowledge must be used, and she mentions specific strategies for gathering information to answer questions, as well as the possible need to add or delete information. Moreover, she indicates a sense of audience beyond the teacher, including both her friends and family.

Terry was part of the control group, whose traditional instruction was based on the language arts textbook. His response showed a mechanistic view of writing. When the interviewer initially asked him what he did when he wrote, Terry looked confused. The interviewer prompted, "When you write to compare or contrast something." Terry responded, "I never heard of it." The interviewer then prompted, "When you write a story." Terry's response was as follows:

> When I write a story this is how I first start off, write the title and then write the beginning of it. First step I do is write the major story. And then I go all the way through and stop at periods and when I ask a question I write a question mark. And if it's exciting, I put an exclamation mark. Put a period [at the end].

These students' responses indicate, not unexpectedly, that "what you teach is what you get." They provide further support for combining generalized instruction in the writing process with instruction in specific strategies for composing expository texts. The creation of an environment in which students share their writing can be seen as an important factor in their development of a sense of audience.

Students' Ability to Write Text and to Convey Information

Students were asked both in the fall and in the spring to write a paper comparing and contrasting two people, places, or things. The directions focused on including important and interesting information, and the audience was designated as the student's "best friend." Matthew, the author of the following paper, had not received any instruction in text structures:

> Mcdonalds is a big place it even has a playground for the kids. That's probably why the kids gobble up their food and run outside. The father gets up grab the kid by the hair and says were are you going? He say swallow your food. So theirs a point that Mcdonald is a good place for the kids. Well the only thing I like is the bag mac and the strawberry shake. The other place I'm comparing is burgerking. Burgerking is a place that has the whopper. That's what I like.
> The end

Matthew intended his paper to compare and contrast the two restaurants, but he did not signal his reader very effectively. In fact, the paper began as a discussion of McDonalds, using a narrative structure to describe the effect of the playground on children's and father's behavior. The restaurant itself was barely described. Even when Matthew introduced the second restaurant, he did not clearly describe it in terms of parallel attributes. He attempted to do so, describing his favorite food—big mac and strawberry shake versus whopper—in both restaurants, but the reader is left to make the connection.

The following paper was written by David, a student who had received instruction in text structures:

> I am going to compare and contrast Burger King and McDonalds. The first thing I'm going to compare/contrast them on is there service. These two restaurants are similar in many ways. One is the checkers are very nice. They always say have a nice day. But there also different. Burger King has propted [prompter] service. It takes them about a minute to get my food ready but at Mcdonalds it took them 30 minutes to get my food ready. The second thing I'm going to compare and contrast them on is there food selection. There selection is alike in many ways. One is they both have breakfast, lunch, dinner selection and they both have a wide selection but Burger King has a wider selection than Mcdonalds.

Note that both papers maintain a sense of "voice," are approximately the same length, and are written at about the same level mechanically. However, the paper written by David, who had received instruction in text structures, clearly lets the audience know that this is a paper that compares and contrasts the two restaurants. David uses parallel traits on which to compare the restaurants; yet he makes his preference and implied recommendations very evident. All these features are lacking in the first paper. One impact of the text-structure instruction is that it clearly improves students' ability to organize and convey information.

Students' Attitude toward Writing

How does participating in the program affect students' attitudes toward writing? One concern about the think-sheets used in the program is that they could reduce students' spontaneity in writing narratives of personal experience or lead to stilted, uninteresting text. Robin wrote the following paper in early fall before she began the program:

> I wish I went into the hunted house. The way Tammy describe it, it must of been fun. Speicely when you walk. When they said [here comes some more meat] that is when I ran out. When I hear screams it ges me scared. Why did you all the suden get scared?
> P.S. Please write back.

Note that Robin showed a sense of audience in her question to her reader ("Why did you all of a sudden get scared?") and in her request to have her friend write back. However, she did not provide much context for the reader, nor did she provide any closure.

The following paper, which Robin wrote after participating in the program, shows a marked contrast to her earlier paper. Not only has she included greater detail; she has also set a context, provided insight into the characters involved, and maintained her "voice." It is important to note that she knew that other students would not be reading this paper, that her only audience was the researcher (i.e., "the grown-up who had been helping in her class"). Although she wrote about a very personal experience, she still followed the narrative structure and included key words that signal time sequence throughout.

> When I was little my dad would come home with a box of donuts. He would only give them to me and I couldn't share with my brothers. One day I gave them both one. My dad saw me and give me a wippen and put me up in my room. The next day he didn't geve me some donuts. I felt like he didn't love me. When I was 2 years old my dad told me and my mom that he was to good for us. When he went out the door I thought he was going to come back. I waited near the door a lot. I never seen him again. When I turned 3 years old I moved out of that house. Now I am 11 years old I still go by that house looking for him. But there is no hope.
>
> One day I said to my self, I am going to look for him when I get older.
>
> I don't know if he is alive. All the other kids make front of me when I am at school.
>
> They don't under stand what my problem is.
>
> I know there are alot of kids without a father.
>
> It seems like he taught me how not to share.
>
> That is why I act kind of strange.
>
> Now everytime I eat a donut I think of him.

Robin's paper clearly demonstrates that using think-sheets to guide the writing process, stressing purpose and audience, does not inhibit students' ability to write about personal experience in a meaningful and moving way.

A second concern about the program is whether it inhibits students' desire to write. When the year ended, all students were asked to complete a questionnaire about strategies they used during writing. At the end of his questionnaire, Freddy, a low-achieving sixth-grader, wrote the following unsolicited note; it illustrates what was perhaps the most important effect of the program:

To Dr. R.—
I don't like to write but when you came along I begane to write
I thank you four helping me to starte liking to writing.
from your best friend
Frederick   Thank you!

Teaching expository writing requires a substantial commitment on the part of the elementary school teacher, and exploring ways to improve this instruction requires a similar commitment on the part of researchers. Although still in its developmental stages as a field of inquiry, initial research of this type suggests that expository writing instruction, if conducted within an environment that encourages writing for real purposes and for real audiences, can have a positive impact on students, their teachers, and the researchers who are able to share in the process.

R E F E R E N C E S

Applebee, A. N. (1981). Looking at writing. *Educational Leadership, 38,* 458–462.

Armbruster, B. B. (1984a). Content area textbooks: A research perspective. In J. Osborne, P. Wilson, & R. C. Anderson (Eds.), *Reading education: Foundations for a literate America* (pp. 47–60). Lexington, MA: Lexington Books.

Armbruster, B. B. (1984b). The problems of "inconsiderate text." In G. G. Duffy, L. R. Roehler, & J. Mason (Eds.), *Comprehension instruction: Perspectives and suggestions* (pp. 202–217). New York: Longman.

Armbruster, B. B., & Anderson, T. H. (1980). *The effect of mapping on the free recall of expository text* (Tech. Rep. No. 160). Urbana: University of Illinois, Center for the Study of Reading.

Barnes, H., & Putnam, J. (1981). Professional development through inservice that works. In K. Howey, R. Bents, & D. Corrigan (Eds.), *School-focused inservice: Descriptions and discussions.* Reston, VA: Association of Teacher Educators.

Bartlett, B. J. (1980). *Top-level structure as an organizational strategy for recall of classroom text.* Unpublished doctoral dissertation, Arizona State University, Tempe.

Berkowitz, S. J. (1986). Effects of instruction in text organization on sixth-grade students' memory for expository reading. *Reading Research Quarterly, 21,* 161–178.

Britton, J. (1978). The composing process and the function of writing. In C. Cooper & L. Odell (Eds.), *Research on composing: Points of departure* (pp. 13–28). Urbana, IL: National Council of Teachers of English.

Calkins, L. M. (1983). *Lessons from a child.* Exeter, NH: Heinemann Educational Books.

Day, C. (1985). *Why teachers change their thinking and behavior: Case studies in professional learning through inservice activities.* Paper presented at the International Study Association on Teacher Thinking, The Hague.

DeFord, D. E. (1986). Classroom contexts for literacy learning. In T. E. Raphael (Ed.), *Contexts of school-based literacy* (pp. 163–180). New York: Random House.

Englert, C. S., & Hiebert, E. H. (1984). Children's developing awareness of text structures in expository materials. *Journal of Educational Psychology, 76,* 65–75.

Fitzgerald, J., & Spiegel, D. L. (1983). Enhancing children's reading comprehension through instruction in narrative structures. *Journal of Reading Behavior, 15*(2), 1–17.

Florio, S., & Clark, C. (1982). The functions of writing in an elementary classroom. *Research in the Teaching of English, 16,* 115–130.

Flower, L., & Hayes, J. R., (1982). Plans to guide the composing process. In C. H. Fredericksen & J. F. Dominic (Eds.), *Writing: The nature, development, and teaching of written communication* (pp. 39–58). Hillsdale, NJ: Erlbaum.

Gavelek, J. R. (1986). The social contexts of literacy and schooling: A developmental perspective. In T. E. Raphael (Ed.), *The contexts of school-based literacy* (pp. 3–26). New York: Random House.

Gordon, C. J., & Braun, C. (1985). Metacognitive processes: Reading and writing narrative discourse. In D. L. Forrest-Pressley, G. E. MacKinnon, & T. Gary Waller (Eds.), *Metacognition, cognition, and human performance* (pp. 1–75). New York: Academic Press.

Graves, D. H. (1983). *Writing: Teachers and children at work.* Exeter, NH: Heinemann Educational Books.

Graves, D. H., & Hansen, J. (1983). The author's chair. *Language Arts, 60,* 176–183.

Kinneavy, J. (1971). *Theory of discourse.* New York: Norton.

Kirschner, B. W., Raphael, T. E., & Englert, C. S. (1985, December). *Text structure instruction and process writing programs: Impact on teachers.* Paper presented at the annual meeting of the National Reading Conference, San Diego.

Kirschner, B. W., & Yates, J. M. (1983). *Discovery to discourse.* New York: Macmillan.

Langer, J. A., & Applebee, A. N. (in press). Literacy development and literacy instruction: Toward a reconceptualization. In L. Frase (Ed.), *Review of research in education.* Washington, DC: American Educational Research Association.

McGee, L. (1982). Awareness of text structure: Effects on children's recall of expository text. *Reading Research Quarterly, 17,* 581–590.

McGee, L., & Richgels, D. (1986, April). *Awareness of four text structures: Effects on recall of expository text.* Paper presented at the annual meeting of the American Educational Research Association, San Francisco.

Meyer, B. J. F. (1975). The structure of prose: Effects on learning and memory and implications for educational practice. In R. C. Anderson, R. J. Spiro,

& W. E. Montague (Eds.), *Schooling and the acquisition of knowledge* (pp. 179–200). Hillsdale, NJ: Erlbaum.

Meyer, B. J. F., Brandt, D. H., & Bluth, G. J. (1980). Use of author's textual schema: Key for ninth-graders' comprehension. *Reading Research Quarterly, 16,* 72–103.

Moffett, J. (1968). *Teaching the universe of discourse.* Boston: Houghton Mifflin.

Murray, D. (1982). *Learning by teaching.* Montclair, NJ: Boynton/Cook.

National Assessment of Educational Progress. (1986). *Writing trends across the decade, 1974–84.* Washington, DC: Author.

Raphael, T. E., Englert, C. S., & Kirschner, B. W. (1986). *The impact of text structure instruction and social context on students' comprehension and production of expository text* (Research Series No. 177). East Lansing: Michigan State University, Institute for Research on Teaching.

Raphael, T. E., & Kirschner, B. W. (1985). *The effects of instruction in comparison/contrast text structure on sixth-grade students' reading comprehension and writing products* (Research Series No. 161). East Lansing: Michigan State University, Institute for Research on Teaching.

Raphael, T. E., Kirschner, B. W., & Englert, C. S. (1986a). *Students' metacognitive knowledge about writing* (Research Series No. 176). East Lansing: Michigan State University, Institute for Research on Teaching.

Raphael, T. E., Kirschner, B. W., & Englert, C. S. (1986b). *Text structure instruction within process-writing classrooms: A manual for instruction* (Occasional Paper No. 104). East Lansing: Michigan State University, Institute for Research on Teaching.

Raphael, T. E., & Pearson, P. D. (1985). Increasing students' awareness of sources of information for answering questions. *American Educational Research Journal, 22,* 217–236.

Raphael, T. E., & Wonnacott, C. A. (1985). Heightening fourth-grade students' sensitivity to sources of information for answering questions. *Reading Research Quarterly, 20,* 282–296.

Rogoff, B. (1986). Adult assistance of children's learning. In T. E. Raphael (Ed.), *The contexts of school-based literacy* (pp. 27–40). New York: Random House.

Schallert, D., & Tierney, R. J. (1982). *Learning from information text: The interaction of text structure with reader characteristics.* Final report to The National Institute of Education (NIE-G-79-0161).

Schiffert, J. (1978). A framework for staff development. *Teachers College Record, 80,* 4–22.

Singer, H., & Donlan, D. (1982). Active comprehension: Problem-solving schema with question generation for comprehension of complex short stories. *Reading Research Quarterly, 17,* 166–186.

Spivey, N. N. (1984). *Discourse synthesis: Constructing texts in reading and writing.* Newark, DE: International Reading Association.

Swanson-Owen, D. (1985, April). *Identifying natural sources of resistance: A case study analysis of curriculum implementation.* Paper presented at the annual meeting of the American Educational Research Association, Chicago.

Taylor, B. M. (1980). Children's memory for expository text after reading. *Reading Research Quarterly, 15,* 399–411.

Taylor, B. M. (1982). Text structure and children's comprehension and memory for expository text. *Journal of Educational Psychology, 74,* 323–340.

Taylor, B. M., & Beach, R. (1984). The effects of text structure instruction on middle grade students' comprehension and production of expository text. *Reading Research Quarterly, 19,* 134–146.

Vygotsky, L. S. (1962). *Thought and language.* Cambridge, MA: MIT Press.

Wertsch, J. V. (1979). From social interaction to higher order psychological processes: A clarification and application of Vygotsky's theory. *Human Development, 22*(1), 1–22.

Wood, D. J., Bruner, J. S., & Ross, G. (1976). The role of tutoring in problem-solving. *Journal of Child Psychology and Psychiatry, 17*(2), 89–100.

POSTSCRIPT

Applying an Emergent Literacy Perspective to Early Childhood Curriculum

Dorothy S. Strickland

The lag between research and practice has always been a source of concern among educators. It takes a very long time for new research to reach the schools and even longer for it to take on meaning and influence change. It is apparently far easier to embrace new ideas on an intellectual level than it is to put those ideas into place in the real world of the schools. For this reason, curriculum research that provides us with rich descriptions of efforts to apply research findings is an important way to educate the field both about the research itself and about its curricular implications.

In this book, we have vivid descriptions of classrooms in which new ideas are being applied. Obviously, these descriptions are valuable for those already involved in similar work and those actively seeking change. They may also serve as a point of entry for those who are curious about what new trends in research they might apply to practice and are uncertain about where to begin.

It is not difficult to find similarities among many of the studies described in this book. Teams of researchers investigated and explored models of communication in the classroom. The research teams consisted of teachers, teacher trainers, curriculum specialists, and specialists in young children's language and literacy development. These teams worked in a collaborative and collegial manner to explore a common concern. The questions raised by classroom teachers were just as important as those raised by experienced researchers. The process of investigation thus took on an interactive quality, as research and practice were mutually informed and new questions and solutions evolved.

These efforts were grounded in an emergent literacy perspective, rather than in a traditional readiness frame, and were guided by the need to help teachers support young children's literacy development in ways that are developmentally appropriate. They reflected an implicit awareness of the need to provide curriculum that supports the total growth of children, not just the development of reading and writing.

An important feature of the report of Kawakami-Arakaki, Oshiro, and Farran in Chapter 9, for example, is the notion of the morning message as part of the classroom communication system. Tied to the children's immediate experience, it offers a meaningful and functional text for modeling writing and reading and for teaching concepts about print. Teachers' experimentation with the morning message revealed that it can undergo a variety of modifications and still retain its integrity, an indication of its strength and usefulness. The discussion surrounding the experimentation with the writing process is a candid and valuable description of the struggle to search for answers to complex questions. It is a reminder that no matter how valuable the intervention, change is neither easy nor predictable.

Classroom teachers and curriculum developers will want to know more about how teachers who use the morning message and the writing-process activities meet the needs of varied levels of development within the group. They will also be interested in knowing more about the development of skills or objectives throughout the year. Is a fixed sequence of skills developed through the morning message, or does the teacher tend to focus on what interests the children about a text and what occurs naturally within it? Do teachers combine the two approaches? If so, what are some of the ways teachers make the necessary decisions involved? Future reports of this project might expand on these points.

As described in Chapter 8, Teale and Martinez's notion of connecting writing with functional purposes in the classroom and with reading and of connecting young writers with each other is a powerful and useful tool for curriculum developers. The use of literature as a link to writing capitalizes on its natural potential as a source of content, form, and language models.

Curriculum developers might also want to know how writing was linked to the content areas in these classrooms. Were social studies and science being taught? If so, were children writing about what they were learning? Expanding the current work described in Chapters 5 and 12 to help children link their writing to content under study would yield useful information for integrating the curriculum.

Valuable insights into how an emergent literacy perspective might be applied to the curriculum are highlighted in Chapters 8 and 9 and noted in reference to children's progress in Chapters 3, 4, 5, 6, 10, and 11. They provoke thought about the following issues surrounding such an application:

Teacher Knowledge. Teachers who attempt to apply a process approach to reading and writing instruction need a thorough understanding of those processes, as well as some idea of the scope of behaviors they might expect from a given range of students. To get a sense of what the reading and writing possibilities are and what they mean, they need to examine the work of many children, interact with both children and other adults about work samples, and observe many children at work independently.

Systematic Observation. Equipped with an understanding of the acquisition of reading and writing in young children, teachers need further help with systematic observation of children's reading and writing behaviors. The ability to respond to a child's scribbles and to note the subtle differences between a string of letters with and without the insertion of marks for word boundaries requires an understanding of the course of reading and writing development over time. Broadly defined scales or categories for observing early reading and writing development can be useful in helping teachers become better observers. Although these must never be used as teaching objectives, they serve as valuable resources for tracking children's development.

The Whole Curriculum. In their zeal to apply the new research on early literacy acquisition to classrooms, teachers must keep the entire curriculum in mind. In addition, researchers and curriculum developers must avoid creating models of instruction that appear to promote literacy only for literacy's sake; such models could give teachers the impression that literacy should be taught in one context and that content area topics, such as social studies and science, should be taught in another.

The Whole Child. Teachers must keep the total development of the child in mind. No matter how valuable the exploration of reading and writing is, it must never be offered in ways that are incongruent or detrimental to the child's social, emotional, and physical development. Engaging children in writing-process activities is certainly preferable to using worksheets and workbooks. But forcing children to sit for long periods of time engaged in any kind of paper-and-pencil activity is inconsistent with what we know about child growth and development.

Dictation and the Process Approach. There is a need to discuss the use of dictation, group or individual, within a process classroom. Does it have a place in the teaching of reading? Can it be used for group collaborative writing? Is it ever helpful with an individual reader or writer? If so, should it be used only after the child has independently tried to write or after an adult has modeled the process? Will its use tend to inhibit a child's writing progress in any way? These questions need to be answered because dictation as a writing activity troubles some teachers, especially those who use the language-experience approach to teaching reading.

Meeting Curricular Objectives. As new models for supporting reading and writing development are proposed, curriculum developers must tie the new ideas to their existing objectives or rethink those objectives in light of the new evidence. If they do not, the risk is that teachers and administrators, rather than reshaping the old curriculum into a new mold, will attempt to tack the new strategies onto their existing curriculum.

New Paradigms for Learning and Teaching. Finally, there is a need to address the fundamental differences between what is being advocated from an emergent literacy perspective and the assumptions underlying most kindergarten curricula today. The prevailing view of kindergarten is that it is a period during which children should accumulate a prescribed list of information and skills in order to get ready for formal (real) reading instruction. Congruent with this view is a model of teaching, even at the kindergarten level, that suggests that the teacher knows the needed skills and information and systematically transmits them to the child. In contrast, the new paradigms for learning and teaching suggest that children come to school with a great deal of knowledge about language and literacy, that effective instruction makes use of what children already know about language and supports continued growth of that knowledge, and that all that is known and learned is valued as a significant part of a lifelong continuum of reading and writing development. The role of the teacher becomes one of setting conditions that support self-generated, self-motivated, and self-regulated learning. It is the setting of those conditions that is at the heart of curriculum development.

Author Index

Subject Index